BROTHERS
among NATIONS

BROTHERS among NATIONS

*The Pursuit of
Intercultural Alliances
in Early America,
1580–1660*

CYNTHIA J. VAN ZANDT

OXFORD
UNIVERSITY PRESS
2008

OXFORD
UNIVERSITY PRESS

Oxford University Press, Inc., publishes works that further
Oxford University's objective of excellence
in research, scholarship, and education.

Oxford   New York
Auckland   Cape Town   Dar es Salaam   Hong Kong   Karachi
Kuala Lumpur   Madrid   Melbourne   Mexico City   Nairobi
New Delhi   Shanghai   Taipei   Toronto

With offices in
Argentina   Austria   Brazil   Chile   Czech Republic   France   Greece
Guatemala   Hungary   Italy   Japan   Poland   Portugal   Singapore
South Korea   Switzerland   Thailand   Turkey   Ukraine   Vietnam

Copyright © 2008 by Oxford University Press, Inc.

Published by Oxford University Press, Inc.
198 Madison Avenue, New York, New York 10016

www.oup.com

Oxford is a registered trademark of Oxford University Press

Library of Congress Cataloging-in-Publication Data
Van Zandt, Cynthia J.
Brothers among nations : the pursuit of intercultural alliances in early America,
1580–1660 / Cynthia J. Van Zandt.
    p. cm.
Includes bibliographical references and index.
ISBN 978-0-19-518124-1
1. Indians of North America—History—Colonial period, ca. 1600–1775. 2. Indians of
North America—First contact with Europeans. 3. Indians of North America—Colonization.
4. Cultural relations—United States—History. 5. United States—Ethnic relations.
6. United States—History—Colonial period, ca. 1600–1775. I. Title.
E77.V25 2008
303.48'273009032—dc22   2007051112

9 8 7 6 5 4 3 2 1
Printed in the United States of America
on acid-free paper

For JIM and HANNAH

Acknowledgments

I have incurred numerous debts in writing this book. Needless to say, any book that begins as a doctoral dissertation and then transforms into a rather different work invariably takes several years and depends heavily upon people's generosity in the process. *Brothers among Nations* has benefited particularly from the intellectual interest and assistance of many people, so many, indeed, that I fear it will be impossible to thank them all.

A research support grant from the University of New Hampshire vice president for research and public service, as well as a grant of leave, helped to make it possible for me to conduct additional studies during a crucial period. I am grateful to Dean Marilyn Hoskin and to the History Department for the necessary leave time to carry out further research. In addition, the American Antiquarian Society granted a Stephen Botein Research Fellowship and made available the society's expertise and resources as I delved deeply into seventeenth-century printed works on navigation, society, politics, and intercultural relations.

Many colleagues read portions of the manuscript at various stages of the writing. I am particularly grateful to the anonymous readers for Oxford University Press, who provided a close reading of the manuscript and an extremely helpful critique. I have no doubt that this is a better book as a result of their suggestions. And if I have stubbornly failed to follow some of their very good advice, they are certainly not to blame.

In addition, a number of other colleagues provided both tangible and intangible assistance. Brendan McConville, Walt Woodward, Karen Kupperman, Richard Johnson, and Daniel Richter offered helpful ideas along the way.

Brendan McConville and Ruth Herndon lent support at a critical juncture. Charles Gehring and the New Netherland Institute were supportive of this project from start to finish, and I am very grateful for their help. Jim Rice made insightful suggestions over the years as we discussed our mutual interest in the Chesapeake and its native peoples. David Furlow and Lisa Pennington share my abiding interest in the extraordinary Isaac Allerton, and they have generously shared their own research with me. Karen Kupperman has given vital assistance and wise counsel throughout; I could not ask for a better mentor.

I am indebted to my colleagues in the History Department at the University of New Hampshire. Their commitment to excellence in scholarship and teaching makes UNH a congenial place to work. All of them have helped with this project in one way or another. Several read portions of the manuscript with particular care and offered constructive suggestions; I extend my thanks to Bill Harris, Frank McCann, Eliga Gould, and Jan Golinski for reading parts of the manuscript and book proposal. Nicky Gullace and Lige Gould took time away from their own work to critique cover images. David Frankfurter has always been ready for a lively discussion of intercultural dynamics, and I have benefited a great deal from our conversations.

In addition, Holly A. Rine provided useful research assistance at an early stage of this work. I am also grateful to my undergraduate and graduate students at the University of New Hampshire. I am a better scholar and writer because of them.

The John Carter Brown Library reproduced the illustrations from their extraordinary holdings; I thank them for permission to use these materials. The members of the JCB's imaging staff were extraordinarily helpful and responsive. In addition, Susan Danforth, who is always a model of professionalism and efficiency, responded to numerous queries for increasingly obscure images with enthusiasm and aplomb. The fact that some of them proved elusive is not due to any lack of searching on her part. Similarly, the Library of Congress, the Maryland Historical Society, and the Massachusetts Historical Society responded generously and quickly to requests for similarly obscure images. I thank them all for their assistance.

I presented portions of chapters 1 and 2 to the New England Seminar in American History at the American Antiquarian Society; portions of chapters 1 and 3 to the "Changing and Exchanging" conference on Cultural Contact and Spiritual and Material Conversions at Princeton University; portions of chapter 6 at the Columbia Seminar in Early American History and to the Fulbright American Studies Conference at the University of Canterbury, New Zealand; and portions of chapter 7 at the Boston Area Early American History Seminar at the Massachusetts Historical Society. I am grateful to the participants at all of these venues for their feedback. A portion of chapter 1 was published in *Early American Studies*.

Ultimately, I did not take the advice of everyone who generously offered suggestions, comments, and constructive criticisms, though I am grateful for their intellectual contributions. In the end, however, the responsibility for any errors or omissions is mine alone.

Everyone at Oxford University Press has made publishing this book a pleasure from start to finish. Susan Ferber has a long list of loyal authors for good reason, and she has been a steadfast model of professionalism. I am grateful for her suggestions and technical assistance and above all for her sound good sense and unwavering support for *Brothers among Nations.*

To everyone who kept asking whether the book was done yet, I offer my thanks. Although it is not always a question one wants to answer, it is one that every writer ought to face from time to time. Thanks to my parents for their forbearance during a very long process and for assuming that some day they would really see an actual book.

I cannot adequately express my indebtedness to Jim Rollins. He has been there every step of the way—for every eureka moment and roadblock—and he has faced it all with love and equanimity. And to Hannah, who has had to wait patiently too many times, thank you for deciding that chapter 5 was good enough, at least at the time. Some things should not have to wait; we had waited long enough. This book is dedicated to Jim and Hannah, with love and gratitude.

Contents

BROTHERS
among NATIONS

Prologue

Seventeenth-century Europeans believed that the sins of the father were visited upon the son. They also expected a son to avenge wrongs done to his father, despite the fact that, if they had thought about it carefully, they would have realized that the son's world is sometimes radically different from the father's. Nowhere does this seem clearer than in the heat of a Virginia summer in the last quarter of the seventeenth century. Virginia governor William Berkeley and his council commissioned Major Isaac Allerton Jr. and Colonel John Washington to call out the militia from Virginia's Northern Neck in August of 1675.[1] Major Allerton and Colonel Washington received instructions to investigate a series of recent Native American attacks in the region and to retaliate against the responsible tribe or tribes. Although it was not yet clear in 1675, these events would become entangled in Bacon's rebellion. Allerton and Washington called out the militia while also quickly enlisting the aid of additional troops from Maryland.[2] They had decided (largely incorrectly as it turned out) that the Susquehannocks were to blame for several of the recent attacks.

The joint Virginia-Maryland militia advanced on a Susquehannock fort on the Potomac River. It laid siege to the stronghold for several weeks without breaking the Indians' defenses. But when a group of Susquehannock werowances came out of the fort to offer terms for a peace treaty, the colonial militia leaders saw a chance to end the stalemate. Militia officers agreed to discuss peace terms and led the Susquehannock leaders aside, ostensibly for peace negotiations. Instead they murdered them. When Major Allerton and Colonel Washington were later called to account for the Susquehannock leaders' deaths, they argued successfully that militia officers from Maryland had committed the murders without their approval. In the end Major Allerton and Colonel Washington were formally exonerated of any wrongdoing, though a cloud of impropriety hung over the ugly event for decades.[3]

Major Isaac Allerton Jr. must have been aware of a certain irony in the situation, for his father had had dealings with the Susquehannocks long before Bacon's rebellion and far away from Virginia. The elder Isaac Allerton was a well-known person. In many ways he was the quintessential figure of the early colonial world. He spoke at least two languages, traveled frequently from one community to another, and recognized the essential truth that colonies could survive only through their connections with other communities, including those with people from other cultures. This was in large part based on a realistic assessment of the balance of power in early seventeenth-century North America because Allerton senior's influence peaked during the heyday of the Susquehannocks' power. In 1655, twenty years before his son became caught up in the events of Bacon's rebellion, the elder Isaac Allerton found himself in the middle of the opening events of a war between Dutch colonists and Native Americans called the "peach war." He also found himself the centerpiece of a demonstration of the mighty Susquehannocks' power and influence.

Hundreds of Indian warriors streamed into Manhattan one September day in 1655, when they knew that the Dutch military was away from the settlement, engaged in an action against a Swedish colony on the Delaware River. The warriors mostly came from Munsee and other Algonquian peoples, but they were joined (and indeed led) by a number of Susquehannocks. The warriors paraded through the streets of New Amsterdam that day, breaking into houses and demonstrating that the community was at their mercy if they so wished. But they did not break into every house; they chose their targets carefully. They singled out the influential merchant Isaac Allerton, forced their way into his house and warehouse, and publicly insulted him in the street. Although they did not harm the sixty-nine-year-old Allerton, Dutch accounts of the incident make it clear that it was a deeply disturbing attack, one that Allerton certainly remembered for the remaining years of his life. And it was an attack that his son must also have had in mind as he rushed to lead a Virginia militia against the Susquehannocks twenty years later, when they were no longer quite so mighty.

The son and his generation were able to wield a degree of power that was seldom possible during Isaac Allerton Sr.'s lifetime in North America. In the distance between the world of Major Isaac Allerton Jr. and that of his father, we see a dramatic shift in Native American power on the eastern seaboard and a remarkable change in the ways in which Indians and Europeans lived and dealt with one another. In the elder Allerton's day, the Susquehannocks often had the upper hand in their dealings with Europeans.

However, by 1675 the world of Major Allerton's father was disappearing. As Colonel Washington and Major Allerton led the Virginia militia that year, they could never have imagined that Washington's grandson George would one day lead thirteen united colonies to become a new nation. Similarly, Isaac Allerton Sr. could not have envisioned how different his colonial American world would become during his son's lifetime. The elder Allerton's world, now lost to us and fading even as his son grew to power and influence in Virginia, was an extraordinary moment in time. This book is about that era and the world of Master Isaac Allerton, merchant, and many other people like him who helped shape their part of the early colonial American world.

Introduction

Brothers among Nations is a book about cooperation between people of different cultures. In seventeenth-century European terms, this is a study of common efforts between people of various nations. But because such work was often fragile and the road toward it frequently paved with prejudice and misunderstanding, conflict is also an integral part of the story. Violence and apparent betrayals were often sparked by the breakdown of previous efforts at collaboration. People of different cultures seldom understood one another fully—and rarely wanted to—but they often needed to rely on one another. In the space between the interdependence born of necessity and the suspicion and hatred born of ethnocentrism, Europeans, Native Americans, and diaspora Africans created a world of international alliances. They did so in part by mapping one another, marking the boundaries of cultures, spaces, and worldviews. This book explores early modern peoples' pursuit of intercultural partnerships by focusing on the ways in which they used maps to bridge cultures and in which early moderns mapped peoples, as well as lands and waterways.

In exploring the cultural history of interactions between colonizers and colonized in North America, *Brothers among Nations* challenges our current understanding of each category. In geographical and temporal range, it focuses on the Atlantic seaboard from the Chesapeake Bay region to New England in the years from 1580 to 1660. These were the first eighty years of European efforts to colonize these regions, and the period is remarkable for the scope and degree of cultural and political experimentation people attempted. *Brothers among Nations* highlights the importance of the fluidity inherent in this era of experimentation. It argues that Europeans, Native Americans, and diaspora Africans all continuously mapped one another as they pursued the intercultural alliances that, to a large extent, shaped the early colonial world.

Much scholarship in the history of cartography has shown us that maps are more than just artifacts. They may take the form of manuscripts, published plots, sea charts, or globes. Yet scholars have demonstrated that maps can be cognitive and metaphorical as well. This was particularly true for early modern Europeans, who were engaged in colonial enterprises at the dawn of modern scientific cartography. Captain John Smith's most famous work, for example, is titled *A Map of Virginia*.[1] Smith's title reflects the fact that his book includes an important geographical map of the territory of Virginia, but it also explicitly revealed Europeans' understanding of mapping as an ethnographic enterprise. With one actual map and more than one hundred pages of text, *A Map of Virginia* plots people and cultures, as well as geography.

Native Americans understood mapping in different but no less important terms. Although almost no Indian nation had a word for "map" before European contact, the evidence makes it clear that mapping was a significant cultural practice for native peoples.[2] Not only did Native Americans sketch maps for Europeans in early contacts, but they also regularly charted their relationships with other nations. The deerskin garment known as "Powhatan's mantle" is one such depiction of the peoples in the Powhatan paramount chiefdom, with a human figure at the center surrounded by circles, each representing a member group. Crucially, it does not depict geographical space; instead, it presents a map of social and political relations. For Indian peoples generally, mapping was often more metaphorical than literal. Native Americans, for instance, also had extensive mapping traditions for preserving and explaining cosmological traditions; many Indian peoples mapped the underworld. When Europeans arrived, native peoples sought to map them into their cosmological, as well as political, framework; sometimes such mappings involved ritual performances, while at other times they took more material forms.

Brothers among Nations extends the implications of understanding that maps themselves can be cognitive or performative, as well as material.[3] Mapping in the early modern era needs to be understood as a process that was linked inextricably and explicitly to making sense of social and physical space. Mapping and ethnography, for instance, were intertwined endeavors. Educated Europeans connected mapping and cartography in their writings about politics, colonial expansion, and diplomacy. Because innovations in cartography coincided with colonial expansion, European writers and colonial promoters created a well-elaborated written justification of the connection between ethnography and mapping. Repeatedly they argued that charting the world's lands and waterways also had to include mapping the world's peoples. And men and

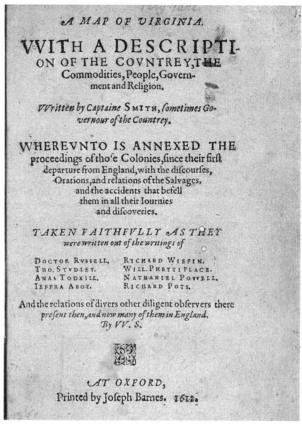

A MAP OF VIRGINIA.

VVITH A DESCRIPTI-
ON OF THE COVNTREY, THE
Commodities, People, Government and Religion.

VVritten by Captaine S M I T H, *sometimes Go-*
vernour of the Countrey.

WHEREVNTO IS ANNEXED THE
proceedings of those Colonies, since their first
departure from England, with the discourses,
Orations, and relations of the Salvages,
and the accidents that befell
them in all their Iournies
and discoveries.

TAKEN FAITHFVLLY AS THEY
were written out of the writtings of

DOCTOR RVSSELL,	RICHARD WIEFIN.
THO. STVDLEY.	WILL. PHETTIPLACE.
ANAS TODKILL.	NATHANIEL POWELL,
IEFFRA ABOT.	RICHARD POTS.

And the relations of divers other diligent observers there
present then, and now many of them in England,
By VV. S.

AT OXFORD,
Printed by Ioseph Barnes. 1612.

FIGURE 1. Captain John Smith's 1612 book about Virginia was titled *A Map of Virginia*. It included an actual map but also pointed out that the long descriptions of the land and the people of Virginia were integral parts of Smith's mapping enterprise. *A Map of Virginia*, Oxford, 1612. Courtesy of the John Carter Brown Library at Brown University.

women who actually went to North America actively charted new peoples, as well as lands and waterways, to make sense of the always-changing social spaces in which they found themselves.

Moreover, Native Americans and Africans also mapped the constantly shifting realities of early colonial North America. Neither left a similarly explicit paper trail, however. Because Indian peoples did not use alphabetic writing in the early seventeenth century and Africans in North America in this period also left virtually no written documents, we have no written evidence that either group made the same epistemological connections between mapping and ethnography (mapping social, as well as physical, space). Yet, the records make it clear that Native Americans and Africans on North America's Atlantic seaboard, like their European counterparts, worked constantly to map their realities—both social and political—in ways that would give them definition, if only temporarily.

In the early colonial period, constant change, shifting alliances, and periodic epidemics and warfare made it imperative that everyone on the Atlantic seaboard map and remap the other peoples they encountered, including their size, strength, customs, and political alliances. To chart social space was to be armed with the knowledge necessary to manipulate and gain some command of a world that seemed to be spinning rapidly out of control. However, different cultures did not map the early American world in the same ways, and they did not understand the process to be the same.

In focusing on the relationship between mapping, ethnography, and intercultural contact, *Brothers among Nations* contributes to an interdisciplinary scholarship. Scholars working in European and Asian history, in particular, have begun to take similar approaches to the cultural importance of mapping in the early modern world.[4] Like those works, *Brothers among Nations* is not about maps per se. It is not about gaining a full understanding of how maps functioned in early colonial North America. Rather, it approaches this period by focusing on mapping as a metaphorical lens.

We can begin to understand more about the ways in which people were connected to one another across regions and cultures if we understand that they were all working in their various ways to chart their realities. Much of this process involved forming intercultural alliances as people sought to fit others into a grid of social space that made sense to them. At other times, mapping included kidnapping individuals who could provide information about the physical and social lay of the ethnographic terra incognita. It included learning other cultures' languages or at least negotiating a trade jargon that allowed for intercultural communication. Native peoples mapped the changes in their world by seeking to place European colonists into existing American kinship, trade, and alliance networks. As a result, Europeans sometimes found themselves in conflict with powerful Indian nations because they became the adversaries of the enemies of their new Indian allies. In addition, enslaved Africans charted the spaces in which they could blunt the oppressive force of slavery's power over them, and slavery in the early seventeenth century provided far more such spaces than existed in later periods.

For most of the seventeenth century, colonial North America was the product of unrelenting contestation by people of many different cultures: European, Native American, and African. This is not to suggest a world of chaos or of unrelieved conflict. To be sure, clashes were frequent and often severe; however, they are best viewed as one part of a larger process of ethnographic mapping, self-interest, and alliance building. Using the theoretical rubric of mapping enables us to understand the ways in which physical mapping, ethnography, the pursuit of alliances, and self-interest all served to connect different cultures across the Atlantic seaboard. It also serves to emphasize that this period cannot be satisfactorily explained as the imposition of European power and culture on native peoples. Even in the case of severely unequal power relationships, such as between Europeans and enslaved Africans, Europeans had no choice but to negotiate elements of the interactions.[5]

The question of what exactly constituted an alliance is an important one. For much of the seventeenth century, intercultural alliances were the raison d'être for mapping. Certainly, not every kind of contact or agreement between various communities or cultures was an alliance, nor were all collaborative efforts necessarily long lasting. For the purposes of this study, an alliance is any interaction that was intended to ensure or influence the course of subsequent interaction, whether for a short or a longer period of time. Indeed, in the late sixteenth and the first half of the seventeenth centuries relatively few such associations continued for long stretches of time without interruption or change, but everyone experimented with "periodic alliances."[6]

The ongoing pursuit of such connections had repercussions far beyond any individual or community. Historians tend to emphasize conflict as characterizing the colonial period. Often we think of European colonization as a kind of inexorable development, with European domination over Native Americans and Africans a tragic but inevitable aspect of colonialism. Certainly, a great deal of important scholarship has shown the importance of seventeenth-century intercultural conflict, and there is no question that clashes between peoples were an ongoing part of seventeenth-century life. Conflict, in a sense, often represented a failure of mapping, a mismapping of the physical and cultural boundaries all parties sought to get right. However, if disputes are one crucial part of the story, their importance has blinded us to another equally significant aspect: the moments in which people got mapping right. We have missed the widespread accommodation that shaped the early colonial period. The pursuit of alliances was among the most important and frequently attempted strategies of accommodation.

With its focus on the significance of accommodation, *Brothers among Nations* speaks to a rich and growing literature on seventeenth-century North America and its place within the larger Atlantic world. Much of the recent historiography of seventeenth-century Native American–European contacts has emphasized that Indian peoples on the eastern seaboard continued to exercise considerable power despite heavy disease mortality and related social dislocations.[7] As a result, Europeans were never able to wield as much power as they desired and were continually forced to accommodate the demands of others.

This is not to say that people liked or understood their allies, trading partners, or neighbors, nor is it to suggest that they took any pleasure in making alliances or even in having contact with people from other cultures. They seldom did. However, an extraordinary mix of people recognized necessity when they saw it and made temporary alliances with people from other cultures.

In every part of the Atlantic seaboard, European colonists repeatedly faced the realities that Native Americans knew the land and its resources better than they did and had extensive trade and communication networks far into the interior of the continent. For their part, Native Americans entered into partnerships with each other and with Europeans for their own specific reasons. In these joint ventures, no side fully understood the other's intentions, nor was there a unified agreement within cultures on how to deal with others. Yet this was a world in which international or cultural isolation could easily lead to extermination for Native Americans and Europeans. Moreover, Africans were as bound into this interdependent world as anyone; uneasy interdependence was a central fact of life in seventeenth-century North America.

In many ways this is a cultural history of the first international coalitions in North America. *Brothers among Nations* does not assume that Europeans were the dominant party in all of their relationships with Native Americans nor even entirely with enslaved Africans. Indeed, it argues that some Native American nations treated particular European colonists as clients and tributaries. Moreover, Indian actions were often determined more by relationships with other Native Americans than with Europeans, especially when inter-Indian alliances and conflicts stretched across territory claimed by European colonies. As a result, Native American alliances and conflicts prompted constant fears and rumors in European colonial communities, despite the fact that, from Indians' perspectives, Europeans themselves were largely peripheral to the issues involved. The effect was that Europeans not infrequently overreacted to perceived rather than real threats from native peoples.

In the early colonial period, the difficulty of intercultural communications highlights everyone's fragile hold on survival—Europeans, Native Americans, and Africans. *Brothers among Nations* emphasizes the importance of knowledge gained from Native Americans, along with the efforts at complex language acquisition and trade jargons that laid the foundation for an array of far-ranging intercultural alliances. These associations, which were formed through frequently jumbled and at times inchoate channels of communication, became essential facts of life for those living in the new colonial world of eastern North America.

The European colonial ventures that changed the American cultural and political landscape were fueled by innovations in cartographic and navigational technologies that not only influenced the details of colonial planning but also had a significant cultural impact during the late sixteenth and early seventeenth centuries. Recently the work of a number of scholars has brought the importance of maps and mapping into the forefront of early modern and colonial North American history. Studies have demonstrated that early modern Europeans began thinking more extensively about space in the context of political and cultural relationships, even as changes in print and cartographic technologies greatly increased their familiarity with maps and mapping concepts. Simultaneously, other studies have demonstrated that Native Americans had their own well-established mapping traditions. As a result of this groundbreaking scholarship, it has become increasingly clear that maps and mapping played a crucial role in shaping the many meetings of European and Indian cultures as intercultural contacts increased in the first half of the seventeenth century. *Brothers among Nations* examines the links between maps and colonial travel narratives in this period of colonial and technological experimentation and demonstrates that maps and mapping provided a necessary, if inconclusive, method of incising political and economic alliances onto physical and mental landscapes.

This is not a study of colonial history as seen only through a European lens; repeatedly and in every part of the Atlantic seaboard, European colonists had to contend with the realities of Indians' knowledge, networks, and power. For their part, Native Americans entered into alliances with each other and with Europeans to meet their own cultural imperatives, just as they provided mapping information to Europeans when it suited their purposes. At times Europeans found rather to their surprise that they also had to deal with Africans' alliances, even when they did not always recognize them.

In the fluid context of early colonial North America, even enslaved Africans were able to carve out some spaces that they themselves controlled, and they did so in part by mapping the relationships among European colonists and between Europeans and Indian nations. Africans' ability to delineate and exploit the weak points in some European colonial communities affected the stability of those groups of people, and in some circumstances European leaders relied upon Africans' assistance to defend a colony against external threats.

No one side fully understood the other's intentions or mastered intercultural communication, despite the fact that this was a world in which international or cultural isolation could easily lead to extermination for both Native Americans and Europeans. All parties quickly recognized this central fact of life in seventeenth-century North America; historians have yet to fully explore its implications.

In its geographical and cultural scope, *Brothers among Nations* takes an unusually broad look at seventeenth-century North America. Such a focus enables us to see clearly the importance of connections that ranged across colonial and regional boundaries, sometimes for hundreds of miles. Many alliances stretched far beyond any one group's territory or colony. Even when these associations were more narrowly contained in geographical terms, they were frequently directed at threats from outside the region. This book ranges broadly in order to capture the full dimensions of these intercultural affiliations. By doing so it makes it clear that webs of alliances shaped all of the regions this study covers and entangled everyone in one way or another.

Historians have seldom considered the implications of the extensive webs of connections that linked people of radically different cultures in the early colonial period. However, people in various regions were influenced by others from quite distant areas throughout the seventeenth century. When colonists in Plymouth, for instance, received news of the 1622 Powhatan attack on English settlers in Virginia, they responded by taking careful stock of the Indians around them. Thrown into a panic by rumors of a Dutch–Native American alliance against New England thirty years later in 1652, the United Colonies of New England held an emergency meeting to consider the rumor and to decide whether to launch a war against New Netherland.

New Englanders' descriptions of the rumored anti-English alliance sound remarkably reminiscent of descriptions of the Powhatans' 1622 attempt to eradicate English Virginia, with one significant difference. This time, colonists in New England feared that other Europeans might join forces with Indian enemies against them. Puritans in New England were not confident that they could trust their fellow European Calvinists in New Netherland to stand with them against all Native Americans. On the contrary, they found it quite plausible that Dutch settlers would make an alliance with Indians to exterminate the New England colonies. Such accounts provide just one demonstration that colonists in Massachusetts Bay, Plymouth, Connecticut, and New Haven felt themselves connected to and sometimes threatened by intercultural alliances throughout eastern North America.

This sense of interconnection helps to explain why everyone worked so assiduously to map all aspects of their surroundings, including peoples and their relationships. Belief in the pervasive reach of interconnections fed the fears and conspiracy theories that constantly circulated among Europeans and Native Americans. Neither the fears nor the intercultural alliances that formed their basis stopped at regional or territorial borders, a fact easily missed in studies of single regions or cultures.

Intercultural alliances took shape in a variety of ways. The Five Nations of the Iroquois League called the Dutch of New Netherland their brothers, and in diplomatic councils with Iroquois representatives, Dutch officials agreed that they were "brothers" of the Five Nations. The powerful Susquehannocks called themselves the protectors of the colonists of New Sweden. Swedish colonial leaders concurred that it was a good thing the Susquehannocks wished to play that role because they were far more powerful than the tiny New Sweden colony. The Swedes had no doubt the Susquehannocks could have destroyed New Sweden had they wished to do so.

In Virginia, Captain John Smith called the Powhatans' paramount chief his father during the early years of the Jamestown colony and established a playful Algonquian-style family relationship with Powhatan's daughter Pocahontas. Years later, when Pocahontas visited England, she reminded Smith of the kinship basis of his relationship with Powhatan and called on him to honor his kinship obligations. Africans in Manhattan formed allegiances and kinship bonds with each other, despite belonging to several distinct ethnic groups and having come to New Netherland from different places in Africa and the Atlantic littoral. Significantly, they used their alliances with other Africans to influence the degree of Dutch control over their community.

This study explains why cooperation across colonial and cultural lines was so necessary along the Atlantic seaboard in the seventeenth century. It is clear that Europeans, Native Americans, and Africans wanted to limit the influence of foreign cultures on themselves. No one in this period desired to become an assimilated and subordinate version of some new and foreign group.[8] If Europeans and Native Americans were often suspicious of other cultures and if they generally sought to limit their influence on them, why then did they also feel compelled to form intercultural alliances?

To some extent, the answer to this question is fairly straightforward. Native American and European communities on the Atlantic seaboard of North America experienced considerable turmoil and instability throughout much of the seventeenth century. European colonies were fragile and extremely expensive and faced periodic supply problems. Native American communities were disrupted by epidemics and the changing balance of power created by those outbreaks of disease and by the arrival of Europeans.

Economic concerns also played an important role. Europeans needed American products to send across the Atlantic to markets in Europe. For much of the seventeenth century, furs and hides were among the most important American commodities that Europeans exported from the colonies, and Native American hunters and traders were the main source of these items. In addition, European colonists needed Indian consumers to buy European-manufactured goods. For their part, Native Americans wanted European-produced articles, particularly metal goods and armaments, and over time Indians came to depend on some of those items. Africans in North America played an increasingly important role in the production of crops for the Atlantic market, and in the early years they were crucial in helping to build and defend European colonial settlements, despite the fact that they were unwilling and often unfree residents there.

Indeed, the kinds of alliances that constituted such an important part of the framework of seventeenth-century North American life went far beyond commodity exchanges. As people from different cultures worked to live with one another and to use one another for mutual advantage, the associations they formed took on a logic of their own. The reasons for intercultural agreements led European leaders to do things with or for their allies that they would not otherwise have done, often with considerable internal dissent and anxiety. Furthermore, it led Native Americans to expand their alliance systems to include new peoples and to try to accommodate the European newcomers' persistent inability to fulfill their proper role as understood by their Indian partners.

Importantly, intercultural alliances in seventeenth-century North America were fundamentally based on an Indian logic rather than a European one. Europeans often struggled against that framework; they usually misunderstood aspects of it, but they were forced time and time again to follow its dictates at least partially, and they did. When they failed to do so, they often found themselves engaged in bloody and destructive wars or facing starvation. Occasionally Africans' logic of collaborations also changed the course of events, although neither Europeans nor Native Americans seem to have understood the alliances of Africans in North America. But even if they failed to understand them, they could not avoid their very real consequences.

One of the crucial questions for understanding this period is why some cooperative relationships worked whereas others often failed. *Brothers among Nations* explores that issue. The book's focus is largely on groups of people—European colonies, Indian nations—but that is by no means the whole picture. To discuss the period only in terms of cultural or ethnic groups would be a mistake because it would suggest that categories such as "the English," "the Dutch," or "the Susquehannocks" were both fixed and easily defined, yet they were neither. Moreover, large-scale diplomatic and commercial cooperation was made possible by the fact that individuals had already formed a variety of relationships across cultural and ethnic lines. The commercial networks and kinship ties developed by individual men and women often formed the basis for wider cooperation between groups. Many individuals communicated in multiple languages and operated in a number of cultural contexts, and those people played vitally important roles in the first half of the seventeenth century.

Men like Plymouth elder Isaac Allerton, for instance, stitched together numerous dissimilar communities by trading in both goods and information. Ironically, the same personal relationships that helped clear the way for intercultural cooperation frequently fueled fears of conspiracies and imminent conflict between groups. Allerton intentionally traded information that fed such anxieties more than once. In recognition of the importance of the links between individuals from diverse social groups in shaping larger intercultural associations, this study explores varieties of alliances by tracing the activities of several European, Native American, and African individuals. These men and women formed many different kinds of relationships with people from other cultural groups. In the process, they reshaped the cultural, political, and economic contours of Early America.

Dating, Orthography, and Outline of the Study

I have chosen to use the hybrid Old/New Style dating system where the records themselves do so, as, for example, January 10, 1645/46. Thus, all dates for the period from the start of the year in the New Style calendar on January 1 up to the start of the Old Style year on March 25 will include the year as reckoned in both calendars, as, for instance, March 1, 1657/58. In North America, this was the solution favored by many English people, who frequently employed the combination notation as a compromise between the New Style, which the United Provinces and other European polities used, and the Old Style, which remained the official calendar of England and its territories. Dutch colonists used the New Style, so the hybrid Old Style/New Style dating system provides a modern, as well as a contemporary, compromise.

Similarly, wherever possible, *Brothers among Nations* uses terms that would have been familiar to seventeenth-century people in North America, thereby relying on their own language to describe the people, places, and events of their time. There are some exceptions to this. Except in quotations, I do not employ early modern terms that offend modern sensibilities, such as "savages" to refer to Native Americans. However, I explore the implications of such language for understanding the ideas and behaviors of people who lived in seventeenth-century North America. I have not modernized the orthography of records that I quote directly. Although some readers may find early modern spelling off-putting, reading words as people actually wrote them rewards us with a deeper sense of their world than if I were to modernize their language.

In cases in which no early-modern term existed, I have relied upon several different expressions. For instance, Native Americans did not have a name for all of the indigenous peoples of the continent. In a study such as this one, it is necessary to generalize at times about broad cultural differences between Europeans and Native Americans. Those discussions alternately use the terms "Indians," "Native Americans," "native peoples," and "Americans" in contrast to "Europeans" or "Africans." None of these is wholly satisfactory or free from colonial residue; however, each makes possible discussions of extensive cultural distinctions. Similarly, although early moderns from central Africa probably did not think of themselves as "Africans" in this period, I use the term to facilitate discussion of wide-ranging cultural and linguistic differences.[9]

In geographical range, this study explores interactions from Iroquoia and northern New England in the north to the Outer Banks of modern-day North Carolina in the south. The bulk of the study's evidence focuses on intercultural contacts from the Chesapeake to New England. In chronological range, I begin with the intellectual background of sixteenth-century Europe in order to explain why European newcomers saw intercultural alliances as essential to their enterprises. It is an intriguing fact of early colonial ventures that Europeans invariably sought to learn about the native peoples of North America rather than just to ignore or conquer them. Understanding why that was so helps us to realize why early intercultural contacts took the forms they did. The book then concentrates on actual intercultural interactions between peoples during the first half of the seventeenth century. In doing so, *Brothers among Nations* pays particular attention to a number of early, short-lived connections and colonies from the first two decades of the seventeenth century.

Although these very early contacts and colonial ventures are well known in general terms, historians have tended to study them either in isolation (for what they can tell us about the early colonial history of a particular town or state) or primarily as examples of colonial failures. And while most of these early colonies or trade ventures did indeed fail, they provide us with a great deal of valuable evidence about the halting steps toward intercultural alliances that Europeans and Native Americans took in the first two decades of the seventeenth century. Their failures paved the way toward later, longer-lasting, and more successful partnerships.

Finally, *Brothers among Nations* uses the term *intercultural* rather than *cross-cultural* in order to emphasize not only the cooperative nature of such interactions but also the limits that were always present. To get at the complex nature of these alliances and to explore the chain of consequences they frequently created require a particularly broad range of source materials. This is especially important because the sources for seventeenth-century colonial history are less extensive than for many later historical periods. Before 1660 Native Americans left almost no documents they themselves had written; the same is true of Africans in North America. Moreover, many European sources that we know once existed have not survived across the centuries.

Accordingly, in order to address the limitations of the extent and types of resources available and to explore the fullest dimensions of intercultural alliances before 1660, this study relies on a wide array of materials. It uses official colony administrative records, colonial court records, records of colonial sponsoring companies, published colonial promotional tracts, geographical treatises, maps, sea charts, travel narratives, and personal letters. The extensive range of sources helps to ameliorate the limitations of any one type. More-over, it would not be possible to trace the full dimensions of many intercultural connections without such a wide range of source material. In the first half of the seventeenth century, people constantly pursued intercultural alliances, but because they did so within the context of a variety of activities and fears, the evidence of their preoccupation and of these affiliations themselves is scattered throughout a great deal of apparently unrelated material.

1

Mapping the Peoples of the World

Geography, Chorography, and Intercultural Alliances

European colonial ventures that changed the American cultural and political landscape were driven by innovations in cartographic and navigational technologies. Those innovations not only influenced the details of colonial planning but also and just as importantly had a significant cultural impact during the late sixteenth and seventeenth centuries.[1] As intercultural contacts increased in the first half of the seventeenth century, for instance, maps and mapping played a central role in shaping the many meetings of European and Indian cultures. Indeed, they lay at the root of political and trade alliances that Europeans formed with Native Americans, particularly in the earliest period of contact. When European colonial sponsors and explorers worked to chart the earth and its waterways, they explicitly sought also to map the peoples of the world. To understand the crucial role that mapping played in forming both European expectations about North America and European actions toward other peoples there, we need to recognize the ways in which maps and mapping began to take center stage in much European culture in this period. As we shall see in later chapters, much of the contact between Native Americans and Europeans in North America was ultimately influenced more by Native Americans' assumptions and expectations, but Europeans initially approached colonization in North America with their own increasingly well-developed ideas about the centrality of mapping and cultural observation.

If we think first of mapping and navigation in their most literal forms, mapping, along with its sibling art, navigation, was a vitally important new tool in European expansion. This is a familiar story, but what is less well known is just how new both were in the sixteenth and seventeenth centuries. England experienced a revolution in mapping and cartographic understanding during the course of the sixteenth century.[2] Maps were quite uncommon and generally not well understood in England at the beginning of the sixteenth century. Throughout the century, maps and their uses became easily recognizable by English people from all walks of life. In his introduction to an English edition of Euclid's *Geometry*, sixteenth-century mathematician and astrologer John Dee famously wrote of the growing interest in maps that was sweeping the kingdom: "Of this Art [geometry] how great pleasure, and how manifold commodities do come unto us daily and hourly: of most men is perceived."[3]

Dee noted that English people were embracing maps as decorations and as tools for studying history. "While some," he wrote, used maps "to beautifie their hals, Parlers, Chambers, Galeries, Studies or Libraries with: other some, for things past, as battles fought, earthquakes, heavenly firings, and such occurrents, in histories mentioned: thereby lively, as it were, to view the place, the Region adjoyning, the distance from us: and such other circumstances."[4] Dee described several other popular uses of maps from the aesthetic to the scholarly to the practical: "Some other presently to view the large dominion of the Turk: the wide Empire of the Moscovite: and the little morsell of ground, where Christendome (by profession) is certainly known.... Some either, for their own journeys directing into far lands: or to understand of other mens travails."[5] He concluded by emphasizing how map crazy many Englishmen were becoming: "Some for one purpose, and some for another, liketh, loveth, getteth, and useth Maps, Charts, and Geographical Globes."[6] Significantly, Dee pointed out that one popular use for maps was to depict the scope of empires. As the first person to write of a British empire, John Dee well understood the connection between maps, colonization, and other imperial ventures.[7]

Even by the end of the sixteenth century, however, it was clear that maps had become better known as decorative objects and general guides to world geography than as the kind of guide for getting from place to place that we now take for granted. Growing numbers of English people may well have appreciated that the innovations in the new discipline of geography were responsible for the expansion of overseas trade that began to change the United Kingdom. However, the practical use of maps was a skill that remained restricted to a relatively small number of people. So few English people understood how to use a map as a functional geographical tool that educated writers saw a growing need to publish instructional manuals.

Thomas Blundeville justified his sixteenth-century guide to the use of maps in just such terms: "I Daylie see many that delight to looke on Mappes, and can point to England, France, Germanie, and to the East and West Indies, and to diuers other places therein described: but yet for want of skill in Geography, they knowe not with what maner of lines they are traced, nor what those lines do signifie, nor yet the true vse of Mappes in deed."[8] Blundeville promised that his book would help fill this gap.[9]

By the seventeenth century maps were everywhere. Printed maps, more than anything else, spread the idea of using maps among the public at large. In the late sixteenth century, Christopher Saxton's maps of English counties were woven into tapestries and reproduced on playing cards.[10] Moreover, European culture increasingly linked ideas about mapping, navigation, and seafaring. Early modern Europeans used them almost interchangeably to discuss a wide range of social and political issues, and they brought their cultural fascination with mapping, navigation, and seafaring to their encounters with other cultures. The growing interest in navigation is not surprising in light of European overseas expansion; however, the cultural and colonial influence of navigation on European culture was extraordinarily powerful. Europeans from all ranks of society were preoccupied with navigation in the sixteenth and seventeenth centuries, and navigation helped them to understand their own world and increasingly to make sense of less familiar ones.

Because systematic observation was an essential component of the art and skill of navigation, navigators' proficiency and their usual goal of trade or colonization were inextricably bound up with Europeans' interest in examining the natural world, as well as people from other cultures. Navigation absorbed the energies and imaginations of mariners, colonial promoters, and overseas merchants, but its influence and appeal did not end there. As changes in print and cartographic technologies increased Europeans' familiarity with mapping concepts and navigation techniques, Europeans extended the language and concepts from the practical problems of mapping and navigation and applied them also to a wide variety of political and cultural relationships.

Mapping and navigational metaphors offered conceptual tools that proved increasingly important in European culture. Authors of political pamphlets, theological treatises, and sermons found mapping, navigation, and seafaring metaphors ideally suited to make their arguments. For example, authors of very different tracts in an early seventeenth-century pamphlet debate each used mapping analogies to drive home points about social and political issues. They argued over the extent to which England needed to increase its foreign trade and colonial efforts, which was a proposition of great interest in the early seventeenth century. In a 1615 pamphlet called *The Trades Increase*, Robert Kayll used a map analogy to argue in favor of greater foreign exchange and to promote policies to alleviate distressingly bad economic and social conditions at home. With an analogy that was becoming increasingly familiar, he pointed out to the English nation the danger of unemployment:

> As the Cosmographers in their Maps, where in they haue described the habitable Globe, use to set downe in the extremity of their Cards, on vnknowne Regions and Climates, That beyond those places they haue noted there is nothing but sands without water, full of wilde beasts, or congealed seas, which no ship can saile . . . so may I write in the map of employment, that out of it, without it, is nothing but sordide idlenes, base condition, filling the minde with a hundred Chymeraes and grosse fantasies, and defiling both body and minde with dissolute courses and actions; like fat ground neglected, that bringeth forth a thousand sorts of weeds, or vnprofitable hearbs.[11]

To ensure that his readers understood that this "map" of unemployment applied to England, the pamphlet continued: "And with this disease is our Land affected, our people infected; whereby so many come to an vntimely & reproachfull death in the Land, & many more liue so dissolutely, and so wickedly on the seas"[12]

In rebuttal, Dudley Diggs wrote a pamphlet called *The Defence of Trade.* Diggs argued that Kayll had exaggerated England's problems; indeed, he implied that *The Trades Increase* was treasonous in its depiction of England's social problems, economic strength, and political will. He went even further and told his readers that such criticism could originate only from England's great enemy, Spain.[13] Interestingly, he used the language of mapping and navigation to make social and political points, just as the anonymous author of *The Trades Increase* had. In each case, the points under discussion in this pamphlet debate were social and economic problems, not actual mapmaking or navigation. Other English writers also found mapping and navigation imagery ideally suited for discussions of trade and commerce, particularly as the century wore on and European trade with other cultures increased. In 1638 Lewes Roberts published *The Marchants Mapp of Commerce*, which freely used both kinds of metaphors.[14] Roberts made it clear that he had written a practical guide to international trade and that he intended his text to be a kind of map.[15]

In the modern era, navigation and mapping have come to be seen as highly technical and specialized skills. Such distinctions did not apply in the sixteenth and seventeenth centuries, however. Navigation, mapping, and their related areas of knowledge indeed required technical knowledge and were certainly understood at the time to call for particular kinds of expertise.[16] Had they not, there would have been no need for geography and navigation instruction manuals. However, in the context of imperial contests and the nearly global expansion of European trade, concepts from navigation, cosmography, and cartography related so clearly to people's understandings of their world that they used metaphors, vocabulary, and concepts drawn from these technical, artisanal skills to discuss all kinds of social practices and experiences.[17]

Other writers, however, referred to navigation and mapmaking more directly as tools of political control. English poet and statesman Fulke Greville, the first Lord Brooke, wrote of maps as a crucial instrument of power available to monarchs. In *A Treatise of Monarchy*, which was probably written during the first two decades of the seventeenth century, Greville laid out the connection between political power, laws, and maps. He was the author of a report on trading conditions in the East and held numerous offices of state, so he well understood the influence of laws and maps. *A Treatise of Monarchy* stresses the necessity of maps to those who would wield political authority successfully:

> Yet in mans darknes since Church rites alone
> Cannot guard all the parts of government,
> Least by disorder states be overthrowne,
> Powre must use lawes, as her best instrument;
> Lawes bring Mappes, and Councellors that doe
> Shewe forth diseases, and redresse them too.[18]

A Treatise of Monarchy not only describes the use of maps as a tool of political authority but also alludes to maps and mapping as means of drawing cultural boundaries, just as laws were. In Greville's poem maps and political advisors ("Councellors") were tools for identifying problems ("diseases") and for finding solutions to them.

A Treatise of Monarchy also warns of the threat of unchecked social disorder. It is significant that Greville saw a clear connection between maps as tools for controlling disorder and establishing boundaries; also, sponsors of English colonial ventures would increasingly draw similar connections. The concern with checking disorder was an obvious one for political leaders, particularly in early seventeenth-century England. Authorities in colonial settings worried even more about how to contain disorder.

A number of scholars have written of the pervasive fear among English people in the first half of the seventeenth century that their society was disintegrating. Widely held perceptions of the growing numbers of wandering poor combined with the religious, political, and social upheavals of the civil war and interregnum to foster this concern.[19] In colonial settlements, political and social authority was often much more tenuous than in home countries, particularly in their early years. Moreover, Europeans were generally apprehensive that their cultures, which they regarded as civilized, would degenerate in uncivilized places where colonies were settled unless the most rigid attention were paid to policing the bounds of cultural mores.[20]

Early modern English people also worried explicitly about religious roots of disorder, and in the seventeenth century they found mapping and navigation metaphors to be especially compelling ways to discuss religious issues. English writers who focused on religious subjects used mapping and navigational concepts to make broad points about Christian cosmology, as well as their worries about spiritual decline and religious disorder. A number of writers described humankind as a map of God's intentions. In 1617 Samuel Purchas, the famous English colonial promoter, wrote that "man therefore was last created, as the end of the rest, an Epitome and Map of the World."[21] More than a decade later George Hakewill echoed Purchas's observation by writing that "*man* presents himselfe vpon this *Theater,* as being created last, though first intended, the *master* of the whole family, & chiefe Commauner in this great house, nay the master-peece, the abridgment, the mappe and modell of the *Vniverse.*"[22] For Purchas, when Caine killed Abel, "God . . . cursed CAINE from the earth, to be a runnagate, and wanderer thereon . . . restlesse in himselfe, hated of the World, despairing of reliefe from GOD, a liuely [i.e., living] Map of the deadly and damnable state of sinne and sinners."[23]

Navigation also served writers well as a way to make religious points, particularly when the metaphor of a journey helped to convey the writer's meaning. Later in the seventeenth century, an admirer of English minister Henry Smith wrote that "he was commonly called the silver-tongued Preacher . . . Their ears did so attend to his lips, their hearts to their ears, that he held the Rudder of their Affections in his hand, so that he could steer them whether he was pleased; and he was pleased to steer them onely to God's glory and their own good."[24]

Navigation, sea voyages, and the fear of shipwreck are themes that appear repeatedly in seventeenth-century English religious writings—in sermons, funeral orations, and exegeses of biblical texts.[25] Many English ministers relied on navigational metaphors to emphasize the need for souls to carefully plot a safe course through the dangers of this world. Many others used less explicit references to navigation itself but relied heavily on seafaring and sailing figures of speech.

In the context of early modern English culture, ideas about navigation and sea travel with its attendant threats of storms, piracy, and loss of life and property became interconnected. Successful sea voyages were not possible without careful navigation, and English people were quite aware of this throughout the early modern period. When they used concepts and metaphors from geography, navigation, and seafaring, they did so with the assumption that the three were integrally related. During that time, navigation not only made oceanic voyages possible but also offered one of the few means within human control of avoiding shipwreck.

Some writers celebrated new developments in navigation and made the connection between navigational skills and tools and mariners' ability to withstand the forces of nature while otherwise unprotected on the sea. In 1630

George Hakewill described the explosion of knowledge and technologies in the early modern period, which had been unknown in the ancient world. Hakewill singled out navigational developments for particular praise. The compass, he noted, changed everything.[26] The assumption that navigation and its tools offered one of the few protections against shipwreck lay beneath many of the sea travel metaphors that were widespread in this period. Even when writers used a metaphor simply of sea voyages or shipwreck, they did so within a context in which people assumed a close relationship between navigation and all other aspects of travel by sea.

Crucially, two momentous developments in English history combined to make mapping, trade, and all things related to the importance and hazards of navigation very appealing to English people in the 1630s, 1640s, and 1650s. The first was the turmoil of the English civil war, which coincided with the second great development, the first sustained English push toward colonies. The 1630s witnessed significant English population growth in both New England and Virginia, the two mainland areas of English colonization in North America.[27] And English writers saw mapping and navigation metaphors everywhere.

Additionally, in the turbulent religious strife of seventeenth-century England, the looming destruction of one's ship (or its preservation) seemed an especially meaningful figure of speech to many writers, as, for instance, in this piece from the 1640s: "The poore afflicted Church . . . grievously and greatly afflicted in sorrowes of all sorts, outward and inward tryalls, as . . . like a Ship tossed in tempests."[28] The same writer described the journey of the Christian soul to salvation as a sea voyage: "But this discovery I confesse is a dangerous voyage, full of difficulties . . . yet . . . we will . . . put forth to Sea with the first faire gale of wind he shall please to fill our Sailes with, and advance forward on this dangerous voyage."[29] Another warned that people who failed to think of their sins while on earth were like a sailor who allowed calm seas to lull him into complacency instead of thinking of the coming storm.[30]

Because careful observation of the weather and sea conditions was an essential part of good navigation, early modern readers would have understood the navigational implications of the failure to follow the practice without explicit reminders. Sins of omission and inattention were frequently compared to a pilot's failure to be alert at sea, leading invariably to the destruction of his vessel. In 1665, looking back on the period of the English civil war and the interregnum, John Spencer complained: "Thus howsoever, the bold Pretences to Revelations, Prophecy, and a greater intimacy with the Divine Spirit, proved the great Evils of those particular Times, causing many . . . to *make shipwrack of Conscience* and a *sound Mind*."[31]

Making an even more direct analogy between Christian and navigational guidance, Robert Mandevill published *Timothies Taske or A Christian Sea-Card* in 1619. Like more prosaic sea cards or navigational charts, the "Christian Sea-Card" offered sailing instructions for the soul's journey "through the coastes of a peaceable conscience to a peace constant and a Crowne immortall."[32] The whole volume followed the navigational premise of its title. Mandevill compared the elements of the Christian tradition to early modern international trade on the seas and incorporated a distinctly Protestant slant: "The Prophets are Gods factors, sent to negotiate in these remote Regions. There traffick is the reconciliation & gain of soules. the Church is the ship wherein they imbarke, the world the sea whereon she floates, the word the card that directeth her course."[33]

As we have already seen, religion was by no means the only subject that lent itself to mapping or navigational tropes. In the third edition of his massive collection of travel narratives, Purchas cast his eye toward English society after more than a thousand pages of text describing the rest of the world and proudly noted that "England presents it selfe to mine eyes, representing to my minde a Mappe of Heuen and Earth, in the freedome of Bodie and Soule, yea where our subiection and seruice is Freedome (which I haue not elsewhere found in all my Perambulation of the World)."[34]

If mapping imagery readily lent itself to discussions of religion and history, mapping and navigational figures of speech also seemed ideal for describing politics and current affairs. In a published sermon, Daniel Dike assured his listeners in 1617 that Christ would weather the storms of earthly turmoil with them. "Why then should wee bee so fearefull, O wee of little faith?" he asked. "Because . . . the sea rageth, and the waues thereof storme, and threaten shipwracke? Yea, but let vs content our selues, Christ Iesus is in the ship with vs."[35] For English people, the power of mapping and navigation phrases continued throughout the first half of the seventeenth century. In 1645, more than thirty years after Daniel Dike's sermon, William Goode preached to the House of Commons and told them "the sooner . . . a Government with Scripture warrant may be fully executed, the sooner you may expect to bring the Ship of the Common-wealth into the harbour of a happy Peace."[36]

It was no accident that the influence of all things related to maps and navigation spread throughout English culture just as England was pursuing colonies and expanded international trade in search of empire, and nowhere is the connection between maps and colonial ventures clearer than in a moment described in the records of the Council for New England. In June of 1623, members of the council presented James I with "a plott of all the Coastes & lands of New England, devided into twenty pts, each pt conteyning two shares. And twenty lotts conteyning the sd [said] Double shares made upp in little bales of waxe, And the names of twenty pattenties by whom these lotts were to be drawne."[37] After members of the council met with the king and presented him with a map of New England, the assembled group drew lots that were keyed to areas depicted on the map. In some ways this is one of the clearest illustrations of the kind of connection between mapping and colonies that we would expect. But there were other kinds of connections as well.

The Council for New England's materials, both the published accounts of their efforts to establish plantations in New England and their manuscript records, discuss Indian affairs and relations with Algonquians in terms of alliances, sometimes explicitly and sometimes implicitly. Moreover, while they also wrote about the eventual desirability of Christian and cultural conversion programs by which New England's native peoples would become Christian English Indians, alliances were to be the foundation of good English-Algonquian relations. Everything else, including conversion, could follow from successful associations. More than that, Ferdinando Gorges (one of the most active members of the Council for New England) and at least some of his fellow council members, saw intercultural cooperation as being absolutely necessary to ensure the success of their colonial venture. Gorges combined his quest for geographical knowledge with his search for methods of establishing intercultural partnerships. He used Algonquian captives as sources of geographical and political knowledge.

When he was around seventy, Gorges looked back on his colonial ventures and wrote "of the use I made of the Natives."[38] He unselfconsciously described the things he had learned from the Algonquian men he held captive in England: "The longer I conversed with them, the better hope they gave me of those parts where they did inhabit, as proper for our uses."[39] He became particularly convinced of the suitability of New England as the location for his colony, "especially when I found what goodly Rivers, stately Islands, and safe harbours those parts abounded with."[40] Not wanting to leave anything to chance, Gorges described how he had his captives prepare maps for him, complete with ethnographic and political information, "and having kept them full three yeares, I made them able to set me downe what great Rivers ran up into the Land, what men of note were seated on them, what power they were of, how allyed, what enemies they had, and the like of which in his proper place."[41]

Having taught the Algonquian men how to make a European-style map, Gorges hoped later to take advantage of skills they already possessed. He planned for his Algonquian tutors to serve as pilots of his ships when they reached New England. Gorges wrote that he trusted the Algonquians' descriptions of New England's waterways more than English navigators' claims because he "understood the Natives themselves to be exact Pilots for that Coast, having been accustomed to frequent the same, both as Fishermen and in passing along the shoare to see their enemies, that dwelt to the Northward of them."[42]

Almost two generations before James I and members of the Council for New England met over a map to divide up sections of New England, Richard

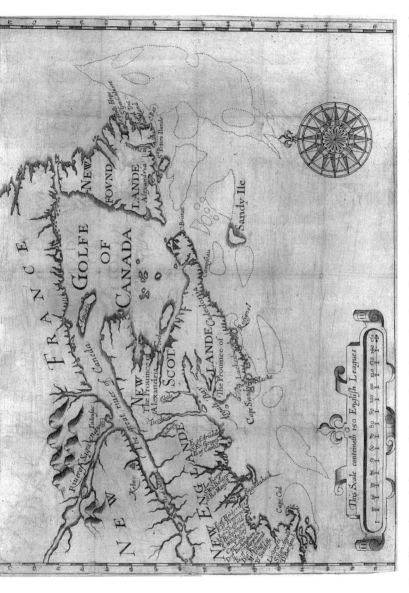

FIGURE 2. Sir William Alexander's map of New England shows the plots allocated to the members of the Council for New England. Ferdinando Gorges's plot is third from the bottom. From Sir William Alexander, Earl of Stirling, *An Encouragement to Colonies*, London, 1624. Courtesy of the John Carter Brown Library at Brown University.

Hakluyt the younger published *Divers voyages touching the discouerie of America*. Hakluyt hoped to promote exactly the kind of North American colonial planning that English sponsors were in fact undertaking by the 1620s, and so he printed a number of tracts originally written for other colonial ventures. One of the most useful of those was a set of instructions that the Muscovy Company had provided to its employees on an earlier venture. The Muscovy Company's merchants insisted that their employees travel with a selection of commodities chosen to impress important people along the way. Maps were among the items the merchants thought were most important, and they did not mean the kinds of maps and portolan charts to guide their employees on the trip.

For these anticipated meetings with new peoples, the Muscovy Company wanted to send maps that represented the territory, wealth, and market power of the English kingdom. "Take with you the mappe of Englande set out in faire colours, one of the biggest sort I meane, to make shewe of your Countrie from whence you come," they advised. To make sure that their factors conveyed the company's potential as a trading partner, the Muscovy Company merchants believed the ships should take a second map: "and also the large mappe of London, to make shewe of your Citte. And let the river bee drawne full of shippes of all sortes, to make the more shewe of your greate trade and trafficke in trade of merchandise."[43] The Muscovy Company recognized that maps could bridge cultural differences without relying on language, and that made maps themselves important aids for establishing intercultural trading relationships.

In the sixteenth and seventeenth centuries, maps and all things related to mapping took on a wide range of uses and meanings for Europeans. English people absorbed ideas about mapping and seafaring and used them to make sense of many things that appeared scarcely related to questions of geography or the technical problems of oceanic sailing. Colonial expansion was of course much more directly dependent on the technical information that maps, sea charts, and navigation manuals provided. However, here, too, people extended ideas from mapping and navigation far beyond practical questions of distance and location.

When European colonial sponsors and explorers worked to map the earth and its waterways, they explicitly sought also to map the peoples of the world. George Hakewill spelled out the connection between navigation and the gathering of information about other peoples and nations. He celebrated the fact that "by meanes of it are the commodities of all countries discovered, trade, and trafique, and humane societie maintained, their severall formes of government and religion observed."[44] Hakewill asserted that navigation was enabling God to bring all nations into a single commonwealth. According to Hakewill, the objective of all of the developments in navigation was the expansion of Christendom. Nonetheless, what is most interesting for our purposes is his assumption that ethnographic observation and navigation were integrally linked. Like Hakewill, promoters of English imperial and economic expansion increasingly urged mariners and travelers to collect information about other cultures they encountered. Mapping and navigation, in other words, also had to take careful accounting of new peoples.

Writing in the late sixteenth century, William Bourne laid out many of these objectives, and Bourne's assumptions would become widely shared by Europeans involved in international trade and colonial expansion throughout the next century. In the preface to his readers, Bourne urged travelers to systematically observe the countries and cultures they encountered. Among the categories Bourne believed essential were knowledge of any fortifications and defensive capabilities of the particular community or nation, how its rulers raised and maintained a fighting force, whether it had access to navigable waterways, the names of its rulers and its form of government, their allies and enemies, and the kind of trade in which they participated.

Bourne urged his readers to note, for instance, "when that you do come into any Citie or Towne, view of what manner of grounde it standeth vpon, and what it may be or is subiect vnto, and in like maner how it is fortified and prouided, and how it is maintained, and whether it standeth vpon any hauen or riuer, that hath vent vnto the Sea."[45] Just as importantly, Bourne advised his travelers "also to learne what nation, Country, Citie, or Towne that may most annoy them, and also what Countrye, Citie or Towne doth most pleasure them, and by what trade or Marchaundize they are principallest maintained by."[46] Alliance systems, defensive capabilities, local customs, and trade networks: the pursuit of this type of information would shape European activities throughout the early modern world, including those in North America. Throughout the late sixteenth and seventeenth centuries, a wide variety of European materials focused on the need for Europeans to make contacts with new peoples and to gather and preserve information about them.

Navigation manuals, like maps and colonial promotional narratives, focused readers' attention on making contacts with new groups of people, as well as on learning about new lands. In the fifteenth century, changes in shipbuilding, mathematics, and astronomy began making oceanic navigation possible. Subsequently, the success of Portuguese and Spanish seafarers, traders, and colonizers in using oceanic navigation as a means to great personal and national wealth sparked enterprises in other countries designed to move in on the expanding imperial and commercial opportunities revealed by Portuguese and Spanish successes. This interest in navigation operated at several social and conceptual levels. Although navigation itself was not considered a subject worthy of university attention, elite men were nonetheless interested in it as a practical application of the latest mathematics and astronomy that had tremendous potential for personal and national glory and wealth. Well-to-do women were interested in participating in seagoing ventures as patrons, and a number of them were financial backers of voyages, colonial ventures, travel narratives, and geographical treatises.[47]

For common men and women, the expansion of interest in navigation often created greater employment possibilities, either in colonies accessible by sea or, for men, aboard ship. Moreover, published books of instruction, especially navigation manuals and sea grammars, targeted men from many social levels and explicitly reinforced the expectation that an enterprising man could use such knowledge to go on voyages of discovery, thereby earning honor, glory, and riches for himself and perhaps for family and monarch as well. Sea grammars and navigational manuals were often unambiguous about their author's expectation of reaching men from many social levels, including privileged men. In the dedicatory epistle to his book, *An Accidence or Path-way to experience*, Captain John Smith noted that he did not intend his book of instruction for mariners or sailors, who probably did not need instruction. Rather, he hoped to reach "many young Gentlemen and Valient spirits of all sorts" because they "do desire to trye their Fortunes at sea." For them, Smith's book provided "an intraduction for such as wants experience, and are desirous to learne what belongs to a Sea-man."[48]

In our minds and theirs, colonization related to all of this. Navigation, however, had more than just those applications we would consider practical. It related directly to ideas and practices of colonization in several ways. Because sea voyages were undertaken as an essential step in expanding trade or in the imperial control of a kingdom or republic, the practice of navigation included certain skills thought necessary for colonial enterprises; principal among them was the art or practice of observation. Colonial sponsors, for instance, sometimes hired artists for exploratory and colonial expeditions and supplied them with detailed instructions that explained what they should observe. The advice also described how expedition artists should observe and record what they saw so that others could share their knowledge.

Humphrey Gilbert's planned 1582 or 1583 expedition to the east coast of North America included an artist named Thomas Bavin.[49] Bavin received highly detailed directions to record and describe specific items as realistically as possible.[50] Although the expedition did not actually occur, the instructions to Bavin remain one of the best examples of a kind of colonial planning that was widespread in the late sixteenth and early seventeenth centuries, although few samples have survived intact. His directive included sixty-eight separate points to guide this North American prose and drawing survey. His sponsors directed Bavin to "drawe to lief one of each kinde of thing that is strange to us in England . . . all strange birdes beastes fishes plantes hearbes Trees and fruictes."[51] They did not stop at flora and fauna, however, but told him to observe people just as carefully. They wanted him to draw "also the figures and shapes on men and woeman in their apparrell as also their manner of wepons in every place as you shall finde them differing."[52]

Systematic observation and recording of sights and local customs were widely promoted as the patriotic duty of travelers, not just of those hired as employees on colonial ventures. In a book promoting travel, for example, Thomas Palmer advised that merchants who traveled with letters of marque should "be carefull to set downe in their seuerall Sea Charts, euerie thing of speciall note; as Countries, Hauens, Creekes, Iles, Rockes, Gulfes, Shooles, Sands, Shelues, and such like: whereby others after them may make vse thereof, to the profit of the Common-weale. And when these shall returne, to make a true relation (if they be demanded) of euerie accident durring their voyages."[53] Travel accounts built on one other, as each included new information about coastlines, sea routes, land travel, local languages, customs, political networks, and alliances.

For Europeans, the effort to amass such information became increasingly global in the late sixteenth and early seventeenth centuries. European expeditions to Asia and Africa were part of this exploration and data gathering, and many of the people who promoted colonization in North America also reviewed and promoted works by travelers and expeditions to other regions of the world, all using similar fact-gathering techniques. Willem Lodewijcksz's *Teerste Boek, Historie van Indien* provided drawings of people, flora, and fauna in various regions, including Madagascar, Java, and the Cape of Good Hope.[54] Lodewijcksz's account is very similar to the kind of survey Thomas Bavin was to have undertaken and that Thomas Harriot and John White did undertake in the 1580s in Roanoke.

Seafarers who traveled widely were in a particularly good position to acquire valuable geographic and ethnographic knowledge. Some of the most influential navigation manuals presented observational skill as an essential component of the art of navigation. One of the best known manuals, *Het Licht der Zeevaert* [The Light of Navigation], was written and published by Willem Blaeu, who worked for several years as cartographer under the patronage of the Dutch West India Company, the sponsor of the Dutch North American colony of New Netherland. *Het Licht der Zeevaert* incorporated the very latest technical and theoretical ideas about navigation. It included Tycho Brahe's astronomical observations and revisions in coastlines and channel depths. Blaeu's ongoing efforts to update his navigation guide with the latest data in each reprint set his work apart from that of others.

Blaeu, however, had to overcome considerable prejudice against printed materials. In the early seventeenth century, most Europeans still assumed that printed maps, rutters (sailing directions), sea charts, and navigation manuals were inferior to manuscript materials. Printed materials were thought to fall quickly behind the most up-to-date knowledge, which changed constantly on the basis of new reports.[55] Blaeu, then, sought to persuade seafarers that his work was different and more current than any other sources, manuscript or printed.[56] One of the most important methods he used to ensure that his charts and maps contained the very latest knowledge, drawn directly from experience, was to confer with seafarers themselves.

Blaeu's shop was on the Damrak in Amsterdam, where he had constant access to pilots and seafarers, from whom he could obtain the most recent reports on changes in channels, as well as new routes and new places. However, to persuade people to buy his navigation manuals, Blaeu confronted the prejudice against printed materials head-on. In the process, he also described how he worked to ensure accurate knowledge: "Amongst manie Pilots there is an opinion, that they had rather use the written Cardes, then such as are printed, esteeming the printed Cardes to be imperfect, and say that the written Cardes are much better and perfecter, they meane the written Cardes that are dayly made by men, are everie day corrected, & the printed never."[57]

Blaeu went on to correct this misunderstanding: "But herein they are not a little deceived, for the printed Cardes in each respect are as good, yea & better then the written, for that the printed Cardes are once in everie point with al care and diligence made perfect, in regard that they serve for many."[58] In fact, not only did he argue that the printed versions were better because they were more accurate, but he also took issue with the idea that handwritten sea charts were updated more quickly: "The Sea-cardes that are written can not be made so sound nor with such speed, because so much cost for one peece alone were to much, but are all one after the other, with the least labour copied out, and many tymes by such persons that have litle or no knowledge therein."[59] In the end, he insisted that it was as easy and as efficient to correct printed sea charts as handwritten ones and that the former were more accurate and more expertly revised.

According to Blaeu, direct experience was the key to accurate knowledge. His success was based on this belief, and his firm was known for interviewing mariners as soon as they docked in Amsterdam. He repeatedly emphasized the necessity of careful observation and urged seafarers to combine the use of reliable maps and sea charts with personal experience. Blaeu understood that knowledge changed: winds shifted; harbors silted up; governments rose and fell and with them access to markets. Basic navigational skills were of course essential for seafarers, but Blaeu's navigation manual, the most famous in all of Europe, recognized that such proficiency was only the beginning. He conceded that a good pilot must understand degrees of the compass, the constellations and how to navigate by them, the use of the cross-staff and astrolabe, depth soundings and how to take them, and the meaning of changes in wind, water, and coastlines. *Het Licht der Zeevaert* provided instructions for all of these essential skills. Yet for Blaeu, mastery of these techniques was only the foundation of good navigation, not the sum of it:

> These aforesaid rules although that they are so necessarie & needfull for a Pilote to know, that without the knowledge of them he can be no good Pilot, to goe anie long voyage, yet are they not sufficient to make a good Pilot, that is al are not good Pilots that understand them well. For first a good Pilot must besides them be expert at Sea, as the principall thing, which no man can learne by any speculation, but by his own experience.[60]

Secondhand knowledge, whether acquired from books, maps, sea charts, or other seafarers, had to be mixed with considerable personal experience to allow for "good gessing," one of the most crucial abilities of the best early modern pilots.[61] Seafarers had to be able to learn from each experience and to reapply the new knowledge on their voyages. The ability to reproduce observed experience in the form of maps, charts, and drawings was as crucial to the art of navigation as making the observations in the first place because memory alone might fail. In this respect, navigational skills carried over quite readily into colonial planning and intercultural contacts. Blaeu, for instance, directed pilots to record their observations carefully, and his instructions echoed those that colonial sponsors gave to their employees: "Likewise when you passe by an strange Countrie, and sayle along so near by it that you may plainly see it, then take the counterfeit or forme thereof with a penne, to knowe in what manner they shewe themselves upon such strokes of the compasse."[62] Mariners should also take depth soundings and, most important, record their findings: "& there let the lead fall, to see what depth and ground is there, which for your memorie you must also note, for that which you marke in that manner will staye longer by you, then that which you have but simplie seen, and heard of an other."[63]

Advocates of the art of navigation and observers of new places also described the act of creating representations of their observations as "counterfeiting." Today we associate the term with something essentially false and designed to deceive, as in the case of counterfeit money. That meaning was also conveyed in early modern English and early modern Dutch by the word "conterfeytsel"; however, another now-archaic meaning was also widely used by early modern speakers of English and Dutch and is the one implied in Blaeu's instructions. Thus in the context of seafaring and colonial observations, "counterfeiting" implied falseness only to the degree that early moderns who used the term were noting explicitly that representations of things were not the things themselves.[64]

Indeed, for early modern Europeans the best representations re-presented experience. Navigation manuals, travel narratives, and colonial promotional materials reflected Europeans' assumption that the best way to recapture and convey experience for others could perhaps include a mixture of visual and textual information. Accurate representations, in other words, could consist of written narrative as an accompaniment to drawings and maps. For instance, in his book promoting travel, Thomas Palmer not only advised travelers to note harbors, waterways, shoals, and other important navigational markers on their sea charts but also urged them when they returned home "to make a true relation . . . of euerie accident durring their voyage."[65] Moreover, because the best representations re-presented experience, the most reliable and authentic approach for written accounts was a plain style because it was thought to resemble an unadorned experience most accurately.[66] People who counterfeited what they saw had an obligation to make their representations adhere as closely as possible to their observations; thus Thomas Bavin was to "drawe to lief" the things he saw in North America. Similarly, Sir Walter Raleigh's artist, John White, who accompanied two voyages to Raleigh's Virginia colony, described his work as counterfeiting experience. In the title to his watercolor drawings, White introduced his work as "the pictures of sondry things collected and counterfeited according to the truth."[67]

John White has long been regarded as a gifted artist whose images provided remarkably accurate depictions of the people and natural world of the Outer Banks and the Caribbean. Indeed, the entire endeavor undertaken by Thomas Harriot and John White was a kind of mapping and ethnographic survey, in some ways analogous to Christopher Saxton's county-by-county mapping of England for Elizabeth I.[68] During their ten months in Roanoke, Harriot and White carefully coordinated the information that each collected, and both their assignment and their method of carrying it out were collaborative and comprehensive. Using Harriot's mathematical knowledge and White's artistic skills, they made two maps of the North American Atlantic coastline in the course of their project.[69] In addition, they compiled an impressive survey of information about the language, customs, appearance, and political organization of coastal Carolina Algonquians.

The observations of Thomas Harriot and John White have sometimes been regarded as highly unusual records of an almost unique endeavor. However, theirs was one of many such projects undertaken by Europeans throughout the Atlantic world in the sixteenth and seventeenth centuries. David Beers Quinn, for instance, has estimated that less than half of the journal material from early English contacts with New England known to have existed in 1625 has survived.[70] We know of these enterprises, but unfortunately, many of the records from the late sixteenth and early seventeenth centuries were lost or destroyed.[71] Similar fates befell journals, drawings, maps, and other materials from colonial ventures to other regions. John White himself had already made ethnographic drawings of Inuit peoples, which he probably completed while serving as recording artist with Frobisher's second voyage in 1577.[72] His drawings were greatly influenced by and are often compared with those of Jacques le Moyne, the artist who accompanied the 1564 Huguenot colonial expedition of René de Laudonnière to Florida.[73] However, a number of others also engaged in very similar projects of observation and description of lands and peoples they had seen.

Early modern Europeans considered the need to observe people, their customs, language, political system, military capability, and alliances as part of the same enterprises as making maps, charting new sea routes, or surveying natural resources. It was all necessary information, and it was all part of mapping the world. Another sixteenth-century compendium of drawings and written descriptions of life in the Caribbean, for instance, depicts people, as well as plant and animal species. This collection is known as the Drake manuscript because it may have been compiled by French artists traveling with Sir Francis Drake.[74] The Drake manuscript has been comparatively understudied because it came to the attention of scholars only in 1983, yet it belongs squarely in the tradition of the work that expedition artist Thomas Bavin was expected to do and Thomas Harriot and John White actually did in Roanoke.

Nor were English and French ventures the only ones to undertake early colonial ethnographic and natural world reconnaissance. The Spanish imperial bureaucracy made several attempts to create systematic mapping information of New Spain, and the Casa de Contratación served as an administrative clearinghouse for American and Caribbean maps of all kinds.[75] In addition to that material, Francisco Hernández and a team of painters, a cartographer, and specimen collectors compiled fifteen large manuscript volumes of notes and drawings of Mexico from 1571 to 1577 for Philip II. Unfortunately for historians, all of these volumes were destroyed in a fire in the Escorial in 1671.[76]

Dutch colonial promoters sponsored similar efforts. In the 1640s artists Frans Post and Albert Eckhout, among others, prepared an array of chalk and watercolor drawings and oil paintings of Brazil for Johan Maurits, prince of Nassau.[77] In addition, several Dutch accounts of trade and colonial voyages to Africa, Asia, and the Americas included material very similar to that compiled by Harriot and White and that envisioned for Thomas Bavin to make. Willem Lodewijcksz, for instance, included engraved drawings of native peoples from the Cape of Good Hope and Madagascar in his account of several Dutch voyages. Among other representations, Lodewijcksz presented a sea view of many different aquatic species, as well as an illustration of native dances with various kinds of flora arranged in a row in the foreground; both of these are strikingly similar to some of White's representations of Roanoke.[78]

When Willem Kieft was called back to the Dutch Republic from his position as director general of the Dutch West India Company's North American colony of Nieuw Nederlandt, he carried with him maps, mineral samples, and written descriptions of the region. His materials also included accounts of the colony, many of which would certainly have provided information about Native Americans. The ship on which Kieft traveled went down, however, and all of his records mapping New Netherland and its peoples were lost at sea. The sinking of the *Princess*, the ship on which Kieft was sailing, was considered a great blow to the colony in part because of this loss. When a committee from New Netherland sent a petition for aid to the Dutch States General in 1643, it specifically noted the loss of the *Princess* and its cargo as one of the costly tribulations suffered by the colony: "For in her were lost very exact Maps; fully a hundred different samples of Minerals and numerous Remonstrances and accounts of New Netherland."[79]

Greg Dening has argued that for Europeans the eighteenth century was an age of observing and measuring things, and he has persuasively demonstrated that European imperial activities in the Pacific involved systematic projects of this type.[80] In the sixteenth and seventeenth centuries, Europeans engaged in careful observation and measurement all around the Atlantic, and as they mapped the Atlantic world and its peoples, they constantly looked for opportunities for new alliances. In this, the Atlantic world was merely one part of an almost global effort. It is essential to realize that European colonial activities throughout the Americas were but one aspect of similar imperial and merchant capitalist undertakings in Asia, Africa, parts of Scandinavia, and Europe itself. This explains why Richard Hakluyt assumed that instructions for Muscovy Company employees who might meet the Great Khan in Asia would also be applicable for merchants and colonizers seeking new alliances in North America.

Native Americans and Africans, then, were not the only people who were subjected to the ethnographic scrutiny of European colonists, travelers, and artists. Europeans also made country-by-country surveys of their own continent in which they mapped its peoples. In a treatise published in the early seventeenth century, Robert Stafforde, for example, included cultural and ethnic judgments about people from Spain (united with Portugal), France, Germany, Belgium, the United Provinces, Italy, Hungary, Poland, Turkey, Russia, and Iceland, as well as Africa, China, and America.[81]

Stafforde's assessments of other Europeans were often as xenophobic and critical as those in many European accounts of Native Americans and Africans. Indeed, that was the case with his attitude toward non-English people more generally. Of Spain and Portugal, he wrote that "the inhabitants of it are verie ceremonious, superstitious, proude, hypocrites, laborious, addicted more then any other nation vnto Melancholy, and descended of the Gothes, Saracens, and Iewes."[82] Poland was noteworthy because all forms of religion were thought to be tolerated there, a practice that Stafforde deduced was the source of a popular saying: "If any one hath lost his religion, let him goe into Poland, and he shall finde it." That situation was not unlike the one he described for Africa: "The Inhabitants . . . are generally very black, of countenance rude, barbarous, and of vnciuill [uncivil] behavior, addicted to all sorts of religion, of Gentiles, Iewes, Turkes, Christians, and such like."[83]

Moreover, Stafforde's emphasis on Russian religious and funerary customs was quite similar in interest to many accounts of Native American spirituality. For Europeans in the sixteenth and seventeenth centuries, especially for those involved in international trade or colonial ventures, there was no doubt that knowledge of other people's religion was necessary in order to make judgments about whether they were likely to be friends or foes, allies or enemies. Thus Europeans collected this information from throughout the world. Stafforde's account of Russian religious practices involving the dead echoed many of the concerns that shaped John White's drawings and Thomas Harriot's description of Algonquian leaders' tombs. According to Harriot, "under the tombs of their Weroans, or chief lords, they build a scaffold nine or ten feet high. . . .They cover this with mats and upon them they lay the dead bodies of their chiefs."[84] He went on to describe the process of drying and preserving the remains:

> First the intestines are taken out; then the skin is removed and all the flesh cut from the bones and dried in the sun. When it is well dried, they wrap it in mats, which they place at the feet. Then the bones, still held together by the ligaments, are covered with the skin and made to look as if the flesh had not been taken away. They wrap each corpse in its own skin after it has been thus treated and lay it in its rightful order beside the bodies of the other chiefs.[85]

Finally, Harriot emphasized the religious elements of the interment: "Near the bodies they place their idol, for they are convinced that it keeps the bodies of their chiefs from all harm."[86] About Russia, Stafforde wrote, "They are also very superstitious, having many foolish ceremonies, and absurd solemnities, as the consecrating of Riuers once in a yeare, the burying of their dead with a pair of shoes on their feet, and a staffe in one hand, signifying a great iourney which they haue to goe: and a letter in the other vnto S. Nicholas, for their readier admission into heaven."[87]

Navigation manuals played an important role in promoting the collection of the kind of extensive ethnographic information writers like Robert

Stafforde gathered. Although one might expect that these handbooks would serve a specialized technical purpose by explaining the use of compass, cross-staff, and various other navigational aids, they also discussed techniques that were directly connected to colonial ventures and intercultural contacts, such as specific instructions on how to observe people, as well as land and waterways. Both maps and navigation manuals demonstrated the importance of placing people in several different ways. Europeans wanted, of course, to know where lands were located and people lived, but they also wanted to know the identity and position of each new group's allies and enemies. Early modern Europeans saw mapping and navigation as parts of a larger whole and as explicitly connected to colonial expansion.

In other words, as far as colonial promoters were concerned, alliances formed an integral part of the context of mapping in the sixteenth and early seventeenth centuries. It was not just that maps might serve as useful aids in setting up initial trade alliances or that establishing contacts with new peoples might provide additional knowledge for European maps, although both of these were certainly important. Mapping, navigation, and ethnography were also part of the same, larger, empire-building endeavor for early modern Europeans.[88] Travel narratives, maps, portolan charts, and navigation manuals were all based on the assumption that studying people was part of observing the world and recording that knowledge.

Part of what it meant to observe and map the peoples of the world was to know who lived where, what religion they practiced, and who their allies and enemies were, as well as other relevant customs, especially those regarding trade and diplomacy. Edward Herbert, the first Lord Herbert of Cherbury, wrote about the need to promote greater study of geography in England. He linked geographical knowledge of lands with political knowledge of other cultures, such as their alliances and enmities: "It will bee fitt to study Geography with exactnes soe much as may teach a Man the scituation of all Countrys in the wholle world together with which It will bee requisite to learne something concerning the Governments manners and Religions either Ancient or new as also the Interests of state and Relations in Amity or strength in which they stand to their Neighbors."[89] This is precisely what Ferdinando Gorges had been doing with his Algonquian captives, and it accomplished exactly what Edward Herbert had said the study of geography might enable people to do. Because Gorges had studied American geography and political partnerships not only in books but also with American tutors, the difference was one that explicitly included intercultural alliances.

Similarly, other colonial sponsors, colonists, and explorers were intensely interested in learning as much as possible about North America and the Caribbean. Consequently, from their earliest contacts they sought information about natural resources that could be used as commodities for trade and industry. That was an important part of Harriot and White's mission at Roanoke, as well as what Thomas Bavin's employers had intended him to do. Historians have long understood that Europeans' quest for extractive mineral wealth and other colonial riches played a major role in motivating these European ventures. However, scholars have paid less attention to another critical element in early European enterprises and voyages of discovery. From the beginning Europeans also sought information about the polities of the people living in an area, their likely status as ally or enemy, and their civil and military authorities. Sixteenth- and early seventeenth-century European mapmakers were as concerned with mapping the body politic as with charting lands and waterways. Indeed, the body politic was a central social metaphor.[90]

Many European-made maps of North America illustrate the careful attention that European mapmakers paid to presenting as much information about Native Americans as possible. John Smith's map of Virginia is one good example of this degree of interest: It notes the locations of various Indian peoples in different fonts, while the variation in font size suggested each group's relative strength. The name "Powhatan," for instance, dominates the map, just as the Powhatan paramount chiefdom was the primary power in the region. Names such as "Monacans" were visually much smaller and therefore less dominant, which is also an accurate reflection of their relative influence in the area. Smith's map is particularly interesting because it does not merely illustrate European territorial claims but also clearly presents England's claims within the context of North America and its native peoples.

Smith juxtaposed the Stuart royal arms in the center and larger images that represent Indian political and military presences. For example, the large picture of the warrior in the upper right represents the Susquehannocks' military strength (Smith was particularly interested in establishing trade relationships with the Susquehannocks). Impressed with their size, military strength, and trade items, he decided they were a major power in the region, as indeed they increasingly were.[91] He noted that, when visiting other native groups, he saw "many hatchets, knives, peeces of iron, and brasse . . . amongst them, which they reported to have from the Susquehannocks, a mightie people and mortall enemies with the Massawomeks."[92] Later Smith learned that Susquehannocks were trading with the French, which made establishing an English alliance with them even more important.[93] He feared that a French-Susquehannock relationship presented a rival alliance that could undermine English Virginia as both an economic threat to English-Indian trade and a military danger to English colonial security.

Smith's map also depicted Powhatan political and military power with a cartouche of an Indian king holding audience; the Powhatan image was opposite

FIGURE 3. Captain John Smith's map of Virginia uses Maltese crosses to show the limits of his personal geographic and ethnographic knowledge. Note the prominent placement of the Susquehannock warrior at right; the territory under his feet is designated as belonging to the Susquehannocks. Smith also shows the Massawomecks as having territory above the Susquehannock man, and, of course, Smith emphasizes the power and territory of Wahunsonacock, or Powhatan. Courtesy of the John Carter Brown Library at Brown University.

the Susquehannock warrior.[94] As Smith understood the political landscape of the greater Chesapeake region, the Powhatans and the Susquehannocks were the two major powers in the area. In his use of these images and names in various fonts, Smith clearly laid out his recognition of the Indian civil and political authority over the region. The result is that his map symbolically depicts Indian and English control in Virginia. Indeed, it conveys both Virginia's and England's aspirations for Virginia. It is not surprising that Smith never questioned the Stuart claim to the territory. On the contrary, his map was part of a narrative intended to promote further colonization in Virginia. Yet, despite that (or perhaps as an integral part of that colonial enterprise), Smith also sought to demonstrate that other people lived in Virginia and that their strengths had to be understood and dealt with before England's hopes for the area could be realized.

Captain John Smith's depictions of native people's political organization, social structure, military strengths, locations, and alliances were impressively thorough and remarkably accurate, but they were not unique. John White also mapped social and political authority for Sir Walter Raleigh and future sponsors and colonists. He drew many pictures of Algonquian men, women, and children and took careful note of tattoos, scarification, and body painting that indicated social status and political clout. These images of people were a kind of map of Algonquian social structure and political leadership that provided essential knowledge. In a drawing of warrior marks, White carefully reproduced symbols that these fighters wore raised on their backs.[95] He noted that each symbol represented the warrior's home village or his allegiance to a particular sachem. White did not provide this information so that colonial sponsors in England or readers in Europe could identify a Roanoke or Pomeoc warrior should they meet one, although the knowledge might have been useful for future colonists. Understanding internal Algonquian political allegiances and social status could be crucially important for English colonists seeking to establish new alliances of their own. White's drawing served as a chart or depiction of Algonquian bodies politic as mapped onto the corporeal bodies of Indian warriors.

White also drew images of tattoos and body paint and took careful note of the social distinctions that such decorations conveyed in Carolina Algonquian culture. He drew several representations of elite Indian women and meticulously reproduced their body decorations. White's particular attention to Native Americans' social rank and adornment suggests a parity between English social distinctions and those he and Harriot found in sixteenth-century Virginia. White's illustrations did not represent savagery—quite the contrary. They conveyed the fact that the Indians of Roanoke and the surrounding areas lived in a civil body politic,[96] which meant that they were people with whom some version of diplomatic conventions could be employed to form a new alliance.

Moreover, just as English clothing and ornamentation signaled social status at a glance, so those of the Algonquians provided similar information.

For English people in the late sixteenth century, mapping the body social meant identifying important distinctions in community status. Such images were as much a guide to Indian society as John Smith's map was to the geography of Virginia. In a culture in which mapmaking was beginning to take on central importance in everything from garnering support for expansionist enterprises, to travel, to expressing social fears and anxieties over changing cultural boundaries, ethnographic observation and representation often drew on the realm of cartography. Many European ornamental maps directly illustrated the close connection between cartography, chorography, and ethnographic observations by featuring drawings of men and women from different cultures dressed in typical costume in the margins of the map.

Mapping, navigation, and observation together constituted a constellation of practices that were closely related in European culture. Mapping and navigation were similar technical skills, as well as associated cultural enterprises. In the late sixteenth and early seventeenth centuries, both required systematic observation and record keeping as a way to update information about the safest, fastest, and most profitable travel routes. As an integral part of navigation, observation easily spilled over onto a related sphere of endeavor, one that took on a range of cultural uses. Careful records and descriptions, for example, were essential for transoceanic navigation.

However, at an early date, observation also became associated with the colonial and trade ventures that were the products of long-distance oceanic navigation. The accounts of recording expeditions such as those undertaken by Thomas Harriot and John White in sixteenth-century Roanoke, Jacques le Moyne in Florida, or Francisco Hernández in Mexico, as well as less formal reports such as those recorded by Captain John Smith in seventeenth-century Virginia, reflected the growing emphasis placed on careful observation as a source of information and a way to lay the groundwork for intercultural alliances with native peoples.

Yet, even as Europeans established an intellectual groundwork for the systematic mapping of other cultures, in North America they were soon to find that they too were the object of careful scrutiny. Native Americans mapped European colonists in both cosmological and practical political ways, and even enslaved Africans quickly learned that developing their own map of colonial communities enabled them to maneuver in influential ways despite the strictures of slavery. As we shall see in the following chapters, once Europeans established actual settlements in North America, the lived experience of intercultural partnerships was shaped fundamentally by Native Americans' logic of alliances and the ways they mapped Europeans into them.

2

Laying the Groundwork for Alliances

Language, Maps, and Intercultural Suspicion

European colonial expeditions were given explicit directions for observing new lands and peoples, and these observations provided information that colonial sponsors believed was crucial to the success of their ventures in distant lands. They were not intended merely to provide a template for colonialism and conquest, although they were unquestionably in the sponsors' self-interest. Attempts to acquire systematic knowledge of new lands, waterways, and trade routes also invariably included efforts to obtain information about new peoples and their alliances and political systems. For Europeans active on the North American eastern seaboard, the pursuit of alliances with native peoples was a widely shared goal for well over a hundred years.[1] Many Native Americans shared that goal as they incorporated Europeans into existing kinship and cooperative systems; however, Indian peoples quickly learned that not all Europeans would make trustworthy allies.

The period from 1580 to 1640 was one of crucial intercultural experimentation with collaborative efforts in the region stretching from New England to the Outer Banks of what is now North Carolina. Much of the groundwork for successful cultural interpretation and alliance building was established well before the successful English and Dutch colonies took root in the Chesapeake, Delaware-Hudson, and New England regions. Indeed, Indians and Europeans laid the foundation for some of the most important intercultural relationships before 1640.

This chapter draws on materials from several of the earliest and often ignored European colonial ventures. Most of the colonial expeditions to eastern

North America in the late sixteenth and early seventeenth centuries either were intended to be short-term ventures or, when they were expected to last for a longer period, nonetheless failed as permanent colonies. English and Dutch contacts with Indian peoples in the first two decades of the seventeenth century, for instance, often did not lead to lasting alliances or permanent European colonies. Indeed, they frequently resulted in cultural misunderstanding and violence. Yet these early experiences were crucial for all sides in helping people to determine which tactics succeeded with other parties and for learning how to map new groups' strengths and weaknesses. Indians and Europeans formed trade partnerships whenever each party found such arrangements advantageous.

By the 1630s an increasing number of successful and mutually beneficial intercultural alliances were in place throughout the Atlantic seaboard. As we shall see in the chapters that follow, some successful partnerships began sooner and had already ended before 1630. Yet we can see patterns in the types of alliance-building strategies during the period from 1580 to 1660. Native Americans and Europeans acted toward one another in ways that closed off future opportunities for certain interactions and alliances even as they furthered others. These behaviors foreclosed possibilities that required a high degree of trust; instead, they encouraged those that were based on calculated, short-term, even ruthless self-interest. The period from 1580 to 1620 witnessed a wide range of strategies, many of which were spectacularly unsuccessful and counterproductive as people tried to make contacts with other cultures work for their own maximum advantage.

European strategies in particular tended to alienate Indians in profound ways during this time. Then, by 1630, we begin to see a shift in the ways in which people approached intercultural contacts. After the 1620s a narrower range of strategies shaped most Indian-European contacts, and each side tended increasingly to rely on tactics with a proven record of success—if not with the current group, then with another one believed to be similar. All of the successful alliances of the 1630s benefited from the earlier period of experimentation, even (or especially) when previous models were disastrous failures. The later collaborations reshaped the early American cultural and political landscape, but they rested on earlier unsuccessful attempts.

For Europeans, many of the contacts with Native Americans before 1610 were influenced by the assumption that successful alliances would be possible only when Europeans retained a defensive or military advantage.[2] While European colonial sponsors and early colonists carefully considered how they might establish working associations with native peoples, they also worried about the military power of Native Americans, and they never trusted Indians' early overtures as being sincere. Treachery, Europeans assumed, surely lay behind each seemingly friendly gesture. The only sane response, to their way of thinking, was to be prepared for conflict, violence, and betrayal.

For many people the best preparation for expected hostility was to attack Indians first. English colonists and explorers in particular frequently adopted preemptive strikes as a way to show native peoples that Europeans would defend themselves and their property. Just as often, anticipatory attacks were a strategy to draw Indians' attention away from Europeans' weakness and vulnerability.[3] Yet nothing else was as damaging to early attempts to form intercultural alliances as the legacy of these tactics. Interestingly, the pursuit of alliances and the effort to strike the first blow were approaches that both Europeans and Native Americans used, and they were followed virtually simultaneously despite their apparent incongruity.

Precautionary strikes grew out of an impulse for self-protection, both for Europeans and for native peoples. The former were especially likely to assume that a strong show of force would effectively protect them from hostile acts when first meeting a new people. It is not surprising that Europeans in a strange land would interpret actions they did not understand as hostile. Most Europeans in North America before the late 1620s were keenly aware of their vulnerability. They had little room for error because, if they misjudged and missed the signs of a surprise attack even once, the consequences could be devastating. Europeans' numbers were small, and they seldom understood much of native languages; as a result, they were rarely sure they comprehended either Indians' actions or their motives. They also worried constantly that Native Americans would form pan-Indian alliances against the small European settlements. These were real fears, even if they often were not necessarily accurate ones.

Soldiers and former soldiers played an especially important role in the earliest colonial ventures. They generally interpreted North American events in light of both early modern military theory and their own experiences in European wars. We can see their influence and the degree to which it had a dampening effect on the prospects for lasting intercultural alliances in Europeans' actions on the ground in North America and in European promotional materials. Sir Walter Raleigh's Roanoke ventures in the 1580s are particularly clear examples of the ways in which English attitudes and strategies sometimes made the quest for intercultural alliances go disastrously wrong, despite the expeditions' desperate need for reliable Indian allies. The first Roanoke colony suffered considerably from the consequences of its leaders' "first strike" tactics. Coastal Algonquians near the colony suffered even more.

During the course of the first Roanoke colony (1585–1586), colonists made sure they attacked any Indians who might present a threat before the Indians could assault them. Moreover, Roanoke's leaders made certain that they punished any perceived slight against the colony, fearing that if signs of disrespect were allowed to stand, then Indians would quickly view the colony as weak and move against it. One of the most infamous examples of English insistence that any perceived slight must be punished came in the middle of July 1585.[4] On July 11 a number of colonists and soldiers set out to explore the coast along the Carolina Outer Banks in four boats under the leadership of Philip Amadas.[5] They stopped at several Algonquian towns along the way, several of which they were visiting for the first time. On July 13, two days into their scouting trip, the ships stopped at the town of Aquascococke and the following day sailed on to the town of Secotan, where they "were well intertayned."[6] At some point the colonists discovered that a silver cup was missing from one of the ships.[7] Amadas took this loss as a direct challenge and insisted that those responsible for taking the cup return it or face harsh retaliation.

Thus on July 16 the expedition turned around and sailed back to Secotan, where the rest of the men waited as Amadas took one of the boats to Aquascococke.[8] No account from Roanoke ever explained why Amadas and others were so certain that the cup had been stolen rather than lost and that someone at Aquascococke had taken it. Yet Amadas and his men acted as though they were convinced that this was the case and that the entire community was mocking the English by refusing to turn over both the silver cup and the thief. The account of July 16 says only that "one of our boates with the Admirall [Amadas] was sent to Aquascococke to demaund a silver cup which one of the Savages had stolen from us."[9] The anonymous author reports that the thief did not give back the cup to Amadas even though someone had promised its return.[10] As much as the theft itself, this failure (particularly after someone had guaranteed the cup would be restored) seems to have ignited English fury.

The rest of the account reveals in chilling detail the Roanoke colonists' determination to show no weakness. Just as clearly, it demonstrates why such a strategy often created a barrier to intercultural cooperation. When Amadas and his men discovered that the silver cup was nowhere to be found and realized that no one was going to come forth to either return it or be punished, they lashed out. Faced with no silver cup and an evacuated town, Amadas and his men burned the settlement and the villagers' major food crop, destroying both food and homes in a single attack. One writer reported in his journal account for the day that "we burnt, and spolyed their corne, and Towne, all of the people beeing fledde."[11]

The Roanoke colony is one of the starkest examples of the vital importance of intercultural alliances for the survival of European colonists. The long series of misunderstandings and betrayals experienced by native peoples and English colonists during the first exploratory expedition and subsequently during the two trial settlements at Roanoke illustrates the extraordinary difficulty that both sides faced in trying to establish terms that were acceptable to one another. In some ways, the later story of the Roanoke colonists may well offer us the most dramatic example of successful intercultural collaboration.

If the colonists actually migrated north to the Chesapeake Bay and lived among the Chesapeake nation (as many people believed at the time and as many scholars do now), then they would have spent fifteen years or more reaching a successful accommodation with the Chesapeakes.[12] Although colonists everywhere in later decades also realized that their survival depended on intercultural alliances to one degree or another, the Roanoke colonists had no other choice. They knew this at Roanoke and would have lived with the same realization at the Chesapeake Bay, where they would have lived among a larger, more powerful Indian nation. In the Outer Banks, as would have been the case in the Chesapeake Bay, all of the Native American communities around the colonists knew it. The small band of English strangers had too few members and was too isolated from other English people to have any other option.

Yet the Roanoke colonists were not unique in this respect. Their situation was more extreme to be sure, but the difference was a question of the degree of isolation and vulnerability. Before 1650 no colony was completely immune from similar pressures, and none before that date could isolate itself from the shifting web of intercultural alliances. Crucially, colonists and native peoples alike all understood this reality of the early colonial period. However different their situations, all of the early colonial expeditions and settlements emphasized the need for aggressive displays of force as a way of dealing with the threat presented by powerful Indian nations and the uncertainty of shifting coalitions.

Promotional tracts frequently stressed the need for North American expeditions to prepare carefully for possible conflict with native peoples. The growing record of early conflicts between Indians and European expeditions reinforced the call for an early show of force. In 1604, for example, George Waymouth wrote *The Jewell of Artes* to persuade James I that he had the necessary engineering, navigation, and leadership skills to direct a new voyage to North America.[13] In deference to recent reports that had reached London that the Roanoke colonists were still alive, Waymouth reminded King James of how vulnerable colonists were to Indian attack: "that countrie being as but weakely planted with the English, and they more weakely defended from the invasions of the heathen, Amongst whom they dwell or subiect vnto manifolde perils, and dangers."[14]

Waymouth's tract explained the kinds of abilities that members of a northwest passage expedition should have. He argued that those making such a journey ought to be able "to vse all possible meanes, to preserue both them selues, and theire companies not only from rouers, pirates and men of warre at sea: but also from the furie of the sauages on lande, where with many strange contries are replenished and by whose rages And crueltie many christans haue lamentably been destroyed."[15] He described the need for expeditions to include a surveyor who could select the most defensible location for a fort or fortified settlement, and he offered advice on how best to strengthen new North American settlements so as to maximize their defensive power even when occupied by only a few individuals.[16]

In 1603, the year before Waymouth presented James I with *The Jewell of Artes*, Martin Pring led a forty-three-man exploratory and trade expedition to North America's North Atlantic coast. Pring sailed along the Maine shore and in Cape Cod Bay, where he and his men had a number of contacts with Native Americans. His account of these experiences reveals that in both the planning and the execution of the trip, Pring employed the preemptive strike as an important strategy. To be more accurate, he used the threat of this tactic, reporting that he was particularly pleased with the way in which he had adapted a scheme made notorious by the Spanish in North America: the use of war dogs.

The Spanish were infamous among European Protestants for having set war dogs on Indian peoples. Some conquistadors brought them into battle. Others, such as Hernando de Soto, sadistically used the expedition's mastiffs for sport by pretending to release Indian captives, only to let the dogs loose to hunt them as hounds would chase a fox or other game animal in Europe.[17] In 1603 Martin Pring used his expedition's dogs as a constant threat to Indian visitors, and he wrote that the tactic was extremely effective. Moreover, the Roanoke and Plymouth colonists also brought mastiffs with them to North America for similar reasons. At Roanoke, Ralph Lane had two mastiffs that served as war dogs; however, the colonists reached such straits that they were forced to eat them after their alliance with their Algonquian neighbors broke down.

In the opening years of the seventeenth century, however, Martin Pring made much greater use of his war dogs. He bragged that his expedition included "two excellent Mastiues of whom the Indians were more afraid, then of twentie of our men."[18] He claimed that one member of the expedition had traveled for six miles into the interior, unaccompanied except for one of the mastiffs, and that no Indians had bothered the lone traveler at all. Pring attributed his safe trip to the Indians' fear of the powerful animals. If Pring's physical description was at all accurate, these would have been terrifying animals by any standard. He claimed, for instance, that one of the dogs could carry a seven- or eight-foot-long half pike in its mouth, which would mean that it was exceptionally large and strong.[19]

Moreover, Pring apparently threatened to set the dogs on visiting Indians at a whim; he may even have done so, although his account is somewhat ambiguous. He reported that, "when we would be rid of the Sauages company wee would let loose the Mastiues, and suddenly with out-cryes they would flee away."[20] There is nothing ambiguous about either the threat or the level of aggression it represented. What is less clear is whether Pring or his men actually had the dogs attack native peoples. If they had done so, it is difficult to imagine that the mastiffs would not have chased, attacked, and killed the fleeing people, but the record tells no more than we see here.

Whether or not Pring's mastiffs actually attacked any Native Americans, the expedition's use of war dogs was not conducive to establishing trust or a mutually beneficial relationship. Indeed, mastiffs were useful in establishing only one kind of connection, one in which the native ally feared the English.[21] This suited English goals at least in the short term because most English people in the early seventeenth century had no objection to Indian peoples' collaborating with them out of fear; in practice, however, such "alliances" seldom lasted very long. Almost invariably they erupted into open conflict sooner rather than later.

Native peoples themselves also engaged in preemptive strikes. Indeed, in the years between 1580 and the founding of Jamestown in 1607, Americans' precautionary attacks against European ships and colonial ventures were remarkably successful at preventing significant or long-term settlement by Europeans. Many of the deterrent assaults recorded in early European accounts were actually retaliation against the actions of a previous European ship, but Europeans seldom realized this because they often had no relationship with the group who had caused offense.

The hope of finding the lost Roanoke colonists continued to guide English colonial ventures to North America for twenty years after the last ship left the colonists on the Outer Banks. One of these voyages set out under the patronage of Sir Walter Raleigh with the twofold mission of establishing trade with the Indians on his behalf and finding his lost colonists left Plymouth, England, in 1603. After their ship was blown away from a location near the mouth of Chesapeake Bay, Bartholomew Gilbert and a party of men went ashore somewhere on the Atlantic coast on July 29. They were trying to explore what they thought was the mouth of a river, but they were attacked by Indians almost immediately.

Several members of the expedition were killed in the attack, including Gilbert.[22] One of the men who went ashore with him, a lawyer named Thomas Canner, wrote an account of the experience. His description does not mention any previous contact with the Native Americans who attacked them; indeed, Canner does not report having met anyone at all since the ship had anchored off the West Indian island of Saint Lucia a month before.[23] Instead, he related that a small group of men went ashore in the ship's boat with Gilbert to explore, leaving the ship anchored a mile off shore. Two young men stayed on shore to guard the boat, while the rest of the group marched inland to look around. The expedition was armed, but they were not able to save themselves from a surprise attack that occurred when, "shortly after [going ashore] the Indians set upon them."[24]

In addition, the Indians also tried to seize the ship's boat, and the two young Englishmen left to guard it "had much a doe to save themselves and it. For some of the Indians roming downe to them, would have haled it on shore."[25] The survivors managed to save the boat and return to their waiting ship, but the attack inflicted greater losses than they could sustain. With a crew of only "eleven men and Boyes in all in the ship" and low stores of food and water, the ship returned to England. In the end they found no traces of the Roanoke colonists, and they did nothing to create new trading relationships with native peoples. Low supplies, food spoilage, and a successful preemptive assault by Indians combined to render the voyage almost entirely ineffective.

The first direct experience that both the Jamestown and the Plymouth colonists had with Native Americans was to be shot at by them. George Percy, for instance, described his first sight of the land around the Chesapeake Bay in 1607 in rapturous terms: "Wee entred into the Bay of Chesupioc directly. . . . There we landed . . . but we could find nothing worth the speaking of, but faire meddowes and goodly tall Trees, with such Fresh-waters running through the woods, as I was almost ravished at the first sight thereof."[26] A group from the ship evidently went ashore to explore this awe-inspiring countryside. However, they were assaulted by a group of native men just as they began to return to the ship that evening, and Percy makes it clear that the attackers were people with whom they had had no contact. The Native Americans came at the Englishmen so as to benefit from the advantage of surprise, and their sudden and brief skirmish was quite successful.

In describing the attack, Percy compared the Indians to animals, implying that they were wild and uncivilized. Yet his description also makes it clear that the warriors were employing a sophisticated strategy. "At night, when wee were going aboard," Percy reported, "there came the Savages creeping upon all foure, from the Hills like Beares, with their Bowes in their mouthes."[27] Percy's account makes it clear that the surprise attack was quite effective, even though he claimed the crew members were able to repel it. The warriors, he told his readers, "charged us very desperately in the faces, hurt Captain Gabrill Archer in both his hands, and a sayler in two places of the body very dangerous."[28]

Although Percy claimed that the expedition's guns drove the attackers away, his account suggests otherwise: "After they had spent their Arrowes, and felt the sharpnesse of our shot," the Indians "retired into the Woods with a great noise, and so left us."[29] Percy would have liked for his readers to think that the English guns had driven off the attackers, but it seems more significant that the warriors retreated only *after* they had used up all of their arrows. Even in the face of English guns, these warriors fought until they had no more ammunition. Moreover, even if the English guns kept them from retrieving their spent arrows to reuse, they pressed the attack and pulled back only after having driven the newcomers back to their ship.

The colonists' use of preemptive strike strategies, even as they also sought intercultural alliances, was one of the crucial factors that shaped intercultural contacts throughout the early colonial period. The two pursuits were inextricably connected, even though they often turned out to be at odds or proved at least to have opposite effects. People were able to see the need for intercultural cooperation and the necessity of precautionary attacks as simultaneous imperatives, in part because they were remarkably unsentimental about alliances and their limitations.

Most intercultural partnerships in the early colonial period were utilitarian and pragmatic; Native Americans and Europeans entered into agreements with one another based on self-interest. When alliances worked, they did so because all of the parties found that their self-interest intersected at a point of mutual need. What each side needed was invariably different, and the ways in which each party understood the meaning of alliance also loomed across a deep cultural chasm. Sometimes people recognized the immensity of this gap, and sometimes they failed to see it for the profound divide that it was.

Another favored strategy of early European colonial ventures reveals just how deep the intercultural split could be and just how far people would have to travel in order to create successful partnerships. Colonial promoters and adventurers relied heavily on kidnapping as a way to accomplish several of their goals. In many ways, kidnapping was a shortcut that would give colonial promoters greater geographical knowledge while also helping them to map the people and networks of political connections in an area. Moreover, for many English colonial supporters, it also seemed a relatively fast and reliable way to begin to build alliances with Native Americans.

While this evidently seemed like a good idea to a number of English promoters and shipmasters, abduction proved to be one of the greatest obstacles to successful partnerships. When beneficial intercultural ties were created, as in the case of Plymouth Colony's famous alliance with Squanto, it was more the result of epidemic disease than of the much earlier kidnapping of Squanto. It took Europeans a remarkably long time to understand that kidnapping people was not necessarily a good way to build a connection with the kidnap victim's community.

This sounds obvious, but somehow the idea that kidnapping was a self-defeating strategy was not as clear to European colonial promoters in the early seventeenth century as we would think. We may wonder why Europeans would persist in taking native peoples captive as a way to gain helpful intermediaries and allies. And yet they did—and did so repeatedly from the 1530s well into the 1620s.[30] Europeans kidnapped Indians sometimes one at a time and sometimes in small groups. They expected their hostages to provide ongoing, accurate information about coastal waters, geography, and the people who inhabited an area, as well as their language, trade, and alliances.

Abduction, in other words, seemed to the leaders of European colonial expeditions to be a good way to seize living knowledge; as we have already seen, Ferdinando Gorges believed this an extremely useful strategy when laying his plans for early colonies in northern New England. Furthermore, Gorges was not alone in his use of captives or in his hopes for what they might offer English colonies. Often Europeans also used the kidnapped people as liaisons for establishing good relations with native communities. In the first two decades of the seventeenth century, a number of European colonial expeditions tried this and discovered their mistake. Although kidnapping could indeed bring them some information and provide a degree of leverage—they did after all have a hostage—it did not lead to grateful natives, lasting friendships, or real alliances. Let us see how this actually unfolded in several instances in New England.

When we last saw the members of the Council for New England, they were standing around a map with James I, drawing lots for the property each member would control in New England. However, if we look beyond this scene of property division and focus instead on some of the council's sponsored voyages to New England during the first two decades of the seventeenth century, we learn more about the ways in which the council planned to deal with native peoples. Records of the Council for New England and accounts of early New England colonization published by Sir Ferdinando Gorges on behalf of his own and the council's interests demonstrate that good relations with the Indians was one of their primary goals. Or perhaps it would be more accurate to say that they assumed that amicable dealings with America's native peoples were essential for the furtherance of their primary goals, which were commercially successful colonies.

The council's materials, both the published accounts of their efforts to establish plantations in New England and their manuscript records, discuss Indian affairs and connections with Algonquians in terms of alliances, both explicitly and implicitly. Furthermore, while the council also wrote about the desirability of eventual Christian and cultural conversion programs for New England's native peoples, alliances were to be the foundation of good English-Algonquian relations. Everything else could follow from successful partnerships. More than that, Ferdinando Gorges and at least several other members of the Council for New England saw intercultural alliances as necessary ingredients for the success of their colonial venture.

Nevertheless, the realities of the council's early New England enterprises slipped quickly out of its control. While Gorges was governor of the fort at Plymouth (Old Plymouth) in 1605, he himself first became interested in the possibilities North America offered. That summer Captain George Waymouth, who was returning to England from an expedition to Monhegan Island, stopped at Plymouth. Waymouth had five Wabanakis with him, three of whom he left with Gorges, apparently for Gorges to do with as he pleased. Although this "gift" of human beings was not exactly common, neither was it unprecedented. In the eyes of many English people active in colonial voyages, Indians, like maps, were valuable patronage offerings. Their value in English people's views was perhaps that they were rare and exotic, but they also offered living knowledge and would be helpful guides on return voyages, when they also could act as emissaries with other native people.

For the next few years, Gorges followed the news of several other voyages and helped to sponsor some of them, but he became more actively interested in North America six years later. In 1611 Captain Edward Harlow returned from a New England voyage and brought with him an Algonquian man from Martha's Vineyard named Epenow.[31] Harlow "gave" Epenow to Gorges. When Epenow arrived, Gorges still had one Wabanaki man whom he had kept as a servant since 1605, a man named Assacomoit (Sassacomoit). After six years with Gorges, Assacomoit was able to speak English. Now, with the arrival of Epenow, Gorges saw expanded opportunities in trying to pool the two men's knowledge and used Assacomoit as an interpreter between himself and Epenow. This took some time because the two men spoke different Algonquian languages.[32]

Ultimately, Native Americans' language differences would prove to be the least of the problems Gorges faced. In the next three years his ambitions for New England colonies and for expanding trade and defensive alliances with Wabanaki and other Algonquian people collided with certain American realities. Among those were the ambition, greed, and unscrupulousness of other English adventurers and upheaval among the peoples of northern New England. And there was another crucial element: the fact that kidnapped Native Americans greatly resented their abduction.

Epenow, who now found himself stuck in England, baited a hook for his English captors. He told them of rich gold mines on Cape Cod, well understanding what they wanted to hear. When his stories caught the attention of several people, Gorges sponsored a voyage to New England in search of the mines and ostensibly also to look for rich fishing grounds. He sent Epenow along on the trip as a guide to the mines, which was, of course, exactly what Epenow had hoped; there were in actuality no such excavations, but their allure had given Epenow his way home. In New England he escaped from the ship and swam ashore, and the venture was off; the ship returned home. The would-be prospectors had obtained no gold and little additional geographical knowledge of the area, and they had apparently lost an interpreter, guide, and emissary. To make matters worse, from Gorges's perspective, Epenow's tales of New England gold had inspired other English enterprises, one of which struck a lasting blow against amicable English-Algonquian alliances that would resonate with Indian peoples for years.

A wealthy young merchant named Marmaduke Roydon (Rawdon) fitted out a small fleet for Captain John Smith, who was now promoting colonial undertakings in the northern part of Virginia (New England), and a shipmaster named Thomas Hunt. Roydon was interested in New England as a promising investment, particularly based on Captain Smith's enthusiasm and colonial experience. Captain Hunt, who recognized an opportunity to acquire a pot of gold for himself, talked his way into the scheme. While Smith and Roydon were looking for various ways to create long-term colonial success in New England, at least one that would reliably pay a profit to investors, Hunt heard about Epenow's stories of gold. What he wanted was for someone else to pay to get him within striking distance of these riches, and Roydon obliged. In the end, English hopes for lasting alliances with New England's peoples also incurred a heavy price.

For his part, Hunt was clearly willing to take his gold in a variety of forms. He set sail before Gorges could send out his ships with Epenow. For a time, Hunt traded with Algonquians along the New England coast. Then, when he was satisfied with the trade he had conducted, he kidnapped twenty-four Algonquian men and sailed off to sell them as slaves. In an account published by the Council for New England in 1622, Gorges's and other council members' disdain and frustration almost leap off the pages. The account notes that a short time before Gorges's ships arrived in New England with Epenow, "it happened there had beene one Hunt (a worthlesse fellow of our Nation) set out by certaine Merchants for loue of gaine."[33]

According to the Council for New England, Hunt could have made a reasonable profit by returning to England with the trade goods and fish he had already procured. However, he chose to indulge his greed. Gorges lamented that "after hee had made his dispatch, and was ready to set sayle (more sauage-like then they) seized vpon the poore innocent creatures, that in confidence of his honestie had put them selues into his hands. And stowing them vnder hatches, to the number of twenty foure, carried them into the Straights, where hee sought to sell them for slaues, and sold as many as he could get money for."[34] For Gorges and the other members of the council, Hunt's actions threatened to undermine all of the Council for New England's efforts.

Ironically, Gorges was rather conveniently overlooking the fact that he himself had benefited for years from the knowledge and expertise of at least five kidnapped Algonquians. We know for certain that English ships had kidnapped Native Americans for years. However, Hunt's actions somehow seemed much worse. In addition, Gorges blamed Hunt for Epenow's escape, and perhaps even more important he blamed him for virtually destroying future good-faith efforts by English sailing crews or colonists to establish peaceful relationships with New England native peoples. Gorges's ship arrived in New England soon after Hunt had been there, and at first the crew explored the New England coast while the Algonquian men acted as pilots: "As it pleased God that they were arrived upon the coast they were Pilotted from place to place, by the Natives themselves, as well as their hearts could desire."[35]

During these excursions, the three Algonquian men onboard the ship evidently heard about what Hunt had just done, and Gorges laments that Hunt's betrayal "being knowne by our two Saluages . . . they presently contracted such an hatred against our whole Nation, as they immediately studied how to be reuenged; and contriued with their friends the best meanes to bring it to passe."[36] Although Gorges could see clearly the harm Hunt's actions caused, he never understood that his own use of kidnapping and holding people against their will also might be barriers to friendship and alliance. On this occasion, when the ship neared Cape Cod, some of Epenow's relatives came aboard, and Epenow later jumped overboard and swam to several waiting canoes and escaped. Because the ship's captain did not have the heart to continue, the ship returned to England.

Several years later Thomas Dermer returned to North America on a voyage that Gorges sponsored. There he encountered Epenow, who "laughed at his owne escape and reported the story of it."[37] Interestingly, Dermer tried to reconcile with Epenow. Gorges reported that "Mr. Dormer [sic] tould him he came from me and was one of my servants, and that I was much grieved he had been so ill used, as to be forced to steale away."[38] Epenow, however, drew a very different message from Dermer's attempts to reestablish contact between Gorges and him. According to Gorges, "This Savage was so cunning, that after he had questioned him about me and all he knew belonged unto me, conceived he was come on purpose to betray him, and conspired with some of his fellowes to take the Captaine, thereupon they laid hands upon him, but he being a brave stoute Gentelman, drew his Sword and freed himselfe, but not without fourteen wounds."[39] These were the fruits of kidnapping—suspicion, hostility, and constant expectation of betrayal, all of which were realistic, given the native people's experiences.

I have said that Gorges's ambitions for the New England colonies and for successful and peaceful alliances with Algonquians in New England collided with a number of realities in these early years, and we have seen some of those unfortunate incidents, but it is important to note two other important

American realities in this period. Wabanakis in northern New England and other Algonquian peoples in southern New England began to be hit by severe disease epidemics around this time. Furthermore, in northern New England, the Mi'kmaqs were at war with the Penobscots and other Eastern Wabanakis, and the conflict was at its height in 1614 and 1615, just as Gorges sent out his ship with Epenow and Captain Hunt made his infamous slaving raid.[40] All of these things exacerbated Indians' suspicion of others and made peaceful alliances increasingly unlikely.

If, in the end, kidnapping seems to have been an extraordinarily ill-conceived strategy, many colonial promoters and explorers nevertheless saw it as useful for a surprisingly long time. Those who regarded abduction as a practical plan were not just the Thomas Hunts of the Atlantic world, the people who happily opted to make a profit by selling Native American captives for the European slave market in Spain. There were indeed other people like Hunt, and they played an important part in the early colonial world, but they were interested neither in cultivating alliances with Native Americans nor in undertaking long-term colonial ventures.

Those who were involved in such enterprises also took people hostage or relied heavily on developing relationships with the kidnap victims. Gorges used Algonquian captives as sources of both geographical and political knowledge. He did exactly what Edward Herbert had said the study of geography could enable men to do, but for Gorges, accurate information about American geography and political alliances would come primarily from living sources rather than from books, from kidnapped Native Americans who had little choice but to provide him with at least some information.

Many years after his plans for a flourishing North American colony had been dashed, Gorges still argued for the integral role of native peoples. His experiences with the Algonquian men he held captive had taught him to respect the abilities and knowledge of North America's native inhabitants. He even distinguished their skills from those of people from England's lower social orders and insisted that "after I had those people sometimes in my Custody, I observed in them an inclination to follow the example of the better sort."[41] As we have already seen, he believed that the geographical and geopolitical knowledge they could offer would be invaluable: "Having kept them full three yeares, I made them able to set me downe what great Rivers ran up into the Land, what men of note were seated on them, what power they were of, how allyed, what enemies they had, and the like of which in his proper place."[42] He also argued that Indians could fill extremely important roles as pilots of his ships when they reached New England, as indeed Epenow and Assacomoit had done in 1614 because they had far more direct experience of New England's waterways than any European pilots.[43]

The fact that his American tutors were captured against their will does not seem to have been a real concern for him. Instead, he worried about the actions of unscrupulous sea captains like Thomas Hunt and the unscrupulous activities of scheming crews of other English ships. Gorges drew a distinction between what he himself did and what unregulated ships' captains did. He readily saw the benefit of kidnapping people whom he could then hold as captives while extracting whatever intelligence could be had from them. Nevertheless, he drew the line between his own actions and Hunt's search for quick profits by abducting people and selling them into slavery. Of course, from the Native Americans' perspective, there was little real difference. Both ventures meant stealing people and carrying them far away into strange lands against their will.

Although kidnapping was a tactic widely used by English speculators in the early colonial period, it seldom led to lasting alliances. Thus, by the 1640s and 1650s English–Native American associations formed in other ways, as Europeans turned to different strategies to map new peoples and lands; during that time few people still resorted to the old stratagem of seizing hoped-for allies. Yet in the early period of European colonial efforts in North America, kidnapping had seemed a clear solution to the crucial problem of language differences. As we have seen, if Europeans could bring one or more native people back to England, where they might learn English and a few select English people might learn some native languages, then they assumed that all of the subsequent dealings between Native Americans and the English would be significantly smoother.

Communication with strangers presented a perennial problem in the early colonial period. It was particularly acute during first-contact situations and so played an especially important role by limiting the extent and nature of alliances in the first few years of American-European contact. Time and more extensive intercultural experiences ameliorated some of the differences of language and culture, but accurate ethnographic mapping and the pursuit of connections between native peoples and Europeans were significantly limited as a result of most people's inability to bridge divides of language and culture throughout the early seventeenth century.

From the outset, Europeans who were trying to establish new colonial ventures in North America well understood that they had to find reliable means of communicating with other people around them; otherwise, they would find themselves isolated and completely vulnerable. Neither dependable trade nor workable political alliances would be possible without some solution to the language problem. For their part, Native Americans also quickly recognized the need to find accurate ways to communicate with European newcomers for similar reasons.

Indeed, in the sixteenth and seventeenth centuries everyone lived in a world in which many people spoke more than one language. This was the case for most Native Americans, and it was certainly so with many of the Europeans who came to North America. Scholars have often quoted Willem Kieft, director general of the Dutch colony of New Netherland, who in 1643 told the Jesuit Isaac Jogues that one could hear as many as eighteen languages spoken on the streets of New Amsterdam.[44]

Historians have been particularly fond of using this observation as evidence that Manhattan was an unusually cosmopolitan North American community in the seventeenth century. It was indeed multilingual and international, but only as a matter of degree. New Amsterdam was unquestionably a cosmopolitan Atlantic world entrepôt, and the number of languages spoken there probably was unusually large for North American communities in the first half of the seventeenth century. However, its polyglot character was typical of the communities that spread along the Atlantic perimeter in Europe, Africa, and the Americas.

If we broaden our perspective to the larger North American Atlantic coast region, we find people who spoke a wide variety of European, African, and Native American languages. They spoke Germanic, Balto-Finnic, and Romance languages, such as Dutch, German, English, Swedish, Finnish, Latin, French, Spanish, and Portuguese. They also spoke a wide variety of Algonquian languages, a number of Iroquois languages, and different Bantu languages. The complexity of intercultural communication then was more than just a problem between Europeans and Native Americans, but in the relations between Indians and Europeans we see the widest range of early solutions to these difficulties. Moreover, they illustrate some of the most tenacious limitations of intercultural alliances in early colonial North America.

In the early modern world it was not unusual for people to speak more than one language. Many of those who inhabited the rim of the Atlantic were multilingual, and even those who spoke only one language could often communicate with others who spoke related languages such as Dutch and English, Unami and Powhatan, Kikongo and Kimbundu. Moreover, the frequent changes and dislocations of migration in the early modern world prompted people to learn the languages of other cultures and to create new tongues. Within the first twenty years of permanent Dutch settlement in North America, for instance, Lenapes and Dutch colonists had created a trade pidgin, which was a simplified and combined version of Dutch and Unami. This pidgin facilitated intercultural trade and diplomatic negotiation in the early years of colonial contact and settlement.[45]

One of the fascinating aspects of the Delaware trade pidgin is the way in which it simultaneously enabled Europeans and Native Americans in the Delaware and Susquehannock river regions to interact on a regular basis while also making it possible for Lenapes and other native peoples to throw up a linguistic barrier to European intrusions. The Delaware trade pidgin was ideal from the perspective of the Lenapes and other Algonquian-speaking people who had regular dealings with the Dutch and various other Europeans in the mid-Atlantic region. By allowing interested colonists to learn only a simplified version of their languages, these Native Americans protected key elements of their culture. Indeed, linguists now think that the Delaware pidgin was not really a native language at all but a pidgin based on Dutch grammatical structures, with a mixture of Dutch and Algonquian vocabulary items.

This technique worked remarkably well from the perspective of most Europeans and Algonquians. Yet what each side thought worked satisfactorily was not the same thing. The Delaware pidgin facilitated trade, diplomacy, and ongoing neighborly interactions between colonists and Indians, but only to a point. There were clear limits to how much either party could learn about the other by relying on the pidgin. Apparently the Europeans seldom noticed this, presumably they did not always want to know more about their Indian neighbors and trading partners. Moreover, many colonists seem to have assumed that they understood much more about Lenape or Algonquian culture and language than they actually did, on the basis of successful exchanges using the trade pidgin. Native Americans, by contrast, appear to have been much more aware that the pidgin had limitations, which was what they wanted.

In willingly embracing the clear limits on communication that a Euro-Algonquian trade pidgin created, Algonquians in the mid-Atlantic were adapting existing strategies for using language codes around enemies. Indian peoples, for instance, devised other linguistic innovations (such as trade jargons) to protect secret or valuable information. Some Native Americans, for example, developed a code to use when they went to war so that warriors could communicate without letting their enemies understand what they said.

Although the Delaware trade pidgin lasted for years and was more enduring and more complex than any of the temporary war codes, it nevertheless served a similar protective purpose. In other words, the same pidgin that allowed people to communicate between cultures also placed boundaries on the subjects about which they could converse. In many ways, this may have been precisely why the Delaware trade pidgin was so effective for everyone. Neither Indians nor Europeans shared information without considering the implications of losing control of the knowledge they shared.

Numerous European-produced documents clearly demonstrate concern over the security and intelligence properties of knowledge, and many European accounts show both Indians and Europeans approaching intercultural boundaries with careful negotiation of the value to be gained from cultural knowledge. In 1628, for instance, Dutch minister Jonas Michaelius wrote from New Netherland to a minister at home in the Dutch Republic about the hardships he endured in the colony. Michaelius complained at length about the hopelessness of converting Indians to Christianity. As part of his explanation, he penned a long diatribe about native peoples' inferiority and blamed them for his failure to produce converts to Calvinism. "As to the natives of this country," Michaelius grumbled to his fellow clergyman, "I find them entirely savage and wild, strangers to all decency, yea, uncivil and stupid as garden poles, proficient in all wickedness and godlessness."[46]

Not only did Michaelius insist that Indians lacked the intellectual ability to grasp Christianity, but he also feared that their attachment to paganism and especially to the Devil was deeply rooted. Having told his friend how "uncivil and stupid" he found native peoples, he went on to describe considerable skill and sophistication in native beliefs, even as he failed to recognize what he was seeing. Michaelius wrote that he knew that it was futile to try to convert Indians because they were "devilish men, who serve nobody but the Devil, that is, the spirit which in their language they call Menetto; under which title they comprehend everything that is subtle and crafty and beyond human skill and power."[47]

He told his correspondent that he could not understand why church authorities in the Dutch Republic were convinced that Indians could be readily brought into the Christian fold. He was at a loss for what else he might do: "How these people can best be led to the true knowledge of God and of the Mediator Christ is hard to say."[48] Ultimately, Michaelius decided that the root of the difficulty lay with Indians' essential character and language. Both explanations excused his own failure to reach them and instead placed the blame squarely on native peoples' incapacity for what he believed to be the higher elements of European culture.

He confided that he believed church officials in the Dutch Republic had been duped into believing made-up stories: "I cannot myself wonder enough who it is that has imposed so much upon your Reverence and many others in the Fatherland, concerning the docility of these people and their good nature, the proper principia religionis and vestigial legis naturae which are said to be among them."[49] His own experience among Hudson Valley Algonquians, he confessed, contradicted such expectations: "I have as yet been able to discover hardly a single good point."[50] The only encouraging thing about Indians, according to Michaelius, was that they were not as blasphemous as Africans he had met. He claimed that he had found almost nothing positive to report "except that they do not speak so jeeringly and so scoffingly of the godlike and glorious majesty of their Creator as the Africans dare to do."[51]

For Michaelius, as for many Europeans, people's basic intellectual and moral capacities were reflected in their languages, and he judged Native Americans accordingly. For prospective converts fully to grasp an entirely new cosmology, they had to have a cultural and linguistic framework that could express the ideas accurately. Concepts that could not be articulated would remain outside any meaningful frame of cultural reference. In other words, ideas that could not be stated could not be thought, at least not by people who were approaching a culture that was dramatically different from the one into which they had been born. Thus the Reverend Michaelius speculated that the simplicity of Indian languages was a principal impediment to native peoples' conversion because it made it nearly impossible to communicate the complex ideas essential to understanding Calvinist theology.

The implications of this linguistic obstacle were clear to Michaelius. Without more radical transformation, there could be no meaningful meeting of the cultures, certainly not on terms dictated primarily by Christians. Yet from Indians' perspective, barriers raised by language differences were often valued as a desirable state of affairs. Many native peoples had no wish to listen to Europeans' long harangues about religion, nor did they desire to be subjected to intrusive questions about the spiritual world. In this context, the limitations of the trade pidgins provided an important intercultural buffer for native peoples.

The Reverend Michaelius's letter made it clear that he never questioned the need to draw distinct cultural boundaries between Dutch Christians and Indian pagans, even if they were different from those Indians themselves would draw.[52] Interestingly, however, his letter also stated that many other Dutch colonists did not approach intercultural relationships in the same way. Many were busily engaged in trying to learn Native American languages and willingly made regular contacts with Indians. Yet Michaelius's letter also suggests that Native Americans wished to control and limit even more prosaic interactions with Europeans. If he proved to be an extremely xenophobic judge of native culture, Michaelius was also a shrewd observer of more secular exchanges between Algonquians and Dutch colonists. Even as he complained about what he described as the inherent poverty of Indian languages, he noted that many colonists readily tried to learn them.

Michaelius knew that language was an obstacle that Europeans would have to tackle and reported that "their language, which is the first thing to be employed with them, methinks is entirely peculiar."[53] Although he had earlier claimed that Algonquian languages were too simple to allow discussion of complex, abstract ideas, now he acknowledged that they were extremely difficult for Europeans to master, even for secular purposes. He admitted that "many of our common people call it an easy language, which is soon learned, but I am of a contrary opinion."[54] Indeed, he made fun of colonists' efforts and claimed that most could barely pronounce Algonquian words correctly: "Those who can understand their words to some extent and repeat them, fail greatly in the pronunciation, and speak a broken language, like the language of Ashdod."[55]

He claimed that the difference in pronunciation between Dutch and Algonquian was just too great for Dutch speakers to overcome: "These people have difficult aspirates and many guttural letters, which are formed more in the throat than by the mouth, teeth and lips, to which our people not being accustomed, make a bold stroke at the thing and imagine that they have accomplished something wonderful."[56] He went on to distinguish between trading languages and the more elaborate version of Algonquian that native peoples spoke among themselves: "It is true one can easily learn as much as is sufficient for the purposes of trading, but this is done almost as much by signs with the thumb and fingers as by speaking; and this cannot be done in religious matters."[57]

Michaelius's discontent seems to have had class, as well as religious, dimensions. In the disorienting realm of New Netherland, Michaelius tried to reassert status boundaries within Dutch culture, not only between Dutch and Indians. Although the "common people" may have communicated more easily with Indians than he did, according to Michaelius they made themselves foolish in doing so and never succeeded at the level required for theological ideas. Yet he made it clear that other factors were at work, too. The "common colonists" were unable to learn much of the Indian languages not only because of their own inability to master difficult pronunciations but also because the Indians did not allow them to learn much. Michaelius believed the Indians employed a deliberate strategy to guard their language from European newcomers: "It also seems to us that they rather design to conceal their language from us than to properly communicate it."[58] The only exception Indians made was to teach colonists the language necessary for the "things which happen in daily trade; saying that it is sufficient for us to understand them in that."[59]

For Michaelius, the natives' unwillingness to teach colonists their language was at once suspicious and frustrating, and he asserted that Indians wanted to keep Europeans from understanding them. Even when they taught colonists a language for trade, Michaelius wrote that "they speak only half sentences, shortened words, and frequently call out a dozen things and even more; and all things which have only a rude resemblance to each other, they frequently call by the same name."[60] "In truth," he wrote, this trade language "is a made-up, childish language; so that even those who can best of all spake with the savages, and get along well in trade, are nevertheless wholly in the dark and bewildered when they hear the savages talking among themselves."[61] That was exactly what the native peoples wanted.

Michaelius realized that Indians treated language as an arena of protected cultural knowledge. Communication difficulties, as much as any other factor, proved to be a significant obstacle to the formation of successful alliances. Trade relationships were one notable exception, but even these agreements generally worked best when they operated as a succession of short-term connections and interactions that were renewed each time the parties wanted to trade again. While many Indians were willing for Dutch colonists to learn a little of their language in order to facilitate exchanges, they preferred to teach them a trade pidgin with limited applicability in other contexts and thereby limit their interactions with Europeans.

Trade jargons facilitated business associations and even military or defensive alliances, but they did not lend themselves well to fostering the wholesale assimilation of one culture into another. Protecting their languages allowed Native Americans to maintain them as a distinctive and valued cultural property and to exercise considerable control over information the Europeans desired. Furthermore, as a practical matter it enabled them to communicate privately or secretly during intercultural encounters. As Michaelius pointed out in the late 1620s, colonists who thought they had learned Munsee, Unami, or another Algonquian language found themselves "bewildered" when the Native Americans spoke among themselves.[62] Few other Europeans admitted this disability, at least not in writing; yet the historical record is filled with fragmentary glimpses of ongoing limitations in the extent to which Native Americans and Europeans communicated with one another in the early colonial period.

Recognizing that native languages and Indians' control over them presented a permanent restriction on Europeans' ability to convert Indians, Michaelius devised a plan to make a more radical change. Rather than trying to translate and explain concepts, beliefs, and culture to adults, he would target native children, who could learn Dutch. He proposed taking youngsters away from their families and segregating them in Dutch schools. This would allow Dutch instructors to teach them European languages (presumably Dutch) and Christianity at the same time. In addition, Michaelius suggested that the children should be encouraged to practice their own languages, even as they learned new ones. His goal was not to make them entirely Dutch but instead to create a whole cadre of intercultural translators.

The Dutch-educated children could use their Indian language skills to convert other Indians after they had completed their European education. First, though, they would have to be separated from their native culture: "It would be well then to leave the parents as they are, and begin with the children who are still young. So be it. But they ought in youth to be separated from their parents; yea, from their whole nation."[63] Later, after they had learned to speak, read, and write in Dutch and mastered the fundamentals of Christianity, they would become Christianizing agents of their nation.[64]

In Michaelius's scheme, if Dutch Christians could not master Indian languages, perhaps Indians could master the Dutch language and culture, as well as Christianity, and spread the word themselves. In the end, he was never able to put his plan into effect, and Native Americans continued to keep Dutch colonists from learning important aspects of their languages and spiritual practices.

3

"You Called Him Father"

Fictive Kinship and Tributary Alliances in Tsenacommacah/Virginia

In 1617 London was abuzz with news about a royal visit. The visiting delegation centered around a young woman, a foreign princess, whose family had been allied with England for about a decade. Lady Rebecca traveled with her husband, shockingly an English commoner, and emissaries of her father, whom the English public understood to be a powerful king. Lady Rebecca was, of course, the name given, upon conversion to Christianity, to the Powhatan woman known as Pocahontas, and it was as Lady Rebecca that she married Englishman John Rolfe in Virginia, the land she and her family knew as Tsenacommacah. While in England, Lady Rebecca took in many sights and had an audience with Queen Anne. She became something of an exhibition herself as curious English folk flocked to see the so-called savage princess. Indeed, many people traveled to pay their respects to her. Yet the one Englishman she knew almost as well as her husband and whom she also considered to be kin nearly stayed away.

Captain John Smith had gained tremendous fame as a result of his service for the Virginia Company and in large part as a result of his descriptions of having outwitted Pocahontas's father. In the end, Captain Smith wrote that he was able to pay his respects to Lady Rebecca only very briefly because she arrived in England just as he was on the verge of sailing to New England. When he finally saw Pocahontas, the short conversation he later reported was packed with references to the nature of the Powhatan-English alliance in North America and the ways in which each group was endeavoring to insert the other into its own map of the world as allied but subordinate peoples.

FIGURE 4. This engraving of Pocahontas, taken from a portrait painted during her London visit, conveys something of the poise and grace Smith and others described. It does not suggest a woman who was uncritically accepting of a new culture. "Matoaka Al[ia]s Rebecca Filia Potentiss: Prince: Powhatani Imp: Virginiae." London, 1616. Courtesy of the John Carter Brown Library at Brown University.

Smith and the other Jamestown colonists had depended on the relationship he and Pocahontas had created in the place the Powhatans called Tsenacommacah; however, back in England Smith was quite reluctant to be too closely associated with the celebrated visitor. Eventually "hearing shee was at Branford with divers of my friends, I went to see her," Smith wrote.[1] Almost immediately, he claimed, he regretted his decision because he discovered that the visit would not be as easy as he had evidently hoped. Instead, he noted that Pocahontas's behavior puzzled and embarrassed him: "After a modest salutation, without any word, she turned about, obscured her face, as not seeming well contented; and in that humour her husband, with divers others, we all left her two or three houres, repenting my selfe to have write she could speake English."[2]

Although Smith's first recorded reaction was to worry about his own reputation and to fear that people who had read his early account of the colony would doubt him if Lady Rebecca continued to refuse to speak English, the problem was not her knowledge of the language. Smith was confronted with a Powhatan woman who was in fact showing her strong displeasure at Smith's failure to meet his kinship and alliance expectations. Before Smith left that day, Pocahontas made sure that he understood the nature of her disappointment and his failures. She not only began to speak to Smith in English but also offered him a rather stern instruction about the alliance obligations he had failed to fulfill. "But not long after" Pocahontas gave Smith the cold shoulder, he reported that "she began to talke, and remembred mee well what courtesies shee had done."[3]

Even as it reaches us through the veil of Smith's reporting, Pocahontas's outrage is evident, as is her decision to explain to Smith how very badly he had abused their alliance. According to Smith's account, Pocahontas continued: "You did promise Powhatan what was yours should bee his, and he the like to you; you called him father being in his land a stranger, and by the same reason so must I doe you."[4]

In Powhatan terms, the logic of their past association made it clear that the fictive kinship ties they had formed in Tsenacommacah must hold in a reciprocal fashion while Pocahontas and her delegation were in England. Yet Smith reacted with evident panic because the English context was bounded by an entirely different set of rules. His immediate worry almost seems to have been that someone would overhear Pocahontas call him father, and he hastily tried to persuade her that such a relationship would not do in England, where the differences in their social status overrode any other connection between them. Smith explained that his reaction was not really about his own preference; instead, it was a clear recognition of English norms. Having Pocahontas call him "father," he explained, "which though I would have excused, I durst not allow of that title, because she was a Kings daughter."[5] However much he aspired to social advancement, some things could not be changed. John Smith was born a commoner, and although Pocahontas may have been an Indian, she was of royal birth.

Nonetheless, Smith's explanation did not sit well with Pocahontas, who called Smith to task for his past and present behavior. In addition, she did more than just scold him for his blunder. She also made a clear statement in defense of his obligations under their alliance and as someone who had accepted kinship status. Again, her insistence that Smith was bound by Native American rules of kinship and alliance comes through in Smith's account of the conversation. He even described the way Pocahontas's displeasure showed on her face as she explained his obligations to her people. Smith tells us that "with a well set countenance she said, Were you not afraid to come into my fathers Countrie, and caused feare in him and all his people (but mee) and feare you here I should call you father; I tell you then I will, and you shall call mee childe, and so I will bee for ever and ever your Countrieman."[6]

Even Smith's cowardice, Pocahontas suggests, did not cancel his responsibilities. To him she insisted that Powhatans and English were now bound to one another, and he had been instrumental in the binding. Her remarks also reveal that, after Smith returned to England, the Jamestown colonists sought to avoid obligations incurred by his policies and agreements. They had even told Wahunsonacock that Captain John Smith was no longer alive. Pocahontas's description reveals how little trust was left in the relationship without Smith. "They did tell us alwaies you were dead," Pocahontas reported to Smith, "and I knew no other till I came to Plimoth; yet Powhatan did command Uttamatomakkin to seeke you, and know the truth, because your Countriemen will lie much."[7]

By anyone's account, then or now, Captain John Smith and Pocahontas had a complex relationship. For historians, one of its most interesting aspects is that we are able to see how their bond and even their interpretations of it shifted as the context changed. By examining elements of their interactions (mostly through Smith's own accounts), we see glimpses of the ways in which their relationship changed. This is not ideal, of course; one would wish for a broader range of sources. However, Smith's writings are both important and useful. Moreover, other kinds of evidence help us understand how Pocahontas and her father, Wahunsonacock, known as Powhatan by the colonists, regarded their alliance. Even Smith's own writings provide clear echoes of Powhatan voices. Sometimes his confusion as to why Wahunsonacock or Pocahontas spoke or behaved as they did comes through quite distinctly. Even in his uncertainty he tells us more about their attitudes and actions than he realized.

During Pocahontas's celebrated trip to England in 1616–1617, Captain John Smith cautiously tried to capitalize on their past connection. Having written that Pocahontas had saved his life when she was still a child, he could not ignore her when she was actually in England. After all, if he had truly been so closely linked to the Powhatan princess and her powerful father, then how could he not pay his respects to the most celebrated royal visitor England had seen in many years? Yet Smith was keenly aware that the context in England was dramatically different. What worked as the basis for a mutually beneficial association in North America now seemed like the worst kind of social climbing and posturing.

In England, Smith's pretensions to be Powhatan's equal and to be kin to Pocahontas and her father were wildly inappropriate. While she was there, what mattered most was that Pocahontas was Native American royalty; she was of gentle birth. In the eyes of the English public and court, she may have been exotic; to them she was after all a savage princess even if one who had converted to Christianity, but above everything she was a princess. Smith remained a commoner, however, and no amount of bragging about his shrewd colonial and military strategies could change that fact.

After they finally met, Smith wrote about their reunion. In his posturing and prudent caution, we can nevertheless see traces both of Pocahontas's insistence that Smith's behavior in England was inappropriate and that his conduct in Tsenacommacah and Virginia had become suspect to her as a result. We also see Smith's confusion about how to handle the meeting within the English context when he knew that Pocahontas was correct in characterizing their past relationship. Smith tells us, as he reportedly told Pocahontas, that the difference in their social rank made it inappropriate for him to address her in kinship terms.

Certainly he wanted his readers to see that he had not chosen to participate in an improper association. He had not overstepped his station; rather, the misunderstanding was a cultural miscue. However, there was more to the issue than Smith's insistence that he had behaved correctly. In reporting the conversation he also makes it clear that kinship had indeed formed the basis of much of the Powhatan-English alliance that Smith and Pocahontas had helped to create. As Pocahontas and Smith faced one another in England, both seemed to realize that the ties of fictive kinship they had claimed years earlier had not really survived. The alliance that had served both parties for a time in North America was no longer needed by England's colony; thus it was no longer a reality for the Powhatans.

Pocahontas's reproachful words to Captain Smith in England are fascinating for several reasons. Her assertion about having heard that Smith was dead implies that the continuation of the alliance was somehow dependent on Smith and that it would survive as long as Smith himself was alive. At the very least her report suggests that the English in Virginia may have understood the association in those rather personal terms, which may be why they told Powhatan that Smith was dead. Regardless of whether the Virginia colonists truly understood the partnership in those terms, Pocahontas's speech to Smith makes it clear that the Powhatans understood it to have been cemented by a bond of kinship. In England, Pocahontas insisted on acknowledging that relationship, much to Smith's discomfort.

In many ways, when Captain Smith encountered Lady Rebecca on his home territory rather than on hers, their meeting marked the beginning of the end for an era of English-Algonquian alliance in Tsenacommacah. Until that point, however, both sides had tried a range of strategies to make the relationship work and to do so to their own advantage. Kinship was one of the most effective and enduring approaches for the decade-long Powhatan-English alliance.

The paramount chief Wahunsonacock first tried creating fictive kinship ties with Jamestown English colonists, and his daughter eventually established literal familial ties with one of the colonists. Throughout the first two decades of the Powhatan-English connection, kinship was one of the Powhatans' most important strategies to map the English newcomers into the Powhatan world. By creating family ties with the Jamestown colonists, the Powhatans could secure an alliance with the English at Jamestown. Furthermore, under Captain John Smith's leadership, the English colonists agreed to both the metaphor and the alliance.

All of the existing evidence suggests that Wahunsonacock (rather than any English colonial leader) first offered kinship as a means of binding the two peoples together. Yet early modern Europeans well understood the importance of family attachments as a means of establishing and expanding alliances. European families, commoners and royalty alike, had long used marriage to unite families, trading enterprises, and kingdoms. Early English colonization was fueled by these networks.

In the late sixteenth century, English colonial ventures in North America were driven in part by family networks, most notably in the voyages of Sir Humphrey Gilbert and his half brother, Sir Walter Raleigh. In the seventeenth century, Sir Ferdinando Gorges, along with his son, nephew, and grandson, tried for decades to secure his plans for a successful colony in northern New England. In southern New England, families like the Winthrops and the Saltonstalls used kinship connections to link their interests throughout the region and beyond in the early modern Atlantic world. Moreover, in the Chesapeake, the Calvert family's kinship ties helped to ensure the success of the Maryland Colony.

Thus, although specific kinship patterns and the obligations they entailed almost certainly differed for early modern Europeans and Native Americans, the former would have recognized them as an important means of establishing and expanding alliances. In addition, when Native Americans such as Wahunsonacock used kinship terms to characterize ties between colonists and Indians, the metaphor resonated with Europeans. For each group, kinship offered a way to place the other in the complex social space of colonial North America. This is not to say, however, that kinship ties, metaphorical or otherwise, meant the same things to both peoples. Indeed, the fact that each party often meant something different when it used the same metaphor was one reason that kinship was a powerful tool for alliance: Its meaning was flexible.

For the Powhatans and other Americans in the Chesapeake, kinship was an effective means of establishing a partnership, and the Jamestown colony arrived on the scene at a moment when the alliance patterns in the region were undergoing increasing consolidation. The Powhatans, for instance, were a large group of approximately thirty culturally similar Algonquian-speaking bands who joined together politically in a paramount chiefdom. The paramount chief had many names, but he was known to English colonists and perhaps to most outsiders primarily as Powhatan. Most modern scholars now prefer the name he seems to have used most often among his own people, Wahunsonacock. Although virtually all accounts indicate that Wahunsonacock was an unusually influential leader, he could not force compliance with his will and ruled instead through persuasion and consensus.

In the early seventeenth century—when English colonists arrived at Jamestown—the Powhatan chiefdom was an expanding power, and Wahunsonacock himself exercised the greatest degree of influence over those members of his paramount chiefdom who were closest to his capital town, Werowocomoco. Those who were living on the outer reaches of Tsenacommacah were more likely to deal with other Indian and European nations independently of Wahunsonacock and at times even against his wishes.[8]

Tsenacommacah ranged across much of what is now eastern Virginia. Scholars continue to debate the question of which peoples should be counted as part of the Powhatan paramount chiefdom. Christian Feest's conservative estimate limits it to those who lived in the James and York river basins and excludes the Chesapeakes and Chickahominies. However, Helen Rountree contends that Feest's interpretation is based on a fundamentally European model of ethnicity and political organization because it requires evidence of full assimilation of member peoples and total loyalty to the paramount chief. By contrast, Rountree argues persuasively that such European models cannot adequately explain seventeenth-century Algonquian life. Accordingly, she offers a more expansive interpretation of the extent of the Powhatan paramount chiefdom by suggesting that it included all of the Algonquian-speaking peoples of the coastal plain of what later became Virginia.[9] In this interpretation, the chiefdoms located nearer to the older, more established centers of the Powhatan paramount chiefdom were more fully integrated into the expanding polity, while those farther away tended to be newer, less fully absorbed additions. However, all of them can be counted as Powhatan peoples.

The Powhatans were not the only Algonquians in the Chesapeake area to have formed a paramount chiefdom. The Piscataways also had one that seems to have predated that of the Powhatans, and the two peoples had a wary relationship and were sometimes enemies. Each followed similar strategies of incorporating linguistically related groups so as to build up their strength in the face of threats from one another, as well as from the Mannahoacs and the Iroquoian-speaking Massawomecks and Susquehannocks.[10]

Powhatan relations with many of the peoples along the northern fringes of Tsenacommacah were usually friendly, as were those with people from the lower Potomac River and the Patuxent River.[11] The Powhatans were aware of the Susquehannocks to the north but do not seem to have had much direct contact with them. They did, however, endure periodic raiding by the Massawomecks, and their shared enmity with the Massawomecks may have helped to keep communications networks open between the Powhatan and Piscataway paramount chiefdoms.[12]

In turn, the Iroquoian-speaking Massawomecks played a major role in the Chesapeake area during the first three decades of the seventeenth century. They drop out of the historical record by midcentury, after which time they do not seem to have maintained an important presence in the area. However, in the early seventeenth century, the Massawomecks were important fur-trading partners of Virginia and Maryland colonists, and they also traded with some of the Chesapeake Algonquians, though they raided many more of them, including the Powhatans and Piscataways.[13]

Most scholars agree that the Massawomecks spoke an Iroquois language, and James Pendergast has suggested that they were the same people whom the French called the Antouhonorons. Pendergast argues that, from the late sixteenth century until the first decade of the seventeenth, the Massawomecks lived in the region east of the Niagara River, between Lakes Ontario and Erie, where they were allied with other Iroquois peoples. From this homeland in the first decade of the seventeenth century, the Massawomecks periodically traveled south and harassed the Susquehannocks on the lower reaches of the Susquehannock River, as well as the Nanticokes, Piscataways, and Powhatans on Chesapeake Bay.

In the first decade of the seventeenth century, when European colonial settlements began taking hold, the Powhatans were an expanding people, as were the Piscataways. As for European nations that aspired to create empires, Native American expansion also brought with it material goods and wealth, along with growing political and cultural influence and power. In the early seventeenth century, alliances between Indians and Europeans helped each party to expand.

Accurate sources of information were crucial in this process, and Europeans arrived in North America to discover that Indian peoples had well-established and sophisticated networks covering tens and sometimes hundreds of miles. The peoples of Tsenacommacah were linked to each other and to more distant peoples by trade and information networks. Often these functioned according to baton-passing principles. The Powhatans, for instance, had relatively little direct contact with the Susquehannocks, but they knew of them and could learn more through their contacts with Patuxent River peoples. Similarly, Piscataways could tell Powhatans about the Massawomecks' activities because they were a common enemy.

Ultimately the threat the Massawomecks presented to Chesapeake-area Algonquians was so great that thwarting it outweighed other rivalries. Powhatans and Piscataways might mistrust one another in many contexts, but they were more likely than not to cooperate in the face of Massawomeck incursions. Furthermore, if the Piscataways formed the first line of defense against the Massawomecks, then, for their part, the Powhatans were well placed to tell other, more distant, peoples about the English colonial presence, which was spreading through Tsenacommacah.

Because they depended upon reliable sources of information, many alliances were primarily mechanisms to ensure active communication networks. Native American–European connections, as much as those between native peoples, included a number of efforts to maintain an open flow of information, but cultural differences made all such attempts particularly challenging. One way to ensure reliable communication systems while avoiding cultural misunderstandings was to exchange children.

In some ways this idea was rather similar to the kidnapping strategy we have already seen, with the crucial difference that the exchange was usually voluntary on the part of each community's leaders, if not of the children themselves. In Tsenacommacah some English boys were sent to live with the Powhatans, while some Powhatan boys were sent to live among the English in Jamestown. Children's ability to learn new things and their nonthreatening age made them appealing to each side. They could learn the other culture's language and customs and act as cultural and linguistic interpreters when they were older.

Wahunsonacock used this strategy in a particularly effective way. He combined the technique of using children as intercultural mediators and interpreters with that of ongoing, systematic cultural observation. His most effective means of learning about the Jamestown colonists was not through elaborate meetings and negotiations over which he actually presided. Nor did he depend solely on English or Powhatan boys sent to learn a new way of life. Rather, Wahunsonacock used his daughter Pocahontas as his eyes and ears in the English settlement and instructed her to conduct extensive ethnographic observation for him.

The bare outline of what we know about Pocahontas is quite brief. She was a daughter of Wahunsonacock, and she was born sometime between 1595 and 1597. One of her names was Matoaka, but the English colonists at Jamestown came to know her primarily by one of her nicknames: Pocahontas.

Some sources, particularly the accounts of Captain John Smith, suggest that she was Powhatan's favorite daughter. She was only ten or eleven years old when she first encountered Captain Smith and the other English colonists. Nevertheless, the young girl made a strong impression on Smith, a soldier and veteran of European wars, who was not easily impressed. Pocahontas seems to have had frequent contact with the Jamestown colonists for several years, often bringing gifts and messages from her father. Her ongoing connection with the Jamestown colonists ended when she reached puberty, and around 1610 she married a Powhatan warrior named Kecoum.[14]

In 1613, when Pocahontas was about eighteen, she was lured aboard an English ship and kidnapped in a captive-for-diplomatic-ransom version of the by now long-tested kidnapping ploy. She was held prisoner as part of a protracted struggle between the Jamestown colonists and her father, Wahunsonacock. As a result of growing discontent between the Patawomeks and the Powhatans, Pocahontas was captured when a Patawomek leader colluded with an English colonist to ambush her. She was thus caught in the tangled lines of shifting alliances.

During her captivity, John Rolfe confessed to Sir Thomas Dale, governor of Jamestown, that he had fallen in love with Pocahontas. Rolfe began courting her, and, with Powhatan's permission, they eventually married, after which she converted to Christianity. The name given to her at her baptism was Lady Rebecca. She and Rolfe had one son, and the family traveled to England soon after their marriage, where as we have seen, Pocahontas received considerable public notice. When she was about to return to Virginia and to Tsenacommacah in 1617, Pocahontas fell ill and died. She was buried in England, never having made it home to North America.

This brief sketch of her life is merely the barest outline. It does not adequately explore the role that Pocahontas played in mediating between Powhatan and English peoples in the early seventeenth century. Nor does it consider the extraordinary project of ethnographic observation she undertook, beginning as a girl, with a break during puberty, and then resuming again as a woman.

From the time John Smith first began writing about his experiences in the land known to English people as Virginia and with the people of Tsenacommacah, scholars have continued to interpret and reinterpret Pocahontas and the symbol she presents for her age and their own.[15] Pocahontas is most interesting not so much as an Indian princess who married an Englishman and traveled to England or because John Smith believed she saved his life when her father sought to execute Smith. These aspects of her life have received considerable attention. But Pocahontas is also a fascinating subject because she played a vital role in early Powhatan-English efforts at accommodation and alliance.

Perhaps we should understand John Smith's story of how Pocahontas saved his life in more metaphorical terms. Certainly the Powhatans used a rich vocabulary of metaphors to discuss important issues, as all Algonquian peoples did. However, where many scholars have argued persuasively, as we shall see, that the death intended for Captain John Smith that day was to be a symbolic loss of his former identity, they have focused only on the metaphorical meanings of that specific event for the Powhatans. There is, however, another way in which Pocahontas might be said to have saved Smith's life, regardless of whether he ever fully understood it, for Smith and the entire Jamestown colony survived because of the ongoing diplomatic role played by a ten- or eleven-year-old Algonquian girl.

It is well known that, during the early years of virtually all English colonial efforts, colonists had difficulty growing enough food to sustain themselves. As a result, they were heavily dependent on provisions from the Indians either as gifts or through trade; sometimes the colonists even stole foodstuffs outright when the Indians said that they had none to spare. The issue of stolen goods and of English dependence on the Indians' supplies was extremely important in shaping Indian-English relations.[16] It was not clear to either English settlers or Indian peoples that the colonies would survive and become permanent settlements. Nor did anyone know that the settlements would spread and eventually drive Indian communities away violently and involuntarily.[17]

In this early colonial setting, English colonists and Native Americans experimented with a variety of strategies that might enable them to learn more about each other and about the threats and opportunities they presented. It was thus essential to have individuals who could move between the cultures by interpreting or gain the colonists' trust and also communicate with and understand native peoples. In some ways, this seems to have been the type of role that Ferdinando Gorges had envisioned for some of his Algonquian captives.

Pocahontas filled this role in Jamestown by frequently visiting the colonial settlement and bringing messages and gifts from her father. Unlike Gorges's unwilling go-betweens, however, in Tsenacommacah, Wahunsonacock and his daughter created the role and controlled it. Pocahontas was trusted more than many other Indians in Jamestown, probably because she was a girl and therefore considered less of a military threat and less important to her people. In other words, because English people in the early seventeenth century believed that girls were of little significance and because they could see that only men were warriors in Powhatan culture, they assumed they could allow Pocahontas access to their fort. The advantage to them (or so they hoped) was that they could learn things by having more extensive contact with her than they would risk with someone who held a more threatening social position within an English context.

Because it was extremely useful to him, Wahunsonacock permitted and encouraged Pocahontas to maintain contact with the Jamestown colonists and approved of her treatment of John Smith as a father. According to Smith's account, Pocahontas sometimes called him a "father" to her, and they apparently had a playful adult-child relationship.[18] This would have been consistent with the father's role in a matrilineal Algonquian culture. It was rather different from the father's role in English culture, however, although Captain Smith did not seem to have understood the important difference. Because the Powhatans were matrilineal, issues of genealogical descent and clan membership were reckoned through the mother's line, not the father's, as in English culture.

In Powhatan society, the mother's responsibilities in child rearing were extensive, but the role of a Powhatan father was unlike that of an English father. The mother's brother was the adult man who helped her rear her child. Because they belonged to his clan and not to their father's, he, not the child's father, had the task of teaching and disciplining his sister's children. A child's father, by contrast, played a role more like an uncle in European culture. He was usually thought of as a playful figure who indulged the children.[19]

For Pocahontas to call Smith her father implied an adoptive relationship. However, it did not recognize the degree of authority that the term involved in English culture, even if Pocahontas eventually came to understand its meaning and importance in the context of English society. Furthermore, Pocahontas's relationship with her biological father was unusually complex in ways that may well have confused the English colonists with regard to the meaning of kinship terms like "father." Wahunsonacock was the preeminent spiritual and political leader of an expansive paramount chiefdom, and his children were also his people.[20] As a powerful leader who wielded great spiritual and political authority, Wahunsonacock could exercise considerable control over Pocahontas, although his influence was not primarily as her father.

Thus, Pocahontas charmed Captain John Smith and the other colonists, gained frequent access to the innermost areas of the Jamestown fort, and generally did things for Wahunsonacock that he could not do for himself. As the paramount leader of Tsenacommacah and an extremely influential spiritual leader, he would have lost dignity and authority if he had gone to Jamestown, and he certainly could not make the kind of frequent and casual visits that Pocahontas made.

Those visits gave her great opportunities to observe the colonists informally in ways that were very helpful to Powhatan. Moreover, any negotiations that Powhatan personally conducted with the colonists carried a different weight and were treated accordingly by the colonists. So, for some matters, he sent his daughter rather than going in person or sending warriors as messengers.[21] Because the colonists thought of Pocahontas as Wahunsonacock's favorite daughter, they took her seriously as his emissary and understood that her presence on formal diplomatic visits was symbolic of Wahunsonacock's good intentions.

However, as a child, and especially as a girl, Pocahontas had more flexibility in negotiating and in observing activities in the English settlement. As a little girl she was not risking as much dignity or power.[22] And although Captain Smith often wrote of Pocahontas's friendship with him and the Jamestown colonists, even Smith wondered whether she was acting for her father. Smith openly admitted that, "were it the policie of her father thus to imploy her, or the ordinance of God thus to make her his instrument, or her extraordinarie affection to our Nation, I know not."[23]

When Pocahontas was older and held captive in Jamestown, John Rolfe sought to marry her. Their marriage served both sides, and in agreeing to marry Rolfe, Pocahontas was securing the bonds of kinship between the two peoples in a way she knew the English would understand and that would benefit her father and her people. Marrying John Rolfe allowed the adult Pocahontas to continue to have a degree of access to the English colony that she otherwise could not have and that Wahunsonacock himself could never have. Both sides regarded their union as a powerful, symbolic end to the violence that had raged between them, and it allowed Wahunsonacock to continue to gather extensive knowledge about the English and their colony.[24]

Wahunsonacock tried many strategies aimed at neutralizing the English and making it possible to live with them by incorporating them into his sphere of influence. One of the most important and enduring tactics he employed involved extending kinship protections and obligations to the Jamestown colonists. In using kinship ties as an approach, he attempted not only to establish a secure alliance with the English colonists but also to do so by integrating them into Algonquian culture. When that plan eventually broke down, his daughter tried the same strategy in reverse. She would establish a kinship relationship that even the literal English would understand, and she would do so by adopting English culture.

The famous story that Captain John Smith told in which he claimed that Pocahontas interceded with her father and saved Smith's life concerned one of Wahunsonacock's early attempts to incorporate the Jamestown settlers into both Algonquian culture and the Powhatan paramount chiefdom as kin. Smith's description of Powhatan's desire to execute him is the only record that we have of this event.[25] His account, however, provides a great deal of information that has led modern scholars to conclude that the events he described were part of an adoption and initiation ceremony through which Smith would become a member of the Powhatan community.[26]

Smith wrote that he was feasted, and then, in Wahunsonacock's presence, he was forced to put his head on two large stones. He wrote that several Powhatan men stood ready to beat his brains out with their clubs when Pocahontas laid her head on top of Smith's and pleaded with Wahunsonacock for Smith's life. Smith wrote that he was brought to a great house in the woods two days later, where he was left alone for a while and then was joined by Wahunsonacock, whom Smith described as being dressed and painted in "the most fearfullest manner."[27]

In this house Wahunsonacock told Smith that he should go to Jamestown to get two great guns and a grindstone to give Wahunsonacock as gifts. In turn, Wahunsonacock would give Smith a tribal territory and consider him a son. This made it clear that Wahunsonacock was offering not only an alliance with the Jamestown colonists but also a particularly close association based on bringing Smith into Wahunsonacock's kinship network.[28] Smith either failed to understand what Wahunsonacock had offered or chose to stress the threatening aspects of his ordeal for his later English readers. Rather than exploring the implications of an adoptive relationship with the Powhatans, Smith provided a rather different slant. He expected, he told his readers, to be put to death at any time, probably to be eaten by the Powhatans. He never understood these events as rituals adopting him into Powhatan culture.

However, Smith's description of what actually happened to him in these ceremonies is consistent with what scholars know about Algonquian adoption rituals. Moreover, as Helen Rountree has pointed out, Smith's account is not consistent with evidence of Powhatan executions. Instead, when Smith was forced to place his head on the stones with warriors standing over him at the ready, he was participating in a ceremonial enactment of an execution, not an actual one.

The ritual signified his death to the assembled Powhatan community, but it was the demise of Smith's old identity, not of his physical body. When Pocahontas laid her head over Smith's and pleaded for his life, she was making a symbolic request for Smith's new existence as a member of the community.[29] In that capacity, Wahunsonacock would give him a position of status within the chiefdom, in the process neutralizing Smith and the colonists under his authority and ensuring peaceful coexistence under his control. All of this was done in Wahunsonacock's domain and after John Smith had been brought to him; Pocahontas's participation in the ceremony may have symbolized Smith's adoption directly into Wahunsonacock's own family, as well as into the community as a whole.

In offering to make Smith a werowance, Wahunsonacock used a tactic against the English that had succeeded with other Indian groups in and around Tsenacommacah.[30] He tried to absorb them into his expanding chiefdom as a subsidiary tribe in much the same way that the Powhatan paramount chiefdom had incorporated other less powerful Indian nations. Although Smith was unwilling to accept the offer and Wahunsonacock was never able to take in the English colony of Virginia as a tributary colony, Wahunsonacock considered the incorporation of the newcomers to be a viable tactic in the early years of English colonization. As we shall see in later chapters, it was a technique that other Native Americans also employed in their efforts to neutralize various European colonies.

Even as Wahunsonacock tried to incorporate the English into his domain on his own terms, the Jamestown colonists and their supporters were attempting to incorporate Wahunsonacock within King James's domain. Like the Powhatans, Jamestown's leaders tried a range of strategies to accomplish this. Initially, they focused on the language and symbolism of political subordination and tributary status. However, if Captain John Smith failed to understand the full implications and obligations of Powhatan kinship, Wahunsonacock himself comprehended the essential symbolism and implications of vassalage. This becomes painfully, almost comically, apparent in accounts of English-Powhatan negotiations in 1608.

Christopher Newport arrived from England as Virginia's new governor in 1608 and brought with him gifts for Wahunsonacock and orders to crown him as a vassal of King James I and VI. Newport sent Captain John Smith to persuade Wahunsonacock to travel to Jamestown for the coronation ceremony. Refusing to comply, Wahunsonacock told Smith that "if your King have sent me Presents, I also am a King, and this is my land: eight days I will stay to receive them. Your father is to come to me, not I to him."[31]

Wahunsonacock demonstrated his willingness to wait for English emissaries to visit him, but otherwise he refused any requests that failed to recognize his authority. Newport had badly misjudged Wahunsonacock, somewhat to Smith's delight. Newport had arrived in the colony to take over from Smith, and he did not exhibit much interest in learning from Smith's expertise. He should have listened to Smith in this case, however, because Smith was always aware of the aura of majesty that Wahunsonacock cultivated. In this case, Wahunsonacock was unyielding, and the new English colonial governor had to acquiesce to his wishes. Because Wahunsonacock refused to travel to Jamestown to meet Newport and receive King James's gifts, Newport was forced to go to Wahunsonacock, bringing with him the gifts, which included a scarlet cloak and a crown.

When Newport finally made the trip, the scene that ensued was not so much a dignified presentation to the head of a tributary state as a contest of wills with comic overtones. Wahunsonacock agreed to participate in the ceremony but declined outright to go along with some parts of it. He refused, for instance, to kneel while the colonists put a crown on his head. Some of the colonists finally leaned so hard on Wahunsonacock's shoulders that he was pushed off balance and stooped just a little, at which point three Englishmen hastily pushed the crown onto his head.[32] Captain John Smith wrote about the ceremony and described Wahunsonacock's refusal to follow the English script. In his account, the colonists' frustrations and Wahunsonacock's unshakable dignity in the face of a ceremony that took on increasingly farcical overtones come through clearly: "But a foule trouble there was to make him kneele to receive his Crowne, he neither knowing the majesty nor meaning of a Crowne, nor bending of the knee, endured so many perswasions, examples, and instructions, as tyred them all; at last by leaning hard on his shoulders, he a little stooped, and three having the crowne in their hands put it on his head."[33]

In the end, we learn not that Wahunsonacock failed to understand the meaning of a crown or the significance of kneeling. It is evident that Wahunsonacock understood all too clearly the elements of subordination contained in the English gifts and especially in the presentation ceremony. He reciprocated by giving Newport his old shoes and his mantle. Although the symbolism of the shoes is unclear, scholarly interpretations of the mantle strongly suggest that the shoes must also have carried an important symbolic message.

A deerskin garment now held in the collections of the Ashmolean Museum seems to hold a key to understanding the ways in which Wahunsonacock used mapping in his dealings with the English.[34] Although it is impossible to know for certain, the evidence strongly suggests that the deerskin mantle in the Ashmolean is indeed the one that Wahunsonacock gave Christopher Newport in 1608. On the mantle are images of a central human figure surrounded by circles that represent a map of Wahunsonacock's domain, a map, in other words, of Tsenacommacah and of the peoples who composed the Powhatan paramount chiefdom.

Wahunsonacock had previously given Smith a geography lesson in the layout of Tsenacommacah. Then, following Newport's attempt to incorporate him as a vassal of King James, Wahunsonacock presented the colonists with a mantle that was also a map. Wahunsonacock had done what the Muscovy Company had ordered its ships to do: He had presented a powerful foreign king with a map of his sphere of influence. Unlike the English maps the Muscovy Company described, which would have shown the city of London and its harbor full of ships, Wahunsonacock's map showed political and perhaps spiritual authority, as well as alliance connections. The fact that he gave the gift in the context of Newport's ceremony allowed Wahunsonacock to make a strong statement that he was sovereign over his domain and that he would be King James's ally but not his vassal. He might be willing to incorporate the English into his map—to add them as another circle on the mantle—but he would not be subsumed within their realm.

Wahunsonacock presented a symbolic statement with a powerful visual representation, one whose meaning should have been apparent even when language proved inadequate. In short, Wahunsonacock too was using a map to represent existing alliances and to establish new ones. The English colonists should have recognized the strategy; however, there is no evidence that they did so. Instead, their focus under Newport was on creating a hierarchical alliance that would firmly establish Wahunsonacock as an English tributary leader.

While Newport succeeded in crowning Wahunsonacock supposedly as a vassal of England's monarch and Smith insisted that Wahunsonacock did not understand the majesty of either a crown or the English coronation ceremony, it was Wahunsonacock's power and dignity that carried the day. If anything, it was the English colonists who appeared ridiculous as they struggled to get Wahunsonacock to bend until "he a little stooped." Wahunsonacock's refusal to go to Jamestown and his insistence on maintaining a majestic demeanor in all of his dealings with the colonists made Pocahontas's regular, casual visits with the English very important to him.[35]

Although Wahunsonacock was making a cooperative gesture when he gave his mantle to Newport as a reciprocal gift, that action clearly demonstrated his authority to Newport and to Newport's king, who had sent him a scarlet mantle. In addition, he made it clear that he would go no further in meeting the wishes of the English. After the exchange of presents, Wahunsonacock refused to provide Newport with the information that he most desired about the nearby Monacans. Smith noted that Wahunsonacock "gave his old shooes and his mantell to Captaine Newport: but perceiving his purpose was to discover the Monacans, he laboured to divert his resolution, refusing to lend him either men or guides more then Namontack; and so after some small complementall kindnesse on both sides ... we returned to the Fort."[36]

Wahunsonacock was unwilling to provide too much information to the English, and they regarded him with a similar degree of distrust. In the midst of English rituals designed to portray Wahunsonacock's subordination in a symbolic display of hierarchy, Wahunsonacock continued to insist on his own authority, as well as his territorial and cultural boundaries, and he deftly maneuvered to limit English power.[37] It was precisely that absence of both trust and widespread cultural exchange that made it vital for Wahunsonacock to have someone like Pocahontas be his eyes and ears and a nonthreatening reminder of his influence among the colonists.

In this context, Pocahontas's marriage to colonist John Rolfe appears as another way in which she could fill an important role for her father. Pocahontas had stopped going to Jamestown and remained instead in Powhatan villages. Wahunsonacock had probably removed her from contact with the English when she reached puberty. However, as mentioned above, in 1612 Pocahontas was kidnapped by an English ship, when violent exchanges between the Powhatans and the colonists were taking place, and she was held hostage during negotiations with Wahunsonacock.[38]

Pocahontas's capture was made possible by the fact that the Virginia colonists had continued to seek alliances with other Indian nations as their conflicts with Wahunsonacock increased. As early as 1609 the Virginia Company urged its colonists to continue to seek intercultural alliances with peoples outside of Wahunsonacock's network. Specifically, the company advised its settlers to ally with nations who not only could help defend them against the Powhatans but also lived far enough away from the colony to present less of an immediate threat if the alliance should collapse.[39]

The following year, Virginia colonist Samuel Argall made the first steps toward establishing a partnership that would prove crucial in shaping the rest of Pocahontas's adult life and in reorienting the Powhatan-English relationship. Argall established a trade connection with the werowance of Patawomeke. The Patawomekes, situated farther to the north along the Potomac River, represented a rival power to the Powhatan paramount chiefdom and a significant source of trade for the Virginia colonists.[40]

For the next two years, from 1610 to 1612, Argall traded for maize with the werowance of Patawomeke, in the process helping to feed the colonists during their continuing conflicts with the Powhatans and providing the Patawomekes with a good source of valuable European trade goods. The trade relationship soon became more. In 1612, when Samuel Argall returned to Patawomeke, the two parties agreed to a defensive collaboration against Wahunsonacock.

Argall was able to put his new alliance to the test the following year when the colonists learned that Pocahontas was visiting friends at Patawomeke.[41] He gained the cooperation of the Patawomekes' werowance and, with the assistance of his brother, a lesser werowance named Japazaw, lured Pocahontas aboard an English ship, where her Patawomeke hosts allowed her to be captured by the English and taken to Jamestown as a hostage. The negotiations for her release were protracted, and she remained a prisoner for about a year. It was during Pocahontas's captivity in Jamestown that John Rolfe courted her.[42]

Their marriage brought a temporary end to the violence that had dominated relations between Powhatan and English people for several years, suggesting once again that kinship could be a useful means to promote alliance. Their union also brought Wahunsonacock the advantage of once again gaining extensive and intimate knowledge of the English and their colony through his own daughter.

The surviving records indicate that the marriage was not initiated by Wahunsonacock but was instead the result of several English actions, beginning with the capture of Pocahontas. It seems clear, however, that Wahunsonacock agreed to the marriage and that he did so in order to have Pocahontas on the scene as a trusted observer rather than to establish kinship ties with English colonists.

The latter point is suggested by an incident that occurred shortly after Pocahontas and Rolfe were married. Thomas Dale sent Ralph Hamor on his behalf to ask Powhatan for permission to marry another of Powhatan's daughters.[43] In this instance the English were using kinship to anchor an alliance. Dale was already married, but he seems to have assumed that he could give Powhatan's daughter to another, subordinate man to marry, which would also have been consistent with Powhatan culture. However, Wahunsonacock refused the request, and he continued to decline to enter the English settlements. After six years of ongoing experience with English colonists and after Pocahontas had converted to Christianity, Wahunsonacock had learned that, although family ties could be useful, the English could not be trusted completely to comply with or even to recognize kinship obligations.

With Pocahontas established in the heart of the English colony as Lady Rebecca, however, Wahunsonacock could continue to employ kinship as a strategy for controlling the English, even as he prepared for its failure. In the meantime, however, Pocahontas gave him more than just the means to bind the English to his paramount chiefdom by kinship. As Lady Rebecca, she gave her father the ability to learn more about the English and to have someone he trusted watching the colonial community. Once the marriage was a reality, Pocahontas resumed her role as observer of English culture at even closer range.

When Pocahontas and John Rolfe journeyed to England in 1616, Wahunsonacock sent a priest named Uttamatomakin (also called Tomocomo) along with her. Wahunsonacock instructed Uttamatomakin to learn about England and its people, including the size of the population and whether the English were as strong as Smith and other colonists had claimed.[44] Uttamatomakin's conversation with Smith offers more evidence that Wahunsonacock and Smith had created an association based on kinship.

When Smith spoke with Pocahontas and Uttamatomakin in London, Uttamatomakin told Smith that "the King purposely sent him, as they say, to number the people here, and informe him well what wee were and our state." Just as importantly, he told Smith that he was looking for John Smith in England to ensure that he obtained reliable information. He also noted that he did so on Wahunsonacock's instructions. Smith's account describes his meeting with Uttamatomakin as a chance encounter: "Coming to London, where by chance I met him, having renewed our acquaintance, where many were desirous to heare and see his behavior, hee told me Powhatan did bid him to finde me out, to shew him our God, the King, Queene, and Prince, I so much had told them of."[45] Sending Uttamatomakin to have Smith to show him all of those things was an appropriate request of an ally and the obligation of kinfolk. Pocahontas's marriage to John Rolfe made such a scouting trip possible, and, like the trip to Jamestown, this was a journey that Wahunsonacock could not or would not make himself.

Ironically, the England trip made possible by the new intercultural kinship ties that bound Wahunsonacock's family to an English one also marked the end of hopes for a lasting peace. Pocahontas would not survive the trip, and when Uttamatomakin returned home, he could report what he had seen in London, which was rapidly becoming one of the largest cities in Europe. With a population of two hundred thousand people, London would have made it clear to any Powhatan visitor that the English strength lay in numbers, if nowhere else. It is small wonder, then, that after Wahunsonacock's death and within five years of Uttamatomakin's visit to England, Powhatan warriors would rise up and attempt to end English colonization of their territory once and for all.

Pocahontas died in England in 1617, when she was between twenty and twenty-two years of age. She had lived as an English woman, Lady Rebecca, for only a few years. Even then she continued to serve as her father's eyes and ears among the strangers, as she had done while still a child. Moreover, as Lady Rebecca, Pocahontas became a symbol for many English people who pointed to her as the first Native American woman ever to learn English, be baptized, marry, and have a child with an Englishman. To them, Pocahontas represented the way in which all Indians would inevitably become English.

Yet, to Wahunsonacock, Pocahontas was one of the ways he tried to make Englishmen into Powhatan subjects. Pocahontas probably thought of herself as a Powhatan who had become English without abandoning her Powhatan identity or allegiance and who remained a stranger among the English, even if bound by obligations of kinship. Indeed, in the Powhatan world, adoption was as much an adding on as a replacement.

Pocahontas could accept Christianity and Englishness without renouncing her identity as a Powhatan woman and without giving up her filial duties. When Pocahontas met John Smith again in London, she told him things that are extremely revealing. She reminded him that he had been a stranger in Wahunsonacock's country, and she pointed out that she was now in the same position in Smith's country. She explicitly laid out their kinship relation and insisted that it carried lifelong obligations.

When Pocahontas reported to Smith that the colonists had told Wahunsonacock that Smith was dead, she also explained that either those responsibilities had not been extended to other Jamestown colonists or they had failed to honor them. She made Wahunsonacock's distrust of the remaining colonists clear when she told Smith that Wahunsonacock had ordered Uttamatomakin to learn the truth while in England "because your Countriemen will lie much." Smith's account of their conversation in England suggests that Pocahontas continued to think of herself as a Powhatan who had access to English culture and who could move between the two, but her trust and her identity remained with the other Powhatan people in Tsenacommacah.

The Powhatan-English alliance continued to deteriorate over the five years after Pocahontas's death and that of her father. The irrevocable break came when Wahunsonacock's successor, Opechancanough, led a surprise colony-wide March attack in 1622. Shock waves over the breakdown in the Powhatan-English peace spread for hundreds of miles, and with them came the end of any widespread use of kinship to bind the two peoples. The Powhatan-English alliance would not easily be replicated elsewhere. Nevertheless, the imperative to find workable strategies for intercultural cooperation was just as strong in the 1620s and 1630s as it had been at Jamestown's founding in 1607. No single group could yet stop trying to map the others that surrounded it, and none could stand alone without intercultural allies.

4

Alliance Making and the Struggle for the Soul of Plymouth Colony

Plymouth Colony was established only two years before the 1622 Powhatan assault on Jamestown. We often think of Plymouth's colonists as being isolated in the colony's early years, by both design and accident. After all, Plymouth was founded by members of an extreme Protestant sect that took its interpretation of the need to purify the Christian church to levels that made even other puritans uneasy. However, regardless of how much Plymouth's separatists desired isolation, the colony was not cut off from others, nor could it be. As with all other communities, Plymouth's settlers depended upon supplies and information that they could obtain only through regular contact with other people, both Native Americans and Europeans. Their very survival depended upon it. They too had to map the peoples around them. Like it or not, their existence was also dependent upon their ability to contain conflicts to which they themselves were not parties.

When colonists in Plymouth received news of the 1622 Powhatan attack on English settlers in Virginia, they responded by taking careful stock of the Indians around them. They looked for signs of new alliances between New England Algonquian tribes and sent out agents to discover whether any New England Algonquians had kinship or other ties with the Powhatans. They did this despite the fact that Plymouth was more than four hundred miles from Jamestown. Moreover, colonists in Plymouth built their fort partly as a result of fears prompted by the 1622 assault in Virginia.

The colony was only two years old when its residents learned that their fellow English settlement to the south had suffered dramatic casualties in a surprise raid. These earliest years of the colony (and indeed Plymouth's first decade) are best known to us through the eyes of William Bradford, yet Bradford lived as a man threatened and besieged. As we have seen, everyone in Plymouth Colony faced very real threats to their continued survival; however, fear of external enemies was only one of Bradford's anxieties. Wholly committed to his personal and idiosyncratic vision of what Plymouth plantation and all English colonies should be, Bradford fought aggressively against the many people who had different visions of Plymouth's place in the world and of the way in which colonies should expand.

Historians have largely missed those other visions and voices, although they were strong and loud enough in their day to prompt anxious reactions from Bradford. Yet those men and women left traces of their ideas and their lives in the records that survived them. Many appear even in the written product of Bradford's concerted effort to emphasize his own interpretation over those of others. Their lives and ideas appear, with Bradford himself, in Bradford's own history of the colony's early years.[1] Ultimately, however, Bradford's account makes it clear that other colonists saw intercultural alliances as more necessary than Bradford did.

One of those against whom Bradford struggled the longest and most energetically was Isaac Allerton. Allerton the elder played a major role in Plymouth Colony's first decade, and Bradford devoted many pages of his history to depicting Allerton as a misguided man whose greed betrayed the Plymouth community. Bradford's focus on Allerton is fascinating. He quite clearly singled Allerton out for attention and deliberately depicted him as someone whose actions damaged the colony and whom the Plymouth community could no longer trust. Bradford's account of Allerton's place within the colony contains a revealing contradiction because the larger Plymouth community did not share Bradford's assessment of Allerton, no matter how hard he tried to insist that Allerton had sold out the settlement.

Bradford began writing his history in 1630, just at the time when his differences with Allerton were becoming quite intense. The conjunction of dates is significant. Bradford wrote his history of the colony during an ongoing struggle to promote his particular concept of the settlement above all others and especially above the direction Allerton represented. In other words, Bradford wrote *Of Plymouth Plantation* as a way of working out his idea of colonization. He was prompted to do so by community dissension, expanding contacts with Native Americans, and the presence of competing colonies.

Isaac Allerton was involved in all three of these threats as far as Bradford was concerned. Allerton began seeking a wider and more varied array of trade alliances and intercultural relationships than Plymouth had engaged in during its first decade. Although Bradford believed in mapping the peoples who surrounded Plymouth, he did so with the primary goal of defending the colony against them and strongly resisted the attempts of people like Allerton to forge closer connections with different cultures.

William Bradford turned to writing as a weapon in his struggle against Allerton and tried to use his account to shape Plymouth's future by recording the authoritative version of its early history. It was an interesting approach, and it has been remarkably successful. Generations of scholars have accepted Bradford's narrative as one of the central accounts of early colonial North America and as a premier testament of early American history and literature. An eloquent and important work, it presents an important view of early colonial North America, but it was not the only one put forth. In Bradford's own lifetime it was never clearly the predominant vision, and he certainly knew it.

Every region of the early colonial North American world provides evidence of a multitude of voices. William Bradford was keenly aware of this. He did not write only to an adoring audience who shared his views uncritically. He also wrote against many others both within and without Plymouth Colony, including Isaac Allerton. Allerton has received relatively little attention from scholars partly because he lived in several different colonies and so tends to fall out of a study devoted to a single settlement as soon as he left it. When one follows the sweep of his activities in all of the places where he lived or traded, one sees striking differences between his experiences and those of more settled elites like William Bradford.

Although scholars long took Bradford's account as normative, it actually was unusual and quite individual. It was not a complete narrative of most Plymouth colonists' experiences. If Bradford's voice ever predominated, it did so only at the end of his life. After the first generation of English colonists who came to North America as mature adults had passed away, Bradford's account became canonical. His history was picked up more by the next generation of settlers like Isaac Allerton Jr. and after the colonial North American world had changed significantly. But it was not yet so during the years his history encompassed.

Allerton and Bradford began their North American experiences together, and they were closely linked during Plymouth's first decade. For many years other settlers elected the two men to take leading positions in the colony's government.[2] However, they did not approach their lives in North America the same way; their ideas and activities soon began to move in very different directions.

The increasing contrast between Allerton's and Bradford's activities was more than just the divergence of two friends in the new context of colonial North America. Furthermore, their increasing conflict was not merely a matter of two individuals choosing dissimilar activities or routes to power, status, and sometimes wealth. In actuality, Allerton and Bradford acted from different visions of what the early colonial North American and Atlantic world was and should be.

Bradford, for instance, held to a deep commitment to limit and supervise Plymouth plantation's contact with outsiders, even though he recognized that the small community was part of the Atlantic world and could not survive on its own. While Bradford accepted the need for Allerton and others to negotiate with outsiders for credit and goods, he was always suspicious of commercial networks and wanted to maintain control over all negotiations. Indeed, he often insisted on a degree of authority that rendered negotiation virtually impossible. Bradford did not trust the implications of the kinds of flexibility required in intercultural situations or increasingly dictated by the market.

Yet the market and intercultural interdependence and competition frequently coincided in early colonial North America. Those who developed the most successful ways of controlling their markets and expanding trade networks in more than one culture also developed a range of identities from which to choose commercial, political, or cultural strategies and alliances. This capability could often confer considerable power at those points where the needs of diplomacy or the market brought two or more cultures and communities into contact. Allerton began to see the possibilities for this kind of power from some of his earliest experiences in North America.

Allerton's experiences offer evidence of attitudes toward colonization, trade, and identity that were quite different from those that Bradford expressed in his narrative. Perhaps most important, Allerton's activities reveal a very dissimilar set of expectations about the importance of intercultural alliances. It is perhaps significant that Allerton was there from the beginning; in 1620 he traveled to North America aboard the *Mayflower* with William Bradford and a small group of other Leiden separatists. Like Bradford, Allerton lived in North America for the rest of his life.

Unlike Bradford, however, Allerton returned to England several times and regularly traveled to other places throughout the Atlantic world. By the time of his death in 1659, he had lived in four different American colonies and owned property in five. In addition, he had held public office in two colonies, one English and one Dutch, and had established a trade network that encompassed at least eight North American and Caribbean colonies and extended across the Atlantic to Europe.[3]

Taking the experiences of people like William Bradford as their model, modern historians have found both the nature and breadth of Allerton's activities surprising, but to many of Allerton's contemporaries, his intercultural and transatlantic connections were expected. People like Isaac Allerton were to be found throughout North America and the Atlantic world. To develop and maintain extensive commercial, political, and social connections required one

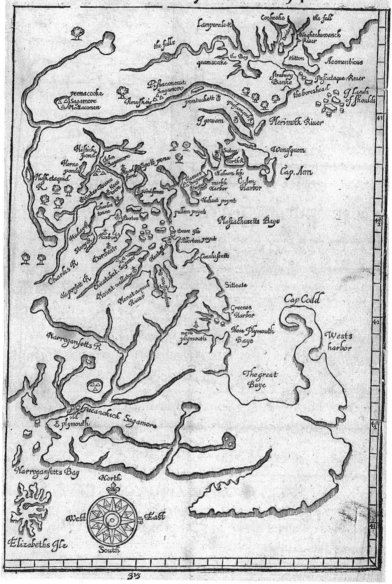

The South part of New-England, as it is Planted this yeare, 1634.

FIGURE 5. Point Allerton, just south of Deer Island in Massachusetts Bay, was named for Isaac Allerton. Although none of his papers are known to have survived, Point Allerton and its representation on maps such as this illustrate both the range and importance of his activities. William Wood's map of New England also shows English settlements, Algonquian and English names for the landscape, and native settlements depicted with triangles and circles. "The South part of New-England, as it is Planted this yeare, 1634," from William Wood, *New England's Prospect*, London, 1634. Courtesy of the John Carter Brown Library at Brown University.

to present oneself in a variety of ways, and Allerton was skilled in doing so. This ability to transform oneself temporarily or to emphasize one identity for the short term was not as unusual or as devious as William Bradford would have had us think, even though to Bradford it was deeply subversive.[4]

Many of Allerton's contemporaries expected him to present complex, multivalent identities. However, as Bradford's suspicion demonstrates, not everyone trusted the implications of Allerton's multivalent identities, but despite their wariness, they understood people like him better than historians have. Allerton's identity has been an enigma to historians who have not known how to reconcile the many facets of his experience and in many cases have been unaware of information about his life in places other than the particular colony they have studied.[5] Yet when we trace all of his activities and connections, it becomes clear that he was widely known and accepted as an important and high-status colonist who understood how to make relations between different groups work by emphasizing mutual advantage.

Early on he foresaw the basic, essential ingredients for successful intercultural alliances. Moreover, Allerton's prominent status and wide recognition demonstrate that men and women who readily crossed cultural, political, and commercial boundaries were part of his generation's expectation of the colonial world. These cultural beliefs helped communities to survive in early and often precarious colonial situations by facilitating the necessary intercultural and intercolonial trade in the first half of the seventeenth century.

As I have mentioned, Isaac Allerton and people like him frequently moved between cultures, and their experiences were as central to early colonial history as those of people like William Bradford. They were so vital to early colonial activities that, after about a decade of colonization, Bradford began to see people like Allerton as increasingly powerful threats to the kind of colonial world he wanted to shape. Bradford began to write *Of Plymouth Plantation* in the early 1630s, just as he was becoming increasingly upset with Allerton's expanding connections.

Before then, however, Allerton was one of Plymouth's separatist elite, as well as one of Bradford's close associates. Historians who have attempted to explain Allerton's shifting cultural and mercantile strategies have often been puzzled by one of his earliest identities—that of an English puritan separatist. Many have contended that puritanism constituted a rigid category with a set of internalized values that completely precluded the numerous identities embraced by people like Allerton.

In studies of the writings of a few elites such as William Bradford, one of the long-standing positions has been that merchant capitalist activity was strictly regulated by the just pricing of a puritan moral economy. This position has largely been modified by the works of Stephen Innes, Mark Peterson, and John Frederick Martin, and few scholars now interpret the relationship between seventeenth-century puritanism and commercial practices in quite the same way.[6] Nonetheless, the older model of the unyielding puritan moral economy long meant that people like Allerton received less attention because they seemed to be anomalous.

It was not just that Allerton's activities did not seem to follow the restraints scholars once assumed operated on puritan economic enterprise; it was more that Allerton presented a number of paradoxes. He was accepted as a member of the church in some of the strictest puritan colonies such as New Haven, where church membership was a highly respected privilege. Accordingly, he was an enterprising merchant entrepreneur whose activities were criticized in Plymouth Colony, yet he remained an important and respected member of several puritan communities.

Allerton continued to be welcomed and accorded high social status in most puritan and Calvinist communities throughout the colonies. His religious identity, then, is a very useful point from which to begin to examine the social position of such people within early American colonization and from there to see that William Bradford sought to portray a colonial world that was narrower and less interconnected than the one in which he actually lived.

Little information survives about his early life, but around 1608, when he was about twenty-two, the English-born Allerton emigrated from London to Leiden in the United Provinces.[7] For a variety of reasons other English men and women immigrated to the Dutch Republic in the first few decades of the seventeenth century. Also in 1608, a congregation of separatist puritans from Scrooby, in Nottinghamshire, immigrated to Amsterdam; a year later they moved to Leiden, and Allerton became affiliated with this community; he lived as one of them for more than a decade and married Mary Norris, an English member of the émigré congregation, with whom he had several children while in Leiden.[8]

Allerton's business skills and perhaps his language proficiency gave him influence within the separatist group, and he was one of those who became a citizen of Leiden. As such, he had a wider range of employment opportunities than most of the other English separatists in Leiden, and he probably worked as a tailor. Most likely he learned Dutch while living in the United Provinces. In Leiden, Allerton's business and negotiating expertise was so valued that he was one of the leaders chosen to plan the venture when the group decided to immigrate to North America and settle Plymouth plantation in 1620.[9]

Although the particular circumstances of the early colonial North American context provided Allerton with an arena in which to thrive as an intercultural mediator, many of the elements that formed his alliance strategies had their roots in European cultural traditions. Born during a period of intense religious conflict, Allerton lived his early life in an environment that included both the necessity of dissimulation and a widespread fear and suspicion of it.[10] For Protestants, lying in all of its forms was associated particularly with Roman Catholics, but others were mistrusted as well.

In a description of the progress of Roman Catholic conversions in Peru and New Mexico, William Castell complained about "all which, and many more, their incredible expressions are fit to be cast off, being in all probability but the subtil fictions of Spanish & Popish Factors who (like travelers) take liberty to lye."[11] Fascination with dissimulation, masking, hidden motives, and secret plots was omnipresent in sixteenth-century court life in England as on the Continent. Expectations of dissimulation spread far beyond the elite realms of court; however, non-elite preoccupation with possible untruths became more widespread in conjunction with the Protestant Reformation and its associated challenges to civil and religious authority.

Perez Zagorin has demonstrated that English people became widely and intensely concerned with the threat of lying and secret plots in association with Southwell's trial and later the Gunpowder Plot. Like Italian Renaissance drama, much Elizabethan drama delighted in themes of disguised truth, altered identities, and plots within plots. Often opposition to the theater criticized acting as the falsification of identity and experience, and indeed dramatists played with these ambiguities. Excessive concern with dissimulation was not only negative, however. Much of the early modern European preoccupation with changes in manners was related to the fear that through gesture, clothing, or body language one could unintentionally convey sensitive information.[12]

This apprehension translated into concrete strategies in North America. As we have already seen, many of the earliest colonial ventures included specific instructions for artists and other employees to observe as much as possible about the people they met. John White's watercolor drawings of Algonquians from the Roanoke area were widely reproduced partly as curiosities but also as important and potentially practical sources of crucial information about Indian cultures.

Religious nonconformity, dissimulation, and a developing merchant capitalism were part of the Plymouth colonists' world in the United Provinces and England and were components of the cultural package Allerton and others took with them to North America. There, dissimulation and masking strategies became particularly significant in intercultural contacts and networks, which were precisely the arenas in which Allerton increasingly operated. For his part, William Bradford worried more and more about treachery and dissimulation on the part of other Plymouth colonists, Native Americans, and rival colonial ventures.

For Bradford, Allerton personified those threats as much as anyone. He became gradually more influential in the early years of Plymouth's settlement, even according to William Bradford's account, and he used his growing power to extend his personal networks in new directions. For more than ten years he was one of the governor's assistants, and he acted as Plymouth's factor, or London agent, for six years.[13] During those six years he engaged in trade on behalf of the colony; he also conducted negotiations for a debt purchase agreement, for a patent for additional land in the fur-rich areas along the Kennebec River, and unsuccessfully for a new colonial charter.[14]

In the course of his travel and business as Plymouth's agent, Allerton gained wider experience in conducting difficult negotiations among many different parties, and he began moving in circles that dealt in ever-larger commercial ventures.[15] For example, Allerton's obligations as the plantation's representative in England took him to the court of Charles I, where he would have witnessed the world of court politics and intrigue and the constantly shifting roles of courtiers vying for favor. There too he would have seen early modern international diplomacy at work, with ample illustrations of the need to pay careful attention to alliances of all kinds.

The authority conferred by his role as plantation agent enhanced Allerton's power in the eyes of those who remained in the colony, as well as with political and financial supporters in England. Thus in England and North America, Allerton participated extensively in the patronage and clientage relationships that were so important to those involved in seventeenth-century trade and colonial ventures. As he did so, he mixed old and new patterns of alliances. While kinship ties formed the foundation of many colonial English and Dutch trade networks, Allerton's contacts were primarily of a different type. Perhaps because he did not have an extensive family network on which to rely, he assiduously created contacts to enter mercantile patronage structures.[16] In the process, he began fashioning an identity as a cosmopolitan with an extensive intercultural, transatlantic network of connections. At the same time, operating from his much more restricted base in Plymouth plantation, William Bradford attempted to limit Allerton's influence and the extent of Plymouth's intercultural ties.

Allerton's cosmopolitanism was not entirely new. In North America he did not choose to become entirely different from the person he had been in the United Provinces. For Allerton, the process of identity building and self-presentation was more complicated than that. Early modern colonialism presented situations that required the kinds of flexibility that people like Allerton possessed and that those like Bradford found threatening. Allerton's many identities developed from his wide-ranging experiences and helped him to fit into and to exploit the diverse settings through which he traveled. He absorbed all of his various identities and emphasized one over another as advantage dictated, and it was this selective presentation of self that made people like Bradford suspicious.

The pattern of Allerton's commercial and diplomatic activities mirrored the process of his identity development because both required flexibility and the ability to represent oneself differently in various settings. In trade, Allerton constantly maneuvered to increase his advantage. His technique was to enlarge his areas of operation and his networks of contacts while retaining the ties that bound him to earlier networks. When confronted with conflict and controversy, Allerton usually responded by traveling elsewhere for a time and developing new connections while the storm abated. Bradford, on the other hand, regarded such conflicts as final conditions that required a permanent break.

Allerton, however, recognized that economic opportunity could result from conflict. He developed a pattern of neutralizing controversy by departing when he became associated with a dispute. As a merchant, people expected him to travel, so it worked to his advantage to sail away to trade just as a particular controversy became too uncomfortable. In the process, he would expand his networks and sphere of activity as a means of allowing the friction to ease. In this way, his area of influence in North America spread outward from Plymouth to Massachusetts Bay, to New Netherland, New Haven, New Sweden, Virginia, and the West Indies.

The seeds of this growing divergence in Allerton's and Bradford's approaches to colonization were present in some of their earliest North American experiences. In his early years in North America, Allerton, for instance, successfully moved across cultures where he was a stranger. In one of the *Mayflower* migrants' early experiences with Americans along the mainland Atlantic coast, a group of Pokanokets greeted them.[17] The colonists had been exploring the coast, looking for a suitable location to build their new colony. In the course of their explorations, they were surprised by the fact that they encountered no Native Americans. They did, however, find evidence of abandoned village sites and went so far as to raid Indian food stores and to pillage Native American burial sites. Now they met a group of Native Americans. In this early meeting with a small group of Pokanokets, the new colonists interpreted the Native Americans' speech and gestures as communicating that their "king" wanted to see the newcomers. Accordingly, "Captain Standish and Isaac Allerton went venturously, who were welcomed of him after their manner."[18]

In this meeting Standish and Allerton represented two of the leadership roles that early colonists would simultaneously honor and regard with suspicion, those of the soldier and the skilled negotiator. Both functions were vitally important for colonists in the pursuit of alliances. As the military leader, Standish represented strength to his own community and potentially hostile groups. Allerton, the negotiator, diplomatically bridged and crossed cultures rather than confronting them militarily. It is highly significant that Plymouth chose to send these men to this early meeting with Pokanoket leaders.

Both roles could be threatening to other colony principals because each type of leadership conferred considerable power in delicately balanced situations, power that threatened to elude the control of intracultural leaders like William Bradford.

Over the coming years, Allerton acted as Plymouth's intercultural agent and its cultural and commercial attaché many times. A few years after sending him to meet the Pokanoket sachem, the other Plymouth colonists sent Allerton to represent their interests at the court of Charles I of England. The intricacies and intrigue of Westminster constituted yet another cultural world whose rules he had to learn. According to another influential Plymouth colonist who came to see Allerton as a dangerous competitor, Allerton adapted to the new power dynamic all too well.[19]

While acting as Plymouth's London agent, Allerton formed an alliance with a group of important players in the struggles at court for control of England's North American colonies. As he did so, the contrasts between his and Bradford's visions of colonial opportunity and colonization led to conflicting demonstrations of power and authority. During the late 1620s and early 1630s, while he was serving as Plymouth plantation's representative in England, Isaac Allerton formed a cooperative relationship with Thomas Morton.

An Englishman who had gathered the remaining members of a small colony near Plymouth, Morton was one of a number of people who developed minor plantations throughout New England. He and his settlement exemplify the fluidity of the early colonial milieu. He established his Merrymount plantation with the remnants of a private colonial venture to Massachusetts.[20] In contrast to the separatists and puritans of other New England plantations, Morton was an aggressively loyal, if not notably pious, church member. In this respect he was more like Sir Ferdinando Gorges and others who had tried to establish earlier plantations and trading ventures in New England.

Morton's plantation openly challenged and provoked the separatists' religious ideology and their sense of political stability. Indeed, the Merrymount colonists' behavior proved so threatening to Plymouth's leadership that in 1628 the latter gathered support from other small English communities nearby and forcibly put Morton on a ship bound for England.[21] Morton personified the worst fears of colonial leaders like William Bradford, whose writings repeatedly stressed his anxiety over degeneracy and the loss of order. In forcing Morton to return to England, Plymouth officials accused him of selling alcohol and guns to the Indians, both acts prohibited by English law. They also accused him and the other men at Merrymount of consorting with Native American women.

The charge of selling guns and alcohol to Native Americans was extremely serious because colonists everywhere feared the destructive threat of Indians who had acquired these items. Accounts from Virginia after the 1622 Powhatan attack on the colony, for instance, stressed that English colonists' willingness to trade guns to the Powhatans and to allow them regular access to English houses was partly to blame for the success of the Powhatans' attack. Ferdinando Gorges complained about the debilitating effects of the alcohol trade on native communities and especially, from his perspective, on the ability of English colonial venturers to establish stable and peaceful alliances with Indian nations.

If Europeans all along the Atlantic seaboard worried about the consequences to their communities of providing Native Americans with guns and alcohol, it was also a reality of the early seventeenth century that some Europeans willingly did so. Moreover, it was a charge against which there was little defense. Although some people everywhere did trade guns and alcohol with Indians, it was usually a contraband exchange. As a result, tracing the goods to their source trader was never easy. Moreover, many colonial officials found it expedient at times to participate in this business themselves or to turn a blind eye to it in order to secure alliances with Indian nations.

However, the colonists at Merrymount threatened too many social and cultural boundaries for men like William Bradford. Their relationships with neighboring Native Americans were too familiar, and their attitude toward plantations like Plymouth was too scornful. Instead of existing as another European colony that could be trusted to join with fellow Europeans against Native American threats, the Merrymount colonists seemed too closely allied with New England Algonquians and too contemptuous of their European neighbors. From Bradford's perspective, Thomas Morton stood behind all of the threats, thereby fostering this outlaw culture so near to the Plymouth settlement. Bradford wrote that Morton's plantation was a "school of Atheism," thus branding him with one of the worst seventeenth-century epithets European Christians could invoke.[22]

What is particularly fascinating about the Plymouth colonists' response to Thomas Morton is that two of their leaders disagreed significantly about what he represented for Plymouth. Allerton clearly did not agree with Bradford's characterization of Morton as a threat and made no effort to hide his opinion. On the contrary, he publicly demonstrated this disagreement in 1629, when he showed everyone at Plymouth that he had formed his own alliance with Thomas Morton. In doing so, Allerton moved his power struggle with Bradford dramatically into public view.

Isaac Allerton returned to Plymouth from one of his London trips with the previously banished Thomas Morton by his side, reportedly as his personal secretary. According to the outraged William Bradford, Allerton defied the other Plymouth colonists by "bringing over this year for base gain that unworthy man and instrument of mischief Morton."[23] Bradford's contention that Allerton had brought Morton back to Plymouth "for base gain" suggests that Allerton was hoping to make use of Morton's experience in the fur trade, where Morton's Native American alliances and knowledge of Algonquian culture and languages would be especially important.

Bradford and certain Plymouth officials were outraged by the dual challenge presented by an Allerton/Morton partnership. Bradford wrote that Allerton was using Morton merely to flaunt his growing contempt for Plymouth's other leaders. He exclaimed that Allerton "not only brought him over, but to the town (as it were to nose them) and lodged him at his own house: and for a while used him as a scribe to do his business."[24]

Bradford and his allies within Plymouth eventually responded by running Morton out of town and admonishing Allerton for bringing this "lord of misrule" into their community. At issue were the personal power and influence of competing elites, but the disagreement went deeper than that. Just as importantly, the dispute over Thomas Morton grew out of conflicting visions of how Plymouth Colony should function in relation to the broader world.[25]

By openly bringing someone considered to be a menace to the colony into its midst, Isaac Allerton symbolically declared that he was part of a wider world. There he had gained power that he would not willingly subordinate to people like Bradford, whose outlook was confined primarily to the boundaries of Plymouth Colony. Perhaps, however, it would be more accurate to describe Bradford's outlook as reflecting his ideas of where the borders of Plymouth Colony lay and of how Plymouth should ally itself with others. Bradford and people like Allerton disagreed on the question of how permeable those boundaries should be. Bradford sought to maintain more precisely controlled public bounds and cultural limits, whereas Allerton accepted the fluidity and permeability inherent in the early colonial setting. Moreover, he consistently tried to use them to his advantage.

In the midst of the growing rift between the two men, Bradford began writing his own interpretation of what was happening in his history of the colony's beginnings. The document upon which scholars have relied as an exemplar of early American history and literature emerged in the course of a colonial struggle for power and authority, when it was one among many competing interpretations of the directions that the colonial North American world should take. Allerton was not the only source of Bradford's growing fears and frustrations. Increasing commercial and territorial competition from Dutch and English colonies, as well as shifting relationships with Native Americans, all combined to persuade Bradford that the colony he sought to control was under siege.

For instance, Bradford regarded the Dutch at New Netherland with suspicion and consistently dealt cautiously with Dutch officials and traders in North America. He seems to have felt the need to guard against charges that the Plymouth separatists rebelled against all English authority by rejecting the church and so may have believed he had to minimize or deny any suggestion that Plymouth had an affinity for the Dutch in New Netherland.[26] Rather than seeking out an alliance with the Dutch colony to the south, Bradford regarded contact and trade with New Netherland as placing the Plymouth colonists in a sensitive situation with respect to their English supporters and the Crown.

After receiving letters and a visit from Isaack de Rasière, who in 1627 offered to establish a trade alliance with Plymouth, Bradford wrote letters reporting the meeting to the Council for New England, which controlled the English rights to the territory that encompassed Plymouth Colony. He wrote directly to Ferdinando Gorges, who was head of the council. In very carefully worded language Bradford told the council about the Dutch contact and also sent them copies of the letters exchanged between Plymouth and New Netherland.

Bradford emphasized that Plymouth had not initiated the contact, that the Dutch had sought out the Plymouth colonists, and that the Plymouth group had made certain to inform the Dutch that their Manhattan plantation stood on territory that belonged to England. In his diary explanation of the reason he notified the Council for New England and Ferdinando Gorges, Bradford wrote about the difficult position the Dutch contact had created for Plymouth's colonists and about their need to defend their English loyalty: "We well knew likewise, that this dealing and friendship with the Dutch (though it was wholly sought of themselves) yet it would procure us envy from others in the land, and that at one time or other, our enemies would take occasion to raise slanders and frame accusations against us for it."[27] To prevent Plymouth's "enemies" from being able to use the incident against them, he reported, "therefore, to prevent their malice, as also to shew the sincerity of our dealing and our loyal and dutiful respect to his Majesty and the Honourable Council for New England; we sent their first letter (with our answer thereto and their reply to the same) unto the Council as may appear more particularly by our letters following."[28]

Bradford was undecided about the contact from New Netherland, and his ambivalence also appears in another highly significant outcome of de Rasière's 1627 visit. The Dutch delegation that stopped at Plymouth that year taught the Plymouth colonists how to use wampum as a trading currency.[29] Bradford described the information the Dutch provided as extremely valuable, and he saw the Dutch offer to trade wampum to Plymouth as an important development. In remembering the 1627 visit, he wrote, "that which turned most to their profit, in time, was an entrance into the trade of wampumpeag."[30] Having been persuaded that wampum could help them trade more successfully for furs, Bradford admitted that the Dutch delegation willingly sold Plymouth some wampum: "For they now bought about £50 worth of it of them, and they told them how vendible it was at their fort Orania, and did persuade them they would find it so at Kennebec."[31]

Interestingly, Bradford explicitly acknowledged that the Plymouth colonists did not know they could use wampum as a medium of exchange; for almost seven years Plymouth's trade with Native Americans had been based on other kinds of barter: "Neither did the English of this Plantation or any other in the land, till now that they had knowledge of it from the Dutch, so much as know what it was, much less that it was a commodity of that worth and value."[32] However, as Indian-European trade changed throughout the Atlantic Coast, wampum became an increasingly important part of intercultural North American exchanges.

De Rasière had offered a valuable gift along with his proposal of alliance and trade relations, and although Bradford quickly recognized its value, he was very uncertain about its implications. Wampum was a gift fraught with anxiety for colonists like Bradford; it proved to be irresistible, but it pulled them more deeply into the realm of intercultural commerce. Plymouth badly needed to expand its commercial activities, but colonists like Bradford greatly disapproved of the connections and alliances they would have to make in order to participate more fully in early modern trade. Wampum, moreover, was even more fraught with potential danger for people like Bradford because it was a means of commerce associated with Native Americans and the Dutch, both of whom Bradford regarded with mistrust.

Isaac Allerton, however, was much less inhibited than Bradford about venturing further into the world of intercultural, intercolonial, and transatlantic trading enterprises. After his first few years in the colony, he began traveling extensively as Plymouth's London agent. He conducted negotiations between the colonists and their financial supporters in England and represented the colonists in patent and charter negotiations. He sailed back and forth across the Atlantic every few months during this period and was away from the Plymouth settlement as often as he was in residence.

While in England in 1628, Allerton acquired a patent for additional territory along the Kennebec River.[33] When he returned to Plymouth, he helped to put the colony's new fur-trading station into operation so that the colonists could expand their first-time dealings in wampum and furs. For Allerton, wampum and Dutch offers of trade and information were welcome tools of support for his efforts to expand his own and Plymouth's networks.

Allerton was also instrumental in setting up a trading post on the Penobscot River.[34] To help with the daily operations at the newly established trading house there, he hired an Englishman named Edward Ashley, who had spent time in Algonquian communities and understood several Algonquian languages. In Allerton's eyes, Ashley was ideal for the undertaking, especially because of his ability to communicate with Wabanaki peoples, who were potential sources of furs. However, Bradford and other Plymouth colonists thought differently. Bradford immediately feared that Allerton had once again brought the wrong kind of person into Plymouth's world: "This business about Ashley did not a little trouble them."[35]

Bradford's concern was not so much that he believed Ashley lacked the necessary skills and experience for the job. On the contrary, he feared that Ashley's encounters with Native Americans made him an unfit associate for the Plymouth colonists. Bradford admitted that Ashley "had wit and ability enough to manage the business, yet some of them knew him to be a very profane young man, and he had for some time lived among the Indians as a savage and went naked amongst them and used their manners, in which time he got their language. So they feared he might still run into evil courses (though he promised beter) and God would not prosper his ways."[36]

Bradford and his Plymouth allies regarded Ashley with suspicion from the beginning of his association with them, and they soon decided that he was selling guns and alcohol to Indians.[37] As with Thomas Morton, Ashley's familiarity with Native Americans was too close to be tolerated by Bradford and others who shared his views. Perhaps as much as their behavior itself, the ability of men like Morton and Ashley (and eventually Isaac Allerton) to move across cultural boundaries with ease made them symbols of everything that Bradford mistrusted.

Bradford may have been right that Morton was a menace to Plymouth Colony. He certainly was a threat to the degree of control that Bradford himself sought. And regardless of whether Morton was really much of a troublemaker in the early 1620s, when Plymouth leaders first moved against him, Plymouth's intractable hostility guaranteed that Morton had become a committed enemy by the end of the decade. Morton's danger to Plymouth did not end in 1629, nor did fears of Allerton's associations with him disappear. After his ill treatment in New England, Morton allied with Sir Ferdinando Gorges in the 1630s against the puritan and separatist colonial officials in Plymouth and the new Massachusetts Bay colony.[38]

In the 1620s and 1630s Gorges remained a key player in the competitive colonial game because he represented the Council for New England. Although the council had originally owned the patent for all of New England, its exclusive rights had been superseded in part by the Massachusetts Bay Colony's grant.[39] Refusing to concede the Massachusetts Bay Colony's authority, Gorges and his influential faction continued to work actively at court to gain control over the entire region of New England from the late 1620s through the mid-1630s. In the eyes of some Plymouth Colony leaders, especially William Bradford and Edward Winslow, Gorges represented a profound threat to the autonomy of the venture to which they were wholly devoted.[40] Allerton broke with Bradford and Winslow over this, too, and his relationship with Gorges became evident several years later when Gorges's efforts to control New England as its governor seemed likely to succeed.

The struggle for control over early colonial North America was waged on many different fronts and was not restricted to a struggle to manage the wealth that natural resources could bring. It was also a contest for political, social, and religious authority, at times conceived in feudal terms and at others in radically new ones. Moreover, it was a competition between various leaders' visions of colonization. In an effort to control all three arenas, Ferdinando Gorges pressed his case at court, where the King's Bench heard the case in May of 1637. Plymouth's old adversary and Allerton's former personal scribe, Thomas Morton, argued the case on Gorges's behalf. During the proceedings Morton struck back at separatist and puritan New England officials.[41]

Having refused to make an alliance with Morton, Bradford turned out to be correct in his insistence that Morton was a threat to all reformed Protestant colonies in New England. The King's Bench issued a quo warranto judgment against the Massachusetts Bay officials. Charles I declared royal control over the government of the colony and appointed Ferdinando Gorges as governor general.[42] The result was one for which Gorges had long hoped and brought him another step closer to securing the claims he had established with James I and the other members of the Council for New England as they stood around a map of New England and drew lots back in 1623. However, the news could not have been worse for the leaders of the Plymouth and Massachusetts Bay colonies.

When Massachusetts governor John Winthrop heard the news, he relayed it to some of his Plymouth allies. Responding to Winthrop's letter and especially to its report of Gorges's success, Edward Winslow privately confided his belief that Allerton's networks lay at the root of their troubles. Hoping against hope that somehow the decision would not be carried out, Winslow wrote back to John Winthrop: "I am bold once more to trouble you, giving thanks for your last remembrance in sending the coppy to me . . . but hope we shall never be troubled with the reality thereof."[43]

He went on to lay the blame at Allerton's feet, lamenting that, if the decision were to stand, "I perswade my selfe it never was without my old neighbor Isaack, whose head is always full of such projects, and hath too great familiarity with our common adversaries."[44] In fact, Winslow complained bitterly about Allerton's growing networks outside Plymouth and linked them to his untrustworthiness, claiming that anyone who dealt with Allerton was destined to be deceived: "But were he as well knowned to yours as us, they would rather have kept him heer then any way have incouraged his going over: but what I write I would not have made publick; but the truth is he loveth neither you nor us."[45] Like many another gossip, Winslow asked his audience not to make his allegations public, while in the same breath he fanned the flames of the rumor fire he had just set.

Winslow was convinced that Allerton, with his intimate knowledge of the situation in the New England colonies, had been instrumental in helping Ferdinando Gorges secure the judgment he had pursued for seven years. Like William Bradford, Edward Winslow used his pen to campaign against Allerton. However, in this case, he made sure to spread the rumor that Allerton was involved, while also insisting that Massachusetts governor John Winthrop treat the information as a confidence. Although Winslow apparently did not mind writing his opinion about Allerton, he drew the line at taking a public stand against him. For in his own day, Isaac Allerton had power, too, and in 1637 it appeared that his more expansive vision of colonization might well win out over Bradford's. The quo warranto judgment against Massachusetts Bay made that very clear. In the end, Winslow's hopes that they might "never be troubled with the reality thereof" turned out to be at least partly correct because several mishaps prevented Gorges from taking over as governor general. Then the matter was soon set aside for the more pressing concerns of the English civil war.

In the meantime, Winslow's "old neighbor Isaack" had taken up residence in New Netherland, where he quickly became a prominent member of the community. However, even though Allerton had established a new base in New Amsterdam, his relationship with New England colonies was by no means ended, nor was his struggle with Bradford. Allerton continued to trade, collect debts, and fulfill other obligations for colonists in Plymouth and Massachusetts Bay. In addition, he now became an influential player in the New Amsterdam mercantile and civic communities. He had moved beyond the immediate circle of conflict while maintaining old contacts. This was one of Allerton's special skills, and it was highly valued in the colonial American pursuit of alliances. Even as he maintained his old connections, Allerton refined his identity to fit the new setting.

His ability to present himself in new ways enabled him to gain access to more trade networks and proved useful to those in his old network who wished to take advantage of Allerton's expanded area of influence. Colonists like Edward Winslow and William Bradford, who made use of but did not trust Allerton's facility for expanding his cultural, mercantile, and patronage networks, expressed their reservations privately for the most part because they knew that many others shared Allerton's vision. Intercolonial and intercultural alliances depended on it.

Indeed, Winslow may not have wanted to make his negative assessment of his "old neighbor Isaack" public in 1637 because Allerton's influence was so far reaching, which Winslow recognized. There is considerable evidence that Allerton retained as much authority as ever among many of New England's elites, even as the Gorges threat was lost in the rising tensions that eventually led to the outbreak of civil war in England. In 1640/1641, for example, a letter from Lucy Downing to John Winthrop demonstrates that, despite his associations with Thomas Morton and Ferdinando Gorges, Allerton continued to exert a great deal of clout among many of the highest-status men and women in New England.

Lucy Downing was an influential English puritan and a cousin of John Winthrop. In this instance, she wrote Winthrop to inquire about training for her son. She told Winthrop that her son was "eager for sea Imployment."[46] As she asked for advice about who might provide her son with the best such experience, she told Winthrop that "my cosen Peters wisht me to put him to msr. Allerton for a while."[47] Downing evidently liked the idea: "So I moved it to Msr. Allerton, and he doth earnestly advise I should rather have him taught first to writ and accoumpt well, and such like, that so he might also be fit for merchandize."[48] Lucy Downing and Hugh Peters were willing to trust Isaac Allerton to train Downing's son because they recognized the value of his experience with and understanding of circumstances in the colonial Atlantic world in ways that William Bradford never did.

It is significant that Lucy Downing asked Isaac Allerton, rather than someone like Bradford, to train her son for work at sea. Although Bradford had not developed such skills himself, Downing's choice of Allerton was an acknowledgment of his extensive knowledge of sea travel, as well as the connections he had cultivated throughout the Atlantic world; these were all aspects of a more expansive understanding of colonization. Allerton's vision had more to offer to a young man in search of a promising future and to a mother who was helping to find an adequate place in the world for her son. Because Allerton was recognized as a respectable puritan and a successful merchant, he could assist Downing's son in gaining worldly training under the guidance of a fellow believer.[49]

Lucy Downing, Hugh Peters, and Isaac Allerton realized that they lived in an Atlantic world in which English men and women in North America were linked to Dutch colonists, Native Americans, and others in England, the United Provinces, and the Caribbean. Contemporaries recognized the importance of the margins of colonial settlements for the center. Everyone relied upon the merchants and mariners who traveled widely and moved across cultural and political boundaries.

Other New Englanders sought to use Allerton's participation in and knowledge of the markets that converged in New Amsterdam to gain access to an increasingly important economic center. They also relied on his intercolonial mobility and familiarity with different colonial legal systems, as when several English colonists appointed Allerton as their attorney to conduct business on their behalf in other jurisdictions. The kinds of matters entrusted to him reflect the respect and high status he commanded. The range of tasks he undertook for others also indicates the colonists' omnipresent need for other people to function on their behalf in other colonies and territories.

For instance, in March of 1638/1639, an Englishman in Massachusetts named Richard Iles empowered Allerton to apprehend a runaway servant "by the authority of any magistrats or governors whatsoever, either Christian or heathen."[50] Iles's willingness to grant Allerton such wide-ranging authority is revealing because it rested on the assumption that Allerton had the ability and the status to operate successfully in a variety of European jurisdictions. Iles's grant makes it clear that colonists like him assumed that Allerton was also able to function effectively in Native American polities. Fellow English colonists recognized the importance of Allerton's expanding intercultural experience.

Moreover, the power of attorney granted by Richard Iles demonstrates more than just the conferrer's faith in Allerton's status and abilities. It also reveals that colonists understood that communities in North America were interdependent and that different settlements and jurisdictions overlapped in important ways. Servants, slaves, and criminals could and did run away to other towns, colonies, and cultures. People like Allerton were able to travel across many of these boundaries and in the process often developed the knowledge and alliances necessary to negotiate outstanding debts and the fate of runaways.

In the first half of the seventeenth century, European colonies frequently tried to make extradition treaties with one another. Alliances that rested largely on mutual extradition of runaways or fugitives were a frequent goal. New Netherland tried to establish such an agreement with Maryland in the 1650s, as did Virginia. Yet collaborative efforts that included extradition of fugitives from other jurisdictions remained an elusive objective throughout the early colonial period. The need for new colonists, more labor, and ever-wider trade networks invariably proved to be a stronger imperative. This reality of early colonial life made people like Isaac Allerton even more valuable because they were able to conduct negotiations on a case-by-case basis, often with successful results. Such informal conferences were far more reliable than more formal intercolonial or intercultural treaties.

Moreover, Allerton's role was particularly widespread. Whereas Richard Iles gave him broad authority to capture Iles's runaway servant wherever Allerton might find him, other English colonists relied more specifically on Allerton's Dutch contacts. One, for example, appointed Allerton as his attorney to recover a debt from an Englishman "now remaining att the Dutch Plantation."[51] Because so much transatlantic and intercolonial trade went through Dutch merchants and markets, Allerton was often asked to intervene in commercial arrangements in New Netherland.

The English civil war made contacts like Allerton even more important in the 1640s. When hostilities disrupted trade networks between the English colonies in North America and their contacts in England, the colonists relied heavily on exchanges with the Dutch, and much of that business was channeled through the community at New Amsterdam.[52] Allerton had positioned himself well, and the facility with which he presented himself as either English or Dutch at different moments enabled him to maintain access to each milieu for the rest of his life.

Allerton understood how to operate in established control centers of the colonial world and in the shifting spaces where power was frequently up for grabs. As the arenas of his trade expanded, he relied increasingly upon an identity that emphasized his role as an intercultural negotiator and interpreter. Over time he became a kind of diplomat at large, helping to ease intercolonial and intercultural tensions while facilitating his own trade. His actions reveal that his vision of the early seventeenth-century Atlantic world was of a place where his personal interests and the larger ones of maintaining intercolonial and intercultural interdependence were all connected.

If Isaac Allerton reacted to the rapidly changing aspects of the early colonial era by cultivating multiple identities and changing with shifting circumstances, William Bradford responded quite differently. Bradford resisted change. He consistently drew boundaries and distinctions between himself and others and never stopped trying to pull people back toward Plymouth Colony. Although willing to expand the settlement's trading interests, he continued to resent other colonists' decisions to pursue non-Plymouth concerns.

Edward Winslow, for instance, became involved in non-Plymouth activities in England after having acted on behalf of the colony during the turbulent 1640s. Bradford lamented that Winslow's absence had hurt the colony, writing that Winslow "fell into other employments there; so as he hath now been absent this four years, which hath been much to the weakening of this government, without whose consent he took these employments upon him."[53] Like Isaac Allerton before him, Winslow became involved in larger networks and issues while in London. Moreover, as he had done with Allerton, Bradford insisted that Winslow should have gotten permission from the Plymouth colonists before taking action. However, such control was never possible, and those who traveled back and forth across the Atlantic quickly realized this. In the end, Bradford never lost his conviction that even the most trusted fellow believers could be seduced by the lure of connections beyond Plymouth, yet he was always disappointed when it happened.

By contrast, as Allerton expanded his trade across cultural, religious, and colonial boundaries, he increasingly emphasized his role as an intercultural negotiator and interpreter. Both functions required considerable initiative on his part and substantial trust by those who engaged him. Allerton's success in presenting mutable identities is particularly clear in situations in which two or more cultures played key roles. He placed himself in those situations frequently during the 1640s and 1650s.

In the 1640s, well after he had left Plymouth, Allerton completed the extension of his trade area, which encompassed New England, the Chesapeake, the West Indies, the Hudson and Long Island regions of New Netherland, and the Delaware regions of New Netherland and New Sweden. As he did so, he acted more and more as a moving point of connection between people in a variety of North American regions.

Allerton's influence and ability to fashion identities that were meaningful in different colonial contexts is illustrated by the fact that in journals, correspondence, and court records, leaders of Plymouth, Connecticut, Massachusetts Bay, New Haven, New Netherland, New Sweden, and Virginia colonies often referred to him simply as "Mr. Allerton."[54] People seldom needed any identification other than this honorific title. Operating at the colonial margins did not isolate him from the more settled centers because center and periphery interacted frequently and on several levels. Alliances and peoples' pursuit of them spilled across them all.

People separated by hundreds of miles knew him. Isaac Allerton traveled and traded in all of the colonies. He gave colonists advice and brought luxury items and necessities, news of illness and disaster, and sometimes information that could affect the fate of a colony. People who were less well known in many different contexts might be referred to by their name and colony affiliation, such as "Edmund Scarburgh of Virginia." That Allerton was seldom mentioned with this kind of qualifying information illustrates again that his identity could not be neatly matched with any one colony or community, unlike William Bradford. Trade and information networks, as well as more formal alliances, depended upon individuals like Allerton. Moreover, the fact that Allerton was readily identified throughout the Atlantic seaboard suggests that his contemporaries understood him in his own broad context and recognized that intercultural alliances required people like him.

By the early 1640s Allerton had simultaneous residences in New Amsterdam and the newly settled English puritan plantation of New Haven. His connection between the two colonies created cultural and commercial flexibility for him and also made him particularly useful to both communities.[55] English colonists and officials sought to use Allerton's contacts with the Dutch, while Dutch colonists and officials hoped to use his connections with the neighboring English colonies. In each case, Dutch and English colonists sometimes attempted to help primarily with commercial and political interests. For his part, Allerton actively and publicly demonstrated loyalty to both colonies, and his dual allegiance was not treated as exceptional.

As long as he was a loyal and civic-minded member of their community, fellow residents in neither colony minded that he also belonged to another community elsewhere. Thus, unlike William Bradford's insistence in Plymouth that community members have a single allegiance and that alliances be kept under strict control, others in the early colonial Atlantic world understood multiple allegiances just as they understood multifaceted identities.

Two events in 1643 illustrate Allerton's ability to operate according to the demands of different cultural settings more or less simultaneously. In that year, New Netherland was immersed in a devastating war with the Munsees, an Algonquian people who lived in the region surrounding the lower Hudson Valley.[56] Allerton was one of eight assistants chosen by the commonalty to advise the director general of the colony during the crisis, a role that was enhanced by his status as a successful merchant.[57] Allerton was not the only English member of the Eight; New Netherland, like the United Provinces, was an international magnet for refugees and merchants from other countries.[58] However, Allerton played a particularly important role because of his affiliation with the New Haven colony. When Director General Kieft decided to request English troops as reinforcements from New Haven, he sent Allerton and an English military officer as messengers to the New Haven general court.[59] They were ideal emissaries because each man maintained residences in both colonies.

To the increasingly desperate New Netherland colonists, Allerton's dual allegiance was seen as an important asset, and the request illustrates that, on a fundamental level, the Protestant colonies in North America recognized that they shared common interests. The tension generated by the fact that they were also competitors was evident in New Haven's response, as is the fact that individual dual loyalties did not always translate into formal group alliances, even though they were almost invariably part of the pursuit of such associations.

In October of 1643 New Netherland sent Allerton and Captain John Underhill to seek English help. New Haven Colony, however, refused to send any men immediately and promised instead to raise the issue the following spring when representatives from the newly formed United Colonies of New England would meet and consider it. New Haven was not willing to deny New Netherland's request, but it was also not prepared to act without the approval of its most important allies, its fellow members of the United Colonies of New England. New Haven leaders must have known, however, that the months between October and spring could mean disaster to the embattled Dutch colonists.

The pursuit of alliances often led to uncertain ground. For many like William Bradford in Plymouth and New Haven's court in 1643, the constantly changing circumstances of the early colonial American world were reasons to worry about the implications of all such connections. People like Allerton, however, took change as it came, often by making a series of short-term agreements. In the same month in which he had requested New Haven's military assistance on behalf of New Netherland, October 1643, Allerton acted again as an intermediary between English and Dutch colonists. This time, however, he acted in support of English interests.

A group of puritan colonists in Virginia had written to John Winthrop in Massachusetts Bay and to John Davenport, minister at New Haven, requesting that the New England puritans send three ministers to Virginia.[60] Because puritans regarded access to preaching as essential, this group of Virginia colonists was quite concerned that they had no puritan ministers. In response, three clergymen agreed to go to Virginia and set out from Massachusetts Bay. When they encountered bad weather while traveling through Dutch-controlled territory, their mission seemed in danger of running aground along with their pinnace. Fortunately for them, Allerton was on hand to intervene.

John Winthrop recorded the events of their journey and Isaac Allerton's role in saving the day: "The three ministers which were sent to Virginia, viz., Mr. Tompson, Mr. Knolles, and Mr. James from New Haven, departed (8)(October)7 and were eleven weeks before they arrived."[61] Their journey took an unusually long time because "they lay windbound sometime at Aquiday: then, as they passed Hellgate between Long Island and the Dutch, their pinnace was bilged upon the rocks, so as she was near foundered before they could run on the next shore."[62] Having survived their shipwreck, they found themselves in Dutch territory with few prospects of assistance, particularly given New Englanders' reluctance to send troops to help New Netherland.

Winthrop noted that although "the Dutch governor gave them slender entertainment . . . Mr. Allerton of New Haven, being there, took great pains and care for them, and procured them a very good pinnace and all things necessary. So they set sail in the dead of winter, and had much foul weather, so as with great difficulty and danger they arrived safe in Virginia."[63] Given his affiliations with New England puritan communities, Allerton clearly understood the importance of the ministers' voyage, but it was his Dutch connections that made his assistance possible.

Without compromising his Dutch alliances, Allerton's actions in this case won him greater favor with key political and religious figures in at least two English colonies. News of his helpfulness, for instance, certainly reached John Winthrop. Winthrop knew Allerton, of course, but he had also been warned by Edward Winslow in 1637 that he should regard Allerton with distrust. The fact that he never acted publicly on Winslow's warnings and that he continued to deal with Allerton over the years tells us much about the critical importance of maintaining intercolonial and intercultural connections.

In addition to acting as a messenger between Dutch and English colonial officials, Allerton, by virtue of his highly visible position in New Amsterdam, played other powerful and profitable roles. He was frequently appointed to serve as an arbitrator of disputes and continued to be exceptionally adept at pursuing his own concerns while emerging unscathed from accusations of wrongdoing.

In September of 1643, for example, a month before Allerton requested troops from New Haven and rescued the shipwrecked puritan ministers, his name cropped up during a controversy over a ship that arrived in New Netherland from the Canary Islands. The *Fortune* resupplied at New Amsterdam and then sailed away after refusing to pay duties. The shipmaster then "dropped down towards Staten Island, where he transferred part of his wines to Isaack Allerton's bark."[64] New Netherland authorities seized the ship and ordered it back to port, but it flouted the order and "sailed in the night."[65] Officials prosecuted and fined the skipper and ordered his cargo and ship confiscated when they could be found, but they did not charge Allerton, and he may have kept the wine.[66]

In another instance, however, the influence Allerton wielded at New Amsterdam brought him into direct conflict with Director General Kieft. As one of the Eight Men, Allerton signed a petition to the Committee of Nineteen of the West India Company, requesting that Kieft be replaced and asking for immediate aid in the wake of the 1643 Dutch-Munsee war.[67] Not surprisingly, this petition earned Allerton and the other members of the Eight the enmity of Willem Kieft, who tried to initiate judicial proceedings against them when Petrus Stuyvesant arrived to be the colony's new director general. By that time, Allerton had gone elsewhere, as he did so often when embroiled in conflict, and Stuyvesant made no determination against him.

Trade through the Dutch markets in the United Provinces and its colonies became increasingly important during the English civil war, and Dutch contacts provided English colonists with much-desired information about the war's progress. Allerton was well placed to receive and pass on communications about events in England. In 1643 and 1644 John Haynes, governor of Connecticut Colony, wrote to John Winthrop to report the latest news:

> There is late news by a vessel that came to the Dutch, and from them to New Haven, by Mr. Allerton. The substance this; that there hath been a great battle betwixt the king's and parliament's forces (since that of Newbery) at Ailsborow in Buckinghamshire, wherein the parliament forces prevailed, pursuing their victory with very great slaughter of the adverse party. Also that the fleet is again out under that noble Earl of Warwick, who came lately into the harbour of some great town held by the contrary party full sail with his fleet, both by bloc-houses and castles, and lands his men, takes the town, sets many prisoners at liberty.[68]

His English and Dutch identities, as well as his intercultural contacts, proved commercially valuable to Allerton. By 1644 he had extended his trade network to the Delaware River valley region and to the small, struggling colony of New Sweden.[69] Allerton and other merchants quickly learned that it was worth the risk to sail to the Delaware despite the challenges that escalating political rivalries in the region presented to travelers.

New Sweden was so chronically undersupplied that it seemed an ideal market for merchants in search of buyers. As we shall see more fully in chapter 7, by alternating his English and Dutch identities, Allerton survived the fluctuating tensions that at times made access to the region difficult. When he emphasized his Dutch identity and his New Amsterdam residence, he gained entry to waterways controlled by Dutch colonial authorities, and when he reached New Sweden's settlement, he identified himself as English. The Chesapeake's English merchants were also active in the Delaware trade, and Allerton's sphere soon encompassed them, too.[70] By the late 1640s Allerton had expanded his trade network to include Virginia, where his son, Isaac Allerton Jr., eventually settled.[71] By the 1640s Allerton senior had regular contacts throughout much of Atlantic North America and the West Indies.

In the 1650s European competition for the region accelerated, and Allerton successfully maneuvered among the rivals for control of the Delaware territory. He did so by forging his own network of individual alliances, which enabled him to operate between two European colonial enemies. Allerton's far-flung contacts could be extremely useful to other colonial leaders, even when they involved competing colonies. Because no one could afford to become isolated in seventeenth-century North America, individuals like Isaac Allerton were indispensable.

In 1651, for instance, Petrus Stuyvesant stopped a number of English vessels on the Delaware River as a way to assert Dutch authority over the region. Stuyvesant forced some of the ships to pay duty to New Netherland for having traded with New Sweden, and a number were assessed several years' worth of back duties. Allerton, however, sailed past Stuyvesant's blockade undisturbed.[72] Stuyvesant and Allerton clearly had a reciprocal relationship. Later that year Stuyvesant traveled to the Delaware and purchased additional land from three sachems. Allerton was one of the witnesses to the Dutch deed that recorded the purchase.[73]

During the last ten to fifteen years of his life, Isaac Allerton mixed his identity as a seasoned Atlantic world merchant with that of an experienced negotiator and diplomat at large, acting in one venue for Stuyvesant and New Netherland and another for New Haven and colonial English interests. In many ways, these years saw the fruition of the networks he had begun to build during his Plymouth years. And whereas Plymouth leaders like William Bradford found Allerton's activities profoundly threatening, other colonists and colonial leaders came to depend on them. Allerton had become extremely useful to others as a go-between who could resolve conflicts between diverse cultures.

His role was especially important and sought after in disagreements that heightened tensions between colonies. As friction between rival settlements grew in the early 1650s, even seemingly straightforward trade disputes threatened to erupt into greater intercolonial discord. Intermediaries like Allerton thus became indispensable. For instance, when Thomas Baxter seized Jan Jansen's bark and sold it to Thomas More of New Haven in 1654 during the first Anglo-Dutch war, Dutch officials exerted heavy pressure for the bark's return.[74] Allerton and Moore settled the intercolonial dispute by offering a bond for the restoration of the bark or its value.[75] Here, as in several other instances, Allerton put forward his own influence and reputation to resolve intercultural and political disputes.

The Anglo-Dutch war was also the occasion of another tense moment in which Allerton's multilayered identity stood out when intercolonial confrontation appeared imminent. In May of 1654 the North American colonies had not yet received the news of the peace between the United Provinces and England. Thinking that the two countries were still at war, Petrus Stuyvesant called his council to discuss a course of action for an impending English attack from Boston. Stuyvesant told his council that rumors that an English parliamentary naval force had sailed into Boston with instructions to attack New Netherland "were confirmed in detail last evening by Dr. Isaacq Allerton."[76]

Oliver Cromwell's navy learned of the peace before sailing to attack New Amsterdam, and a large-scale English assault on New Netherland was postponed until after Allerton's death. To modern eyes, the warning was a remarkable action, certainly treasonous for an English subject. Yet it illustrates the fluid and permeable character of boundaries in the early colonial world and the degree to which everyone relied on individuals who could maintain connections and alliances, even as the boundaries shifted.

Allerton's warning to New Amsterdam reveals some of the ways that flexible strategies of identity and the ability to shift alliances as necessary proved valuable for those who often operated where borders shifted and overlapped. These same techniques were terrifying to those like William Bradford, who always endeavored to make cultural and territorial boundaries clearer and more fixed than they really were. Despite the anxiety that the methods employed by Allerton and others evoked in men like Bradford, Allerton's 1654 warning to New Amsterdam's residents reveals how much colonial officials relied upon people of Allerton's ilk for information, goods, and credit. It is also significant that, on this occasion, as so many times before, Allerton made sure that his position was secure and then sailed away from the conflict. He would not have been as effective at preserving his far-flung alliances if he had ever let himself get too caught up in any conflict.

In the months after warning Stuyvesant of the impending English attack, Allerton learned that a Swedish ship had arrived at Fort Christina with Johan Rising aboard as New Sweden's new governor and moved swiftly to establish a relationship with him.[77] He tried to take advantage of the change of governors to collect outstanding debts, thereby continuing to mix the roles of merchant and ambassador.[78] Here again, Allerton became a kind of commercial peacemaker by working skillfully to keep the intercolonial trade open.

In 1655, for instance, New Haven continued to seek a settlement for its colonists on the Delaware, and in April, Vice Governor Stephen Goodyear set out to negotiate with Governor Rising. On his way to the Delaware, Goodyear stopped at New Amsterdam, where he found one of New Sweden's most prominent officials. Isaac Allerton was there, too. The day Goodyear arrived, the New Sweden official, a man named Elswick, "had a private conversation with Allerton."[79] Goodyear and Elswick then met for the next two days to discuss the situation, while Allerton acted as moderator and perhaps interpreter.

Their final meeting was at Allerton's New Amsterdam house. In this discussion Goodyear asserted that the Swedish settlement on the Delaware could not stand in the way of English claims because it did not involve the Swedish Crown. Allerton seems to have settled the matter by assuring Goodyear that he personally had seen the commission held by Johan Printz, the previous governor and that he knew for certain that Governor Rising also had a royal commission.[80] These negotiations and Allerton's personal assurances kept New Haven Colony from pressing its claims to the Delaware region for a time.

Having once again defused intercolonial tensions, Allerton returned to New Sweden and sold more goods. As would become clear a few months later in the fall of 1655, playing more than one side of the many-sided colonial context was a delicate business and often involved important players who were not necessarily immediately visible. As we shall see in chapter 7, Allerton could not entirely avoid conflict even though he often negotiated it successfully.

Not long after the Goodyear-Elswick negotiations, Allerton left New Amsterdam to trade in New Sweden. Although he had helped to calm the English-Swedish crisis, in the meantime friction had increased between Dutch and Swedish colonial interests, and Allerton found himself in a difficult position. New Sweden governor Johan Rising wrote that "Allerton told us that Stuyvesant had wanted to prevent him from coming here and had said: 'Do you also wish to carry provisions to our enemies?'"[81] Allerton's usefulness and influence were important enough that, although Stuyvesant may have questioned Allerton's actions, he did not stop him from traveling and trading where he chose.

Having turned sixty-nine that year, Allerton continued to demonstrate the resilience that made him a vital and widely known member of the colonial North American world for thirty-five years. He continued to travel, trade, extend credit, and increasingly try to collect debts owed to him. In the summer of 1658, not long after his last petition for recovery of debt in New Amsterdam, John Davenport of New Haven wrote that it was "a sickly time."[82]

Six months later, in early 1659, Isaac Allerton died during an epidemic that swept New Haven Colony. His old neighbor and rival, William Bradford, had died in 1657. Bradford was the architect of a more restricted, culturally pure plan of colonization, one that seldom took hold successfully in any of the colonies along the Atlantic seaboard in the first half of the seventeenth century. In contrast, Allerton's way was much more in the mainstream of early colonial realities. Yet, by the twentieth century, most histories of the colonial period had come to accept Bradford's vision as normative, at least for New England if not for much of the Atlantic Coast. Bradford's decision to sit down and begin preserving his side of the story for future generations had everything to do with later generations' understanding of the seventeenth century.

Allerton did not leave a written narrative among his estate, much of which was such a confused amalgamation of debts and credits that his son refused to handle it. Just as he had lived his life among widely separated and distant communities, Allerton's documentary traces were similarly scattered; there is no cohesive narrative from his point of view.

In contrast, William Bradford left his written interpretation of the first thirty or so years of the Plymouth colonial enterprise among his worldly remains, thereby preserving a coherent report of his life and his vision of colonialism at Plymouth. Increase Mather and Nathaniel Morton used Bradford's account as a resource for some of their writings in the late 1660s and the 1670s, and Cotton Mather drew on Bradford's treatise twenty years later. As a result, Bradford's interpretation of the early colonial period began to shape history writing a decade or so after his death and continued in the early eighteenth century. There was renewed interest in his narrative after the mid-nineteenth-century American rediscovery of the manuscript in Great Britain.[83] In the post–World War II United States, Bradford's history of Plymouth plantation gained renewed popularity with the publication of the modern edition prepared and annotated by Samuel Eliot Morison.

During his lifetime, William Bradford was never sure that his vision or interpretation would win the day. If anything, in the final years of his life, the world of early colonial North America had become overwhelmingly contested and interdependent, and alliances constantly formed and then mutated into new configurations. The map of North America and its many peoples was repeatedly redrawn. By the time Bradford stopped writing in 1650, he had lost even his old friend and ally Edward Winslow to the lure of larger events.

Interestingly, Isaac Allerton did not leave behind the kind of written history that Bradford did, but this is not surprising. Perhaps Allerton wrote journals that have since been lost, though it seems most likely that he lived his life without also recording it. For throughout his experiences in North America, Allerton consistently displayed an unwillingness or an inability to keep clear and accurate accounts and to record his activities. In Plymouth, his failure to do so led to accusations of sharp business practices and cheating.[84]

Having learned through painful experience the importance of maintaining clear written records, Allerton advised Lucy Downing in the mid-1630s that her son should learn to write and keep accounts before acquiring other skills. Yet Allerton himself does not seem to have followed his own advice very consistently. In New Amsterdam, for instance, at times he admitted to not knowing how much money was owed him. Ultimately, forging alliances and networks across cultures, colonies, and interests was Allerton's great skill; writing was not.

Allerton wrote his history in his actions, and while he lived, William Bradford was never certain that Allerton's vision would not prove to be paramount. Bradford's own written narrative is a testament to one man's uncertainty and hopes, but it also contains highly significant glimpses of many people's diverse visions of colonization.

Early colonization and colonialism took many different forms and grew out of a variety of circumstances and visions. This seems obvious, but scholars have often reduced early colonial experiences to only a small number of dominating colonial plans, events, and people. Bradford's history, *Of Plymouth Plantation,* is a clear example of the ways in which only a few such concepts came to dominate historical interpretations with a hegemony they never exercised in their own time.

Bradford's vision has proven to be more appealing to later generations than it was to people in his own era, partly because his written version of events survived him, whereas the strategies and interpretations of many others have not been so clearly preserved. Many, indeed most, competing early colonial strategies and players did not leave the kind of articulate, written testimony that Bradford left, or, if they did, it did not survive for future readers. That does not mean, however, that in their day they were not eloquent exponents and practitioners of activities other than those of which Bradford approved.

The fact that Bradford felt compelled to write his history and that he began setting it on paper while in the midst of what he perceived as ongoing threats to his communal and colonial ideal demonstrates that his voice was not as powerful as later readers have assumed. On the contrary, Bradford's need to write the definitive history of the colony shows the strength and profusion of other voices and possible interpretations of that era. Many of those other voices became inextricably linked to the mapping and constant pursuit of alliances that frequently reshaped the cultural and political landscape of the first half of the seventeenth century.

5

Captain Claiborne's Alliance

During the 1630s Isaac Allerton found himself increasingly at odds with his fellow Plymouth colonists, and the English colonial population of New England exploded. Historians have long noted that New England's colonies took firm root during the 1630s largely as the result of a massive immigration by English protestant refugees who were escaping persecution at home. Equally important for the web of Native American and intercultural alliances that encompassed the eastern seaboard from the Chesapeake to Iroquoia, this was also the decade in which the older English colonization in the Chesapeake finally took hold in far more successful fashion. As in New England, English expansion in the Chesapeake was driven in large part by an increase in the numbers of immigrants, along with reduced colonist mortality.

The story of the 1630s, then, is one of both colonial development and the growth of the intercultural fur trade. Just when New England colonists like Isaac Allerton sought to expand trade networks from their colonies, the Chesapeake settlements also included people who tried to develop networks between Virginia, other colonies, and Indian nations. The increasing number of trade networks during the 1630s depended on intercultural alliances, and establishing these connections was one of the primary reasons that native peoples and Europeans worked so assiduously to map one another.

Before tobacco, the fur trade not only gave Virginia its first major export product but also shaped many intercultural relations for the first thirty years of the colony's history, peaking in the 1630s.[1] Indeed, throughout eastern North America, the 1630s witnessed a great increase in the fur trade.[2] Native

Americans and Europeans increasingly looked for additional or new trading partners as networks spread over greater distances and in new directions. Every trade relationship was evaluated according to its benefits to individual traders and its impacts on political and cultural affairs. In seventeenth-century North America, the fur trade at times provided the nexus for remarkable kinds of intercultural cooperation. In the end the promise of these alliances seldom lasted, but the short-lived nature of many of them was not necessarily apparent to anyone in the early seventeenth century.

The shifting web of alliances spanning eastern North America made it difficult for anyone at the time to foresee which ones would have the greatest staying power. What they were able to see was only that each new partnership had the potential to affect an entire sequence of other relationships. As it turned out, the fact that European settlements changed so dramatically in the 1630s meant that European power dynamics often interfered in otherwise flourishing intercultural connections.

The cultural and political landscape of eastern North America began to alter dramatically in the 1630s, with alliance-changing shifts in several regions. The new colonies of Massachusetts Bay, New Haven, Maryland, and New Sweden appeared on the scene, and colonial populations increased and spread out. Any alteration in the network also invariably threatened a change in political power dynamics, and people became particularly alert to the impact of shifting relations as the movement of peoples accelerated and the fur trade expanded. In other words, intercultural relationships had to survive not only the constant challenge of cultural misunderstandings but also the aggressions of other parties threatened by the new alliance. This is the story of one of the most important intercultural alliances in the early seventeenth century, one that would have far-reaching consequences in time and place.

In the 1630s the Chesapeake became the center of an extraordinary intercultural alliance organized around the fur trade. The Susquehannocks had long been looking for a reliable European trading ally and found one in an English colonist named William Claiborne.[3]

During the decade in which Isaac Allerton faced growing opposition in Plymouth over his trade practices and attempts to expand alliances with Native Americans, William Claiborne faced remarkably similar resistance from his own business partners and rival colonial interests as he worked to achieve a similar objective.

On the surface, William Claiborne was much like Isaac Allerton. He had lived in an English colony from the earliest years of its settlement (in his case, the colony of Virginia). He had held public office there and wielded considerable influence; indeed, he was the secretary of state after Virginia became a royal colony. As a successful early seventeenth-century colonial official, he recognized the importance of cultivating influence at court, just as Allerton had through his association with Ferdinando Gorges.

In the years after the Powhatan-English connection had largely collapsed, Claiborne refused to give up on the premise that alliances with Indian nations could offer English colonists important benefits. At a time when a number of English settlers in the Chesapeake loudly condemned even minimal interaction with native peoples, Claiborne chose a different path, one that sought alliances with native peoples. He soon struck out in search of advantage in the developing intercultural colonial trade.

Rather like Isaac Allerton, Claiborne had considerable personal success; yet, like Allerton, he too eventually had to leave behind part of the life he had made in the expanding colonial trade because of opposition from other colonial leaders. The parallels between Allerton and Claiborne are fascinating and reveal how difficult it was for Europeans not directly involved in trade with native peoples to trust those who were actively cultivating Indian trading partners and allies. In the 1630s both men's business partners accused them of dishonest practices, and both expanded their trade networks by incorporating indigenous peoples.

However, the imperatives and dimensions of those trade associations were completely beyond the control of European partners who were otherwise uninvolved in the venture. In many ways men like Allerton and Claiborne were caught in the middle between the requirements of colonial trade, which were dictated largely by Native Americans and Native American circumstances, and the directives of their English business partners. However, the early colonial economy could not have expanded without them. They stood squarely in the midst of much of the ethnographic mapping and remapping that Europeans and native peoples undertook, and the intercultural and international alliances they established shaped the seventeenth-century colonial world.

Moreover, because Claiborne established an extremely beneficial partnership with the powerful Susquehannocks, another link existed between Allerton and Claiborne, one that went beyond the parallels in their experiences in different colonies. The Claiborne-Susquehannock alliance and the way it ended set the stage for a series of events that would engulf Allerton and the Susquehannocks twenty years later and finally die out with Allerton's son in another twenty years.

The Susquehannock-Claiborne alliance was extraordinarily influential, and its impact had both geographical and temporal dimensions. Geographically, the Susquehannock-Claiborne connection and its demise affected people and events from the Chesapeake to Iroquoia. Temporally, its effects lingered throughout the first half of the century.

The strategies that both parties used to create the alliance demonstrate the ways in which power and advantage shifted fluidly between Indians and

Europeans in the 1630s. Moreover, the Susquehannock-Claiborne association had far-reaching consequences for other peoples from the Chesapeake to Iroquoia, and its disruption by Maryland at the end of the decade transferred the Susquehannocks' attention more fully to the mid-Atlantic and the people who lived there. The change in the Susquehannocks' interests would have significant consequences for Isaac Allerton and others, for, as we shall see in chapter 7, he and the Susquehannocks would meet in the Delaware and Hudson river valleys in the 1650s, long after the Susquehannock-Claiborne partnership had been disrupted.

In the early 1630s, however, the Susquehannocks looked with considerable interest at the English settlements in the Chesapeake, and William Claiborne helped to persuade them that they had finally found a willing and reliable European ally. To understand why such a collaborative effort seemed so beneficial to each side, we need to understand several events that took place in the 1610s and 1620s; indeed, the Susquehannocks' willingness to ally with Claiborne had everything to do with their relationship with the Five Nations or Haudenosaunee. Part of the Susquehannocks' Haudenosaunee strategy was to develop several other alliance configurations in the years before they agreed to one with Claiborne.

Moreover, Claiborne's willingness to ally with the Susquehannocks and the readiness of the Virginia governor and his council to allow it had much to do with the collapse of the Powhatan-English alliance. And in the midst of these shifting Susquehannock and English alignments, Dutch and Swedish colonizing activities helped to create the circumstances that shaped the beginning and the end of the Susquehannock-Claiborne alliance.

In some ways, the Englishman who had played a crucial role in establishing the earlier Powhatan-English alliance also helped to lay the groundwork for a partnership between Virginia colonists and the Susquehannocks. Indeed, before Pocahontas came to call Captain John Smith "father," Smith had spent considerable time exploring the area to the north of Jamestown. As with many of the early voyages we saw in chapter 2, Smith was seeking information about valuable natural resources, rich agricultural territory, and potential native allies and trading partners.

Smith first met a group of Susquehannocks in the summer of 1608, and he reported that they were quite willing to establish a coalition with the Jamestown English.[4] Although much has been made of the report that Smith was awestruck by the Susquehannocks' powerful stature—indeed, he portrayed them as giants—and of his claim that they were in awe of and tried to worship him, ultimately the key information he conveyed was that the Susquehannocks were a powerful nation and were willing to ally with the Jamestown English.

However, the English settlers at Jamestown never really followed through on Smith's early contacts with the Susquehannocks, in part because of the great stresses of Jamestown's early years and in part because of their careful monitoring of their connection with the powerful Powhatans. But over the years English colonists remembered the Susquehannocks and kept an eye on other Europeans' relations with them. In the twenty years after the first Smith-Susquehannock meeting, the English had few recorded dealings with them.[5] Instead, the Susquehannocks made intermittent contact with French and Dutch colonists, priests, and traders and chose to pursue alliances alternately with New France and New Netherland.[6]

The Susquehannocks' comparatively widespread contact with Europeans of different ethnicities resulted from their geographical position, which was almost in the center of the array of European colonial settlements on the east coast from the Chesapeake to the Saint Lawrence. It also resulted from two other factors. The first was the Susquehannock nation's size and strength. They were an Iroquoian-speaking people and, like the members of the Huron and Haudenosaunee Five Nations confederacies, were more populous and militarily more powerful than most of the Algonquian peoples living near European settlements.[7] The second, which helps to explain why the Susquehannocks had wide-ranging contacts with Europeans, was the fact that their network of alliances and enemies coincided in the early seventeenth century with the spread of European colonial settlement. For instance, the Susquehannocks' ongoing enmity with members of the Five Nations Iroquois, or Haudenosaunee, especially the Mohawks and the Senecas, was directly responsible for the Susquehannocks' choices in their dealings with French, Dutch, Swedish, and English colonists and traders. Furthermore, the changing nature of the Susquehannock–Five Nations rivalries also affected the Susquehannocks' relations with Algonquian peoples throughout the eastern seaboard. During the first half of the seventeenth century, the Susquehannocks played a crucial role, culturally, politically, and geographically, between Algonquians, Iroquoians, and Europeans.

Scholars believe that the ancestors of the Susquehannocks, Cayugas, and Mohawks were one people but that the Susquehannocks and Cayugas eventually broke away to become separate groups sometime around the beginning of the fourteenth century.[8] Those who became the Susquehannocks would recognize shared heritage with the Mohawks throughout the next several hundred years, and in the seventeenth century the Susquehannocks maintained kinship ties with the Hurons, who were also Iroquoian people with a shared ancestry. However, the split from the people who became the Mohawks and from those who formed the Five Nations alliance also continued to shape the Susquehannocks' history. Although they acknowledged a common heritage and periodically sought short-term alliances, the Susquehannocks and the Mohawks frequently regarded one another as enemies throughout the first half of the seventeenth century, and the Senecas remained one of the Susqehannocks' most hostile adversaries well into the 1670s.

When the Susquehannocks' ancestors broke away, they moved south. Archeological evidence has shown that by the middle of the sixteenth century they were living in a number of communities along the north branch of the Susquehanna River. For reasons that are not clear, they moved again sometime between 1550 and 1570 and formed one large settlement farther south along the Susquehanna River and then gradually expanded outward from this town and created a number of new communities.[9]

In the early seventeenth century the Susquehannocks continued to extend southward along the Susquehanna River toward the river's mouth, where it empties into the Chesapeake Bay. Their seventeenth-century location put them at an ideal vantage point from which to develop contacts with traders and colonists from New Netherland and Virginia. It also gave them ready access to well-established river and trail routes to the interior of the Great Lakes and Ohio country, which enabled them to travel easily into areas with the best sources of furs and to attack their Iroquois enemies without endangering their own towns.[10] The Haudenosaunee or Five Nations were arrayed just to the north of the Susquehanna River's headwaters, while the Susquehannocks spread out closer to the mouth of the river.

Because they were within relatively easy reach of Dutch and French colonial settlements, the Susquehannocks turned their attention first to them. In the summer of 1615 Samuel de Champlain first learned that the Susquehannocks could be impressive allies. That August, Champlain and Huron warriors were gathering their resources in order to attack the Onondagas. While they were still engaged in preparations, the Hurons received news from their allies, the Susquehannocks, who sent word that they would provide five hundred men to fight with the Hurons and Champlain against the Onondagas and that they desired friendship and an alliance with the French.[11] The Susquehannocks also explained to the French that the Five Nations made war on them periodically and received assistance from the Dutch.[12]

For the Susquehannocks to join in the upcoming strike against the Onondagas would satisfy two important requirements of alliance. First, it would fulfill their obligations to their existing Huron allies. Second, it would enable the Susquehannocks to extend their alliance networks to include Samuel de Champlain and the French newcomers. Champlain and his men must have seemed ideal new allies to the Susquehannocks because they already had sided with the Hurons against the Five Nations Iroquois and could provide both significant military assistance and new trade goods. In the end, the Susquehannocks apparently did not arrive in time for the attack on the Onondagas, but their offer is revealing of how Native American alliance and information networks functioned in the early colonial era and demonstrates that the Susquehannocks were well aware of colonial developments from Iroquoia to the Chesapeake Bay.

Moreover, the Susquehannocks' early overtures to the French had other components. News of one other incident spread among Dutch and French colonists and traders, and the Europeans found the description of barely veiled Susquehannock hostility to be rather sobering. One event that Champlain heard about from the Susquehannocks demonstrates the layers of alliance, threat, and power they conveyed in many of their early meetings with Europeans. In 1615, during the same summer that the Susquehannocks made overtures to Champlain, three Dutch traders met several of the Susquehannocks. Their meeting had consequences not only for them but also for future Dutch and French contacts with the Susquehannocks.

Although New Netherland had not yet been founded as a colony, Dutch traders and seafarers traveled the Atlantic coast during the first two decades of the seventeenth century. During the period from 1614 to 1618 a Dutch trading concern called the New Netherland Company was granted a monopoly to trade in North America, and a number of merchant ships sailed to North America in those years.[13] As with early English colonial ventures, the members of these expeditions sought to explore the lands and waterways of the eastern seaboard and to learn as much as possible about Native American trading partners and alliance networks.

In 1615 a Dutch trader named Kleynties, along with two other men, went on just such an exploratory journey tracing the course of the Delaware River on behalf of the New Netherland Company.[14] Before they finished their explorations, Kleynties and his companions were taken captive by Susquehannocks, who held them as hostages for a year, beginning in the summer of 1615.[15]

The three Dutch traders' appearance in the Susquehannocks' territory was quite unexpected for the Susquehannocks who found them, and the traders quickly found themselves put into the context of the Susquehannocks' expanding alliance network. Although they could not have realized it at the time, this ultimately worked to their advantage because in the summer of 1615 the Susquehannocks were looking for new allies to join them against the Five Nations and hoping to add Champlain's French group to their coalition. Because the Susquehannocks had not yet had many, if any, prior contacts with Dutch traders or colonists, they assumed that Kleynties and his companions were French and belonged to Champlain's group.

As a result, they did not harm their Dutch captives. Moreover, a Susquehannock emissary later told Champlain that they had not harmed the Dutch men because they thought they were his people. The Susquehannocks explicitly placed their treatment of the Dutch traders in the context of the obligations toward allies or prospective ones and of their ongoing enmity with the Five Nations. Most captives, the Susquehannocks told Champlain, would normally be tortured and put to death, but they had chosen not to harm these prisoners.

To make it very clear that they were offering Champlain a valuable alliance, the Susquehannocks stressed that the Mohawks waged war on them and regularly tortured Susquehannock prisoners and that the Dutch aided the Mohawks in this endeavor. When they took Mohawks or Mohawk allies captive, the Susquehannocks reported that they reciprocated the treatment. Those who helped the Five Nations against the Susquehannocks became the Susquehannocks' enemies.

The Susquehannock emissary to Champlain wanted him to understand the context in which the Susquehannocks had shown extraordinary mercy to the Dutch prisoners because they believed them to be with Champlain, who was a supporter of the Hurons, the Susquehannocks' primary ally. Champlain's account of this story illustrates the lesson he was intended to learn. He wrote pointedly that, had the Susquehannocks known that Kleynties and the others were Dutch traders and not associated with Champlain, "these three prisoners would not have got off so easily, and would not escape again should they surprise and take them."[16]

The two versions of this story, one French and one Dutch, have some inconsistencies. They do not, for instance, agree on the date. Champlain's description says that the Susquehannocks took Kleynties and the others captive the year before they made overtures to him. That would mean that the Dutch traders were captured in 1614. However, a Dutch account makes it clear that the men were ransomed in the Delaware region in 1616.[17] Therefore, either the men were captives for more than one year, or they were captured in 1615. One possibility for the discrepancy is that the accounts refer to separate events and to different people. However, it seems most likely that the two versions describe the Susquehannocks' capture of Kleynties and the two other Dutch traders and that some of the supporting details became confused in the retelling of the event.

The evidence is consistent that the Susquehannocks took Dutch traders captive in the middle of the second decade of the seventeenth century, during the period of the New Netherland Company's monopoly. It is also consistent that the Susquehannocks were trying to establish an alliance with Champlain during the same period and that they told Champlain they had treated Dutch captives in an unusual manner—they had not harmed them because they desired an alliance with Champlain.

The further suggestion found in Champlain's account that the Susquehannocks blamed the Dutch for supporting the Mohawks against them as early as the years between 1614 and 1616 is also puzzling. Later in the seventeenth century, after the Dutch West India Company [WIC] established the colony of New Netherland, ample evidence shows that the Dutch and the Mohawks established a durable alliance and the Susquehannocks regarded the Mohawk-Dutch partnership as a thorn in their side. After all, in diplomatic discussions, the Mohawks called the Dutch their brothers. However, no clear evidence confirms that Dutch traders had established connections with the Mohawks in the 1610s.

Dutch records of a treaty with the Mohawks in 1659 report that Mohawk sachems reminded the Dutch that their alliance with the Mohawks had existed for sixteen years, which dates its beginnings only to around 1643.[18] If Champlain's account is true, then it suggests a much earlier origin of the well-known Mohawk-Dutch alliance and of the Susquehannocks' later frustration with Dutch actions. However, at best it is likely to have been true of only a few individuals and not to record a wider alliance between communities.

Another element in Champlain's statement is jarring. He wrote that the Susquehannocks misidentified Kleynties and his companions as belonging to Champlain's party of French colonists "since they had no knowledge of us except by hearsay, never having seen a Christian."[19] However, it is untrue that the Susquehannocks had never before "seen a Christian" because we know that Captain John Smith and a number of English colonists met with a party of Susquehannocks in 1608.

Champlain's version may have meant that the Susquehannocks had never seen Catholic Europeans because they had not yet met any of the French members of Champlain's group. Alternatively, it may have been simply a mistranslation or a strategy on the part of the Susquehannocks to claim ignorance so as to offer the Dutch captives as a bargaining chip in their negotiations with Champlain. For our purposes, we cannot know as much as we would like about the Susquehannocks' early alliance tactics before the 1630s. However, despite some of the perplexing inconsistencies in surviving accounts, the evidence shows us some of the contours of early Susquehannock-European interactions and confirms the Susquehannocks' continuing northward focus before 1630.

The Susquehannocks' most important ally was the Hurons, with whom they reportedly shared kinship ties. Champlain's 1615 account makes it clear that both Hurons and Susquehannocks told him of their well-established "friendship." By midcentury Europeans regarded the Susquehannock-Huron link as so long enduring as to be virtually timeless. Writing in 1649, Jesuit Father Paul Ragueneau described the Susquehannocks' location and strength and noted further that "those people speak the Huron language, and have always been the allies of our Hurons."[20]

Situated between these two allied nations, the Hurons in the north and the Susquehannocks in the south, were the Five Nations Iroquois or Haudenosaunee. Various of the Five Nations were the Susquehannocks' most important enemies and remained so until the 1670s. During the first two decades of the seventeenth century, the Susquehannocks continued to look northward toward their Huron allies for a solution to their ongoing enmity with the Five Nations.

The strength of the Susquehannock-Huron coalition and the magnitude of the difficulties both faced as a result of their conflicts with the Five Nations are evident in Champlain's account of his first experiences with the Susquehannocks. After describing their offer to help fight the Onondagas, Champlain then offered his readers a final assessment of the Huron's old friends: "This nation [the Susquehannocks] is very warlike. . . . They have only three villages, which are in the midst of more than twenty others, on which they make war without assistance from their friends [the Hurons]; for they [the Hurons] are obliged to pass through the thickly settled country of the Chouontouarouon [the Senecas] or else they would have to make a very long circuit."[21]

The Five Nations (especially the Senecas) made it difficult for the Hurons and the Susquehannocks to meet their mutual obligations. This does not seem to have weakened the Huron-Susquehannock alliance; instead it merely provided more occasions for conflict with the Senecas and for revenge attacks. The French newcomers seemed ideally suited for such an enterprise. Establishing themselves near the Hurons and within striking distance of the Five Nations, they formed an early alliance with the Hurons. As time passed, however, several factors converged to prompt the Susquehannocks to look closer to their own territory for new European partners, and no one capitalized on the Susquehannocks' shift more than Virginia colonist William Claiborne.

Claiborne came to Virginia about five years after the Susquehannocks offered to fight with the Hurons and Champlain's forces against the Onondagas. When he arrived in the colony in 1621, he came with an appointment from James I as the colony's surveyor.[22] Significantly, he came with good connections in the Virginia Company and at court and would use them both in the colony and in England in order to set up an extraordinary intercultural trade venture. It is also noteworthy that Claiborne arrived in Virginia on the eve of the final collapse of the Powhatan-English alliance. This too would bring important consequences for Claiborne's trading activities only a few years later.

In the period leading up to the 1622 Powhatan attack, English colonial policy increasingly attempted to undermine the Powhatan paramount chiefdom.[23] Colonial officials sought every means they could to drive a wedge between the Powhatans and their allied nations. Recognizing that Wahunsonacock and his successor, Opechancanough, had the strongest hold on member nations that were geographically closest to the Powhatans, English colonial leaders focused on luring the more distant member nations away from the Powhatan alliance altogether. Although English efforts before 1622 were never completely successful at breaking up the Powhatan paramount chiefdom, the policy had the effect of increasing the degree of attention English colonial leaders paid to the areas farther from the James River.

The Powhatans' 1622 surprise attack did not succeed in destroying the colony of Virginia. However, it did stop English colonial expansion to the west for the foreseeable future, with the additional consequence of prompting English colonists working in intercultural trade to look to the northeast and the Chesapeake Bay as the best route for expansion. They discovered a flourishing exchange there. Indeed, John Pory reported that nearly a hundred European traders were active in the Chesapeake Bay intercultural commerce in the early 1620s.[24] William Claiborne was one of those who quickly saw the promise of joining the English traders' push to the north.

Having survived the 1622 Powhatan attack, Claiborne found his personal circumstances in the colony steadily improving in several ways.[25] In the aftermath of the attack James I rescinded the Virginia Company's charter and made Virginia the first English royal colony in North America. The new imperial structure meant changes in Jamestown, and Claiborne was appointed a member of the new Governor's Council and received additional land grants as partial payment for his new office. These land grants were in addition to the two hundred acres he had received in partial payment of his services as colony surveyor; his first grants were for lands on the eastern shore.

Moreover, Claiborne also had land on the western shore at Kecoughtan, which, by the early 1630s, he was able to use as an auxiliary base for his trading enterprise. Before then, however, his trade path toward the Susquehannocks was cleared as he obtained greater public power in Virginia and another colonial office. In 1625 he became secretary of the colony and received trading licenses as a result of his new office. William Claiborne was well positioned to move into the fur trade.[26]

The following year Claiborne began making tangible moves toward developing trade contacts to the north, and the Susquehannocks began to focus their alliance-seeking efforts farther south than in previous years. Thus, they began to move toward each other in search of new intercultural allies. Armed with his new trading licenses, Claiborne set out on an exploratory trip to the Chesapeake Bay. He stopped to check on his property at Accomack on the way, where he discovered that squatters had taken up residence.[27] Instead of having them either arrested or evicted, Claiborne realized that they might offer him just the additional assistance he would need in developing a thriving trade on the Chesapeake Bay if he were able to find suitable Native American trading partners. Thus Claiborne allowed the squatters to stay at Accomack. Within five years they would move to form a new community and provide crucial support for the Virginia side of the Claiborne-Susquehannock trade relationship.

Also in 1626, very near the time that Claiborne was exploring the possi-bilities for a trade on the Chesapeake Bay, a delegation of Susquehannocks explored the possibilities for a trade alliance with the colonists at the new Dutch West India Company colony of New Netherland. Although Dutch traders and explorers had been active in North America since the first decade of the sev-enteenth century, it was not until the 1620s that a Dutch colony was attempted under the sponsorship of the West India Company.

The first WIC settlement was Fort Wilhelmus on the Delaware, built in 1624, the year before Claiborne became secretary of the colony of Virginia and received official trading licenses. Located on High Island, opposite modern Burlington, New Jersey, Fort Wilhelmus gave the WIC an early entrance into the intercultural mid-Atlantic trade. The Susquehannocks must have heard about the new outpost, because, when Pieter Minuit arrived and shifted the infant colony's center to Manhattan, the Susquehannocks quickly sent emis-saries to deal directly with those Dutch leaders who possessed the authority to make formal alliances.

Unfortunately, they arrived in the midst of disputes over how to interpret the instructions provided by the company for the governance and operation of the new settlement—in other words, during a Dutch power struggle. Claiborne's office-holding counterpart in New Netherland was Isaack de Rasière, who was secretary of New Netherland, and it was de Rasière who reported the Susque-hannocks' visit in a letter to the directors of the Amsterdam WIC chamber.[28]

De Rasière's letter was essentially an official report detailing the early steps the company's employees had taken since a relief expedition arrived in North America that year in the wake of the dismissal of the first director general, Willem Verhulst, who did not go quietly.[29] After his frequent clashes with the council and reports of his overly harsh discipline of the colonists, the council asked Verhulst to resign. He refused and then threatened to seek a position with a rival French or English colony if the council forced him out.

The council outmaneuvered him, however. It voted to banish him from the colony, placed him under house arrest, and, when an available ship was ready, sent Verhulst and his wife back to the United Provinces.[30] In the meantime Pieter Minuit stepped into the breach and took control of the fledgling colony. All of these events happened in the spring of 1626. Minuit made an agreement to buy Manhattan Island sometime during that spring or summer and began consolidating the colony with Manhattan as its base shortly thereafter.

At this point thirty or forty Susquehannocks arrived in Manhattan and proposed an alliance. De Rasière's account of their visit demonstrates, however, that the internal power struggles in New Netherland were not yet resolved when they made their overture. Complaining that his duties as colony secretary were unclear, de Rasière noted that the company's instructions to its employees failed to grant him a vote in the governing council. He protested that this undermined his authority to such an extent that, if it were not redressed, he would prefer to be relieved from his duties in order to focus completely on developing the fur trade. Until the matter was resolved, however, he expected that any action of his would be deliberately subverted by the colony's assistant commissary, Gerrit Fongersz, who, de Rasière claimed, "has sworn to spite me."[31]

Because de Rasière had negotiated with the Susquehannocks and favored the alliance, he insisted that Fongersz would oppose it. Unlike de Rasière, the assistant commissary had an undisputed vote in the council. Knowing that his enemy vowed to block any of his efforts, de Rasière claimed that the profitable new alliance with the Susquehannocks was at risk. Because de Rasière had no vote in the council, whereas Fongersz did, de Rasière argued that a personal rivalry could harm the colony. Furthermore, de Rasière's letter was explicit on this point: "He has sworn to spite me, which he can do not more readily than when I have some request to make to the Council that has to be voted on, as is bound to happen soon, since the Minquaes have been here from the south, some thirty or forty strong, and have sought our friendship."[32]

It is significant that de Rasière first described the Susquehannock embassy as seeking "friendship" rather than trade; the actual word de Rasière used was *vrientschap*, literally "friendship."[33] They clearly desired an alliance for trade, and de Rasière is also explicit about the promise of commerce with the Susquehannocks. However, this was not intended to be just a short-term exchange; it was also an offer of alliance, one with long-term implications understood by both sides. Recognizing the significance of the Susquehannocks' proposal, de Rasière reported that he reciprocated with gestures of friendship. "In return," he wrote, "I showed them as much friendship as I could, so that they begged me that when the season approached I would send them a sloop or a small ship, until whose arrival they would keep the peltries, which I promised to do."[34] The secretary of New Netherland had just made a trade alliance with the mighty Susquehannocks.

The two sides exchanged gifts to commemorate the agreement. The Susquehannocks gave de Rasière ten beaver pelts, and he reciprocated with a fathom of trade cloth, some trade beads, and two hatchets.[35] In each case, the gifts were the kinds of goods each recipient most valued. This was a type of alliance making that followed Native American diplomatic and cultural customs, and de Rasière understood its fundamentals in this meeting. Moreover, he seems to have known who the Susquehannocks were beforehand and did not see the need to explain to the WIC who they were other than that they had come from the south. The Susquehannocks were known to the Dutch by 1626, and an offer of association with them was not to be taken lightly. De Rasière had taken the beginning steps toward an important American alliance, yet he worried that he may have promised more than he could deliver.

In view of the fact that the West India Company held a monopoly until 1648, the only legal fur trade in New Netherland as far as it was concerned was that on its own account. De Rasière knew he would have to send company vessels to the Susquehannocks the following trading season, but he also realized that he needed the council's approval to do so. Unable to resolve the situation in the colony, he wrote to his employers in Amsterdam and told them about the personal vendetta Fongersz was waging against him and suggested that it might hurt the company's interests.

Having described the Susquehannocks' emissaries' visit and the agreement he had made with them, de Rasière pointed out that he could not follow through on his part of the arrangement without some intervention by the company. As long as de Rasière did not have a vote in council, Fongersz stood in the way of the new alliance, and de Rasière was explicit on this point. The Susquehannocks were expecting a Dutch sloop to visit them the next trading season; however, de Rasière told his employers, "as I may not take upon myself to send any sloops where none have been before, unless ordered to do so by resolution of the Council, Fongersz might thwart or oppose me therein."[36] In addition, de Rasière laid out the possibilities for them:

> Since I must propose this and such other matters as concern me in the Council and request a resolution thereon, he could easily bring forward some trivial excuse or other that might spoil a good stroke of business, such, for instance, as that there are not men enough to man a sloop which is to sail to a river where the disposition of the natives is unknown without neglecting other places that have already been visited and are known.[37]

Perhaps Fongersz might raise some other objection; de Rasière reminded the company that giving him a vote in council would make the crucial difference. Without it, Fongersz could make "some other excuse which may readily be found if one wishes to thwart any one in the performance of his duties, especially if the petitioner himself has nothing to say in the matter."[38]

Unfortunately, de Rasière had indeed promised the Susquehannocks too much in light of the circumstances in New Netherland in 1626. It was a question of not only an internal power dispute but also the management of WIC resources. The objections that de Rasière imagined Fongersz might raise to the Susquehannock alliance were genuine problems. The company's employees were already spread thin on existing colonial endeavors; to send people to the Susquehannocks would almost inevitably mean less attention to some other part of the colony. Moreover, it was a risk to send men and a vessel to the Susquehannocks' territory without any guarantees of what they would find along the way.

In the end, the Dutch-Susquehannock alliance did not flourish in 1626 or 1627. The timing was not right for New Netherland's colonial officials. Little did they know it, but they needed to act quickly to secure a place as the Susquehannocks' premier European ally. They had lost a valuable opportunity, one with ramifications beyond a single trading season. Soon the Susquehannocks found themselves entertaining a proposition from a different European ally. The following year William Claiborne received a trading license from Virginia. He was just in time.[39]

Claiborne pursued his hopes of moving further into the fur trade again the next year, in 1628, when he sailed to the Chesapeake on an exploratory voyage.[40] He saw real opportunities for finding a niche in the intercultural fur exchange in Virginia's northern reaches because New Netherland abandoned Fort Nassau on the Delaware in 1628, choosing for the moment to concentrate its resources on building up the colony's Manhattan center. As the Dutch pulled back to the Hudson, Claiborne began lining up the necessary colonial approvals to press outward.

On January 31, 1629/1630, Virginia's governor and council granted Claiborne a commission to trade with the Susquehannocks until April 1. This was quite a limited trading license, though not an unusual one. The fur trading season would eventually stretch from March to June each year. In the Chesapeake Bay region, early English accounts reported that most Indian nations there were not yet accustomed to trading furs each year, and so the "trading season" was not yet a standard intercultural market period.[41] Claiborne's 1629 license may also have been intentionally brief, intended to give him only enough time to prove whether such a venture was likely to succeed.

Having secured a trading license from Virginia and faced with the news that the Dutch settlement on the Delaware was no longer a competitor, William Claiborne established his first base in the Chesapeake region. He selected a small island in the north of the bay, near the mouth of the Susquehanna River, and called it Palmer's Island. This was an ideal preliminary meeting place for Claiborne's initial negotiations with the Susquehannocks. Ultimately, it was not large enough to support a full-time settlement, with all of the necessary supplies for trade and defense, but it was a strategic, neutral meeting ground, and Claiborne made sure he secured Palmer's Island from the outset.

Later the same year, several events affected intercultural alliances in the Chesapeake. The first was the threat of a new colony. After New Netherland pulled away from its settlement on the Delaware (at least temporarily), another English venturer appeared on the scene. Cecil Calvert, Lord Baltimore, stopped in Jamestown after having visited Newfoundland, where he had originally intended to establish a haven for English Catholics. Lord Baltimore found the Chesapeake more inviting, and his visit threw the Virginia colonists into an uproar.

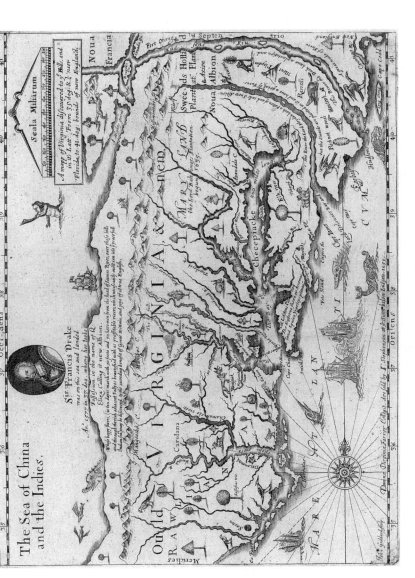

FIGURE 6. John Ferrar's 1651 map of Virginia shows a remarkable understanding of the position of many important groups in eastern North America despite a less-precise understanding of the geography. Ferrar shows the locations of the Virginia, Maryland, New Sweden, and New Netherland colonies, as well as the "Sasquehanokes River." Significantly, he shows Kent Island, which is in the northern part of the bay under the end of the word "Checepiacke." Courtesy of the John Carter Brown Library at Brown University.

Panicking at the thought that Baltimore might try to move in on their colony, Virginia's leaders quickly sent William Claiborne to England to intervene on the colony's behalf and prevent Baltimore from creating another English Chesapeake plantation. Having survived a catastrophic Powhatan attack, epidemic disease, and years of malnutrition and economic failure, Virginia was finally operating on steadier footing. Yet it now appeared endangered from an entirely new direction: It was under threat from an English lord and a Roman Catholic, one with long-standing connections at court.

If William Claiborne seemed to Virginia's leaders to be an ideal choice to plead their case back home in England, the mission provided him with the perfect opportunity to put the financial elements of his trading plan into place. In this, Claiborne was remarkably like Isaac Allerton, who at nearly the same time was working to secure a new patent for Plymouth Colony while expanding his own trade contacts and arranging for additional financing for his growing ventures. Claiborne did much the same thing in 1629. He argued against Baltimore's plans and put forward Virginia's primacy to the region. However, while in England on behalf of the Virginia Colony, he also laid the foundations for his own expansion plan.

With an eye toward cornering the best market on the eastern seaboard south of the Saint Lawrence, Claiborne approached a firm of English investors with experience in speculating in North American trade. He established a partnership with William Cloberry and partners. Cloberry had already invested in the North American fur trade and had connections with the Kirk brothers, who seized Quebec from New France and held it as an English colony for two years. Accordingly, Cloberry knew how lucrative the North American fur trade could be; he needed only to be persuaded that the Chesapeake could offer a reliable source of high-quality furs. In addition, he evidently had already begun exploring that option because he had financed a trading mission in the Chesapeake under the leadership of Henry Fleet.

Claiborne, however, proposed a larger and longer-term venture and suggested using Kent Island as the group's main trading base. Kent Island was farther south than Palmer's Island, but it was larger and more easily defended and would allow for easy access of trade boats and supplies. Using both islands would give Claiborne and his partners ready access to one of the eastern seaboard's most widely used routes into the interior, where the best furs were found. Furthermore, this area was far enough from New France to enable English traders to deal directly with Native American traders, especially if Claiborne could establish a lasting alliance with the Susquehannocks. Cloberry and his partners were swayed, and Claiborne secured the financing he needed. In typical seventeenth-century English entrepreneurial fashion, he ventured his person in the scheme, and Cloberry and the other England-based partners would open their purses.

Meanwhile, back in the colony of Virginia, relations with Algonquians near English settlements continued to worsen. In October the House of Burgesses called for regular military expeditions against the Pamunkeys and other Algonquians who were hostile to the colony and declared that the settlement would organize three strikes against them every year, one in November, one in March, and one in July.[42] The relentless pace of these infrequent but regular attacks was designed to break the Indians once and for all, but it did not signal the end of Virginia's willingness to form alliances with native peoples.

While the new policy showed the hardening attitudes of Virginia's colonists toward many of the Algonquians who lived closest to them (and certainly toward any who had participated in the 1622 attack), it also reinforced the colony's shift in geographical emphasis. Intercultural alliances, particularly for trading purposes, were still of interest to Virginia's leaders, but only with native peoples who lived well beyond the limits of English settlement. As William Claiborne would soon show, the Susquehannocks would fit that bill.

Claiborne finally put all of the elements of his plan together in 1631, and for the next five years he based an interracial trading community on two islands in the Chesapeake Bay and developed a flourishing alliance with the powerful Susquehannocks, whose capital town lay just to the north of the bay on the Susquehanna River. Having persuaded his new English partners that Kent Island was an ideal location for an ongoing fur-trading enterprise in the Chesapeake Bay region, Claiborne returned to the Chesapeake in 1631 and settled Kent Island.

By October the Kent Island settlement had the rough outlines of a defensible colonial town, with a large, timber-framed house and several thatched-roof huts, all surrounded by palisades and four mounted guns.[43] Claiborne's design was typical of early colonial settlements, especially their forts and trading posts. He had buildings in which to store his merchandise and to house and support his colonists, and he considered the importance of defending the community from the outset. Although Claiborne was probably not thinking in these terms, his Kent Island settlement would have looked familiar to the Susquehannocks, whose reputation as a fearsome, powerful nation stemmed not only from their fighting expertise but also from the security of their well-defended and palisaded town.

From 1631 until 1638 Kent Island was the center of Claiborne's enterprise and was closely associated with him and his allies, the Susquehannocks. In 1631 he moved quickly to secure his position in the trade because he soon learned that Dutch traders were back in the region and had established a new settlement in the Delaware River valley in April. The new trading post was called Swaanendael, and Claiborne seems to have decided to neutralize Dutch competition by accommodating it.

In 1631 he received a commission from Virginia governor John Harvey to trade with the Dutch.[44] In the end, Swaanendael did not last; conflict over a stolen tin coat of arms escalated in the chasm of intercultural misunderstanding, and neighboring Indians destroyed the settlement in retaliation for Dutch handling of the incident. Nevertheless, Claiborne knew that Dutch interest in the area and its native peoples would not end with Swaanendael's destruction; his best strategy to overcome this competition was to move quickly and claim a location where he could stay in regular contact with his native allies.

Thus in August the first ship supplied by Cloberry and Company, the *Africa*, arrived in the Chesapeake for Claiborne to use. After stopping first at Claiborne's plantation at Kecoughtan, the *Africa* sailed on into the Chesapeake Bay, and Claiborne and his crew went on to the Susquehannocks to trade.[45] For the next several years, Claiborne's Kent Island crew maintained a successful alliance with the Susquehannocks, one that was quite lucrative for Claiborne but also appealed to Susquehannock interests. Moreover, the Susquehannocks' understanding of their alliance with Claiborne included a broad array of obligations. After Claiborne's community came under threat from Baltimore's new English colony in 1635, the Susquehannocks continued to fulfill their obligations to Claiborne's men for many years, long after Claiborne himself had moved back south of the Chesapeake Bay. But that came later. In the interim, the Susquehannock-Claiborne association had consequences for other Indian nations in the region.

When the Susquehannocks eventually formed their alliance with William Claiborne, various Indian nations around the Chesapeake felt the direct results of the shift in the Susquehannocks' attention. Claiborne and other English traders working with him established Kent Island and Palmer's Island in the Chesapeake Bay as fur-trading centers, which were well within reach of the Susquehannocks' major town at the mouth of the Susquehannock River, where it emptied into the bay. However, Claiborne's development of the trading centers at Kent and Palmer's islands had severe consequences for Indian nations on the upper eastern shore because these hubs encouraged the Susquehannocks to move farther south. Algonquians on the upper eastern shore found themselves largely unable to slow the advancing Susquehannocks.

The much more powerful Susquehannocks pushed the upper Eastern Shore Algonquians south from their early-seventeenth-century homelands into the Nanticokes' territory.[46] They also cultivated a client relationship with the Algonquian Tockwoghs in the early seventeenth century, in which the Tockwoghs were subordinate to the Susquehannocks. In addition, the Susquehannocks and the Piscataways developed a strong rivalry, and Susquehannock warriors raided Piscataway communities.

In much the same way that European colonies were gradually expanding along the Atlantic seaboard during the first three decades of the seventeenth century, so too were several Indian nations. Native peoples, such as the Susquehannocks, who were not devastated by disease epidemics often responded to the changing circumstances by expanding their power base and sometimes by moving into new territories. In other words, the Susquehannocks' movements and their alliance with William Claiborne reshaped native, European, and intercultural politics throughout the region. As we have seen, they were by no means the only Indian nation to expand in this way, nor were they the only one to have such a wide-ranging impact both culturally and geographically. But they were one of the most important players on the North American Atlantic seaboard during the first half of the seventeenth century, and their significance has often been underestimated, both at the time and by later generations of historians.

In the seventeenth century Lord Baltimore and his colonial officials were among those Europeans who failed to understand the strength and range of the Susquehannocks' influence. At first Baltimore truly did not comprehend the value of Claiborne's alliance with the Susquehannocks. Perhaps he believed that it was a relatively unimportant arrangement through which Claiborne and his London partners acquired North American furs.

Although there is little surviving evidence to tell us exactly what Calvert thought about Claiborne's affiliation with the Susquehannocks, the actions of Maryland Colony officials can explain a great deal because, regardless of how Calvert perceived the relationship, the actions of his colonists and colonial officials clearly indicate that they did not understand the larger North American context of alliances into which they had just stumbled.

Maryland's insistence that the Calverts claimed the entire region of the new colony, including Claiborne's island trading bases, failed to give credit to Claiborne's reasonable claims to the area even under English standards. Even more important, it failed to recognize the webs of alliances that already crisscrossed the area and paid no heed at all to the American conventions of diplomacy that governed them. Maryland's response to the Susquehannock-Claiborne alliance is a clear example of the fact that it took actual North American experience and knowledge for Europeans to fully understand the necessity of allying with powerful Indian nations or at least to gain a more realistic appreciation of which Indian nations were the most powerful. This was true despite the fact that many colonial promoters expected some degree of alliance formation. It was one thing to advocate the need to understand and make alliances with native peoples; it was quite another to recognize the real thing when faced with Indian peoples themselves.

The reality was often more extensive and more essential than even the Europeans' theories of colonization and trade asserted. In the case of the Susquehannock-Claiborne alliance of the 1630s, Lord Baltimore also obviously failed to understand that his actions against Claiborne would have consequences that would extend well beyond European control. Instead, Baltimore based his determination more on a sense of his power in England and in relation to colonists in Virginia. Nevertheless, it was a bad decision. As a result, his colony faced war with the Susquehannocks for nearly two more decades, and the legacy of those early years of conflict would reverberate throughout the 1670s.

The experiment at Kent Island did not fail because English alliances with native peoples collapsed. They did not. The Susquehannock-Claiborne alliance ended after fewer than ten years because of intra-English competition for favored status with the Susquehannocks. In the end, Kent Island could not survive the failure of competing English colonial interests to set aside their opposing claims. It was not an intercultural breakdown.

On the contrary, the Susquehannock-Claiborne alliance was extraordinarily successful. In the early seventeenth century, rivalries between Europeans, even those from the same general culture, played as important a role in shaping North America as rivalries between cultures did. In the context of early seventeenth-century North America the offer of alliance could come from any direction, and any new collaborative effort could be immediately challenged by Europeans or Native Americans who were threatened by the new alignment of interests.

The Susquehannocks' search for a reliable European ally and trading partner in the 1620s and 1630s was twice thwarted by internal European power struggles. First, the proposed Susquehannock-Dutch alliance was prevented from becoming more firmly established in 1626, a fact that enabled Claiborne to push himself as the Susquehannocks' primary European ally. Ten years later, intra-European conflict impeded the Susquehannocks again when Lord Baltimore forced Claiborne to abandon his Kent and Palmer's islands trading posts.

In both instances, these power struggles rather than any cultural differences between Indians and European allies were the reason intercultural alliances failed. Yet, to a significant degree, they were unintended consequences of Europeans' preoccupations with their own rivalries and interests. When Europeans focused their attention on mapping other European rivals without paying adequate notice to the webs of Native American connections, the effects could be extremely disruptive for Indians and European colonists alike. As we shall see in the next chapter, their unintended consequences could at times be more powerful than any direct efforts by European colonists to control the endeavors of non-Europeans to create or sustain alliances.

6

Alliances of Necessity

Fictive Kinship and Manhattan's Diaspora
African Community

To a large degree William Claiborne and the Susquehannocks used their alliance for similar ends. Claiborne used his with the Susquehannocks to improve trade and to expand his power base within the political circles of Virginia and London. The Susquehannocks used theirs with Claiborne and Virginia to increase trade and gain advantage over their Iroquois and Algonquian enemies. Many of the intercultural partnerships that formed in North America during the early seventeenth century related to comparable goals. Just as European individuals like Isaac Allerton and William Claiborne and Indian nations like the Susquehannocks developed these associations, others also used alliance-building strategies to strengthen their position, even in some of the most restrictive circumstances.

Enslaved Africans lived under constraints that were different from those that existed elsewhere in North America, but at least in New Netherland, they carefully mapped the social world of the Dutch colony and found a way to use alliances to their advantage.[1] In New Netherland, Africans formed links with one another as a way to influence the degree of Dutch control over their community. Although the circumstances of slavery made these connections rather different from some that shaped seventeenth-century North America, they were also a response to the dangers and flexibility that the uncertain early colonial period created.

The collaborations and conflicts of diaspora Africans sometimes had nothing to do with Europeans but nonetheless fed fears in European communities. In the fluid context of early colonial North America, even enslaved Africans were able to carve out spaces that they themselves controlled. They did not live out their lives in North America merely reacting to Europeans or even to slavery. But if their partnerships were not always necessarily directed at Europeans, they nevertheless affected the stability of European colonial communities. Indeed, in some circumstances, European leaders relied on the assistance of Africans within the colony against external threats.[2]

In 1640s North America, slavery was an evolving institution, and relatively few people were forced to endure it for life. That is not to suggest that early seventeenth-century bondage was a benevolent institution; it was not. However, it was very different from the kind of enslavement that later developed.[3] This state of subjection could last from a few years to most of a person's life. In times of external crisis, enslaved people might be expected to help protect the colony and thus might be given arms by their owners or colonial authorities. They did not always do work that was different from the labor of free or indentured people. Those who were enslaved usually lived and worked while surrounded by free or bound Europeans.

There were as many Africans in New Netherland as there were anywhere in eastern North America north of Florida, and the largest African population in any Atlantic seaboard community in the 1640s was on the island of Manhattan, where the Dutch had built a colonial town they called New Amsterdam.[4] There Africans formed allegiances and kinship bonds with one another even though they may have spoken different languages, belonged to several distinct ethnic groups, and come from diverse places in Africa and the Atlantic littoral.

These alliances gave diaspora Africans a significant degree of influence in the small colonial community. Moreover, they reveal another side of the tension between accommodation and conflict that pervaded the early colonial period. Enslaved Africans in New Netherland successfully utilized these alliances to influence the degree of Dutch control over their community. In the 1640s they also used them to manipulate Dutch anxieties about the threat of growing conflict with Munsee peoples, who surrounded the colony.

The Dutch West India Company (WIC) brought slaves to New Netherland to provide a labor force for company and public work projects. These Africans provided labor for the colony, which was their primary value as far as colonial officials were concerned. However, everyone's lives were much too intertwined for their labor value to be the only important thing to know about these enslaved people and their role in the colony. The enslaved Africans created a distinctively diaspora African community in New Netherland, one that was centered on Manhattan, where the WIC's slaves lived.

Their accomplishment was a particularly Atlantic world phenomenon because the enslaved African community of Manhattan included Africans of different ethnicities and from several regions of Africa.[5] Dutch colonial records indicate not only that Africans in New Netherland formed a community that included people who would never have had contact with one another in their home regions in Africa, but also that Africans in New Netherland were able to preserve some elements of African cultures and to shape them into something distinctly new and Atlantic, if not North American, yet also broadly central African.

They did so despite the strictures of servitude, and the influence of their adaptation and resilience went far beyond New Amsterdam. Africans' ability to create ties with other Africans and Afro-Europeans in New Netherland influenced the lives of non-Africans in the colony as well. This was particularly true in New Amsterdam, where the largest population of Africans and the greatest concentration of colonial Europeans both lived. As a community, enslaved Africans found that they were able to challenge and sometimes shape the power of Dutch colonial officials and institutions of authority. Together, enslaved Africans managed to thwart Dutch officials' efforts even though their power was severely limited.

The surviving records from New Netherland tell us frustratingly little about Africans who were held as slaves in the colony before the 1650s. After 1650, the numbers of enslaved Africans in the colony increased, and the information about their identities and origins also becomes more extensive. And yet, the men and women who lived in New Netherland during its first twenty-five years created one of the earliest diaspora African communities in North America and played an integral role in the web of alliances that crisscrossed the colony.

Indeed, Africans' alliances were important with respect to the question of external coalitions that threatened the colony—both in Dutch perceptions and as borne out by actual events. Dutch fears of internal, intracolonial alliances were always part of larger assessments of external threats; thus Dutch officials were at times more or less willing to accept internal alliances depending on their perceptions of those dangers. In this they were not unique. Throughout eastern North America colonial officials made similar assessments in the early seventeenth century, although relatively few had as large a single concentration of enslaved Africans in their colonies. Accordingly, even the limited information available warrants examination for what it can tell us about the broad array of alliances in this time and place.

In order to learn something of the ways in which enslaved Africans used alliance as a strategy, we need to understand as much as possible about them. We cannot know the exact origin of most of the Africans who ended up in the WIC's North American colony of 1640s New Netherland. However, Dutch colonial records offer significant clues. Even though some enslaved people's names are African place names, for instance, we cannot simply presume they indicate a person's original home.[6] However, we can at least assume that they provide evidence that the person likely passed through that place and may well have come from there.

For instance, slaves with first names followed by "d'Angola," such as Gracia d'Angola, were almost certainly either originally from the Angola region or were bought by Europeans as slaves from the Angolan trading factories. Simon Conge was presumably from the Kongo region of Africa, either as his original home or his point of capture or sale as a slave.[7] Many Africans in New Netherland had names that included either Angola or Congo, which is consistent with evidence about the transatlantic slave trade and the Dutch West India Company's role in it during the early seventeenth century.[8]

Not all enslaved people in New Netherland had names that included African place names, however. In the absence of other documentation about when and how specific individuals came to the colony, it is difficult to know much about their background before coming to America. In some cases, broader knowledge about the early transatlantic slave trade provides important clues, even if they are far more limited than we would wish.

One person who offers a window onto the ways in which enslaved Africans used inter-African alliances to accomplish ends known only to other members of the Manhattan African community bore one such enigmatic name. Jan Premero appeared in Dutch colonial records more in death than in life, and his name offers very few clues about his original home. His name may suggest that he had been enslaved for a relatively long time, perhaps first living in a Portuguese or Spanish colony, if "premero" was used to mean "first." He may have been the first enslaved man called Jan (or Juan or Jao) to live in the colony where he was given the name. Alternatively, the name "Premero" could have referred to an owner's brand on his body, either from the WIC or a private trader.[9] Some traders branded new slaves with numbers when they acquired them, giving each person purchased a consecutive number. Jan Premero may have been branded with the number one.

Most of those taken to New Netherland as WIC slaves came from areas in west central Africa, which, in the seventeenth century, was broadly referred to as Angola. Johannes Postma has shown that the Dutch shipped a substantial number of Bantu-speaking men and women from this region to live as slaves in the West Indies, and some of these people eventually ended up in North America.[10] Indeed, most of the African slaves in New Netherland would have spoken a western Bantu language, probably Kikongo or Kimbundu.[11] Some Africans in New Netherland may have come to the colony from the WIC's other American colony of Brazil. The West India Company had many Bantu-speaking African slaves there, and it was not uncommon for the company to move employees and laborers, including enslaved ones, from one colony to another.[12]

Most enslaved Africans in New Netherland's early years, whether owned by the West India Company or private individuals, were probably taken in raids on Portuguese or Spanish ships.[13] The WIC did not enter directly into the Atlantic slave trade to a great extent until after the Dutch conquest of northern Brazil in 1630 and of Elmina (Mina) on the Atlantic African coast in 1637.[14] Even after Brazil became a West India Company colony in the 1630s, Dutch privateers continued to take Portuguese and Spanish ships and confiscate the cargoes. Privateering actions were construed as part of the company's mission. The WIC was established as a war and trading company and was intended to serve as an instrument of war against the Spanish empire in the Atlantic. After the WIC gained footholds in Brazil and Curaçao, the company sent slaves from those locations to its North American colony.

People sent from these additional WIC colonies had considerable experience with Portuguese and sometimes Spanish Europeans. Although the Dutch conquered northern Brazil in 1630, for instance, the WIC never succeeded in populating the colony with a majority of Dutch colonists. Instead, most settlers remained culturally Portuguese. Even the several hundred Sephardim from Amsterdam who settled in Brazil had retained much Portuguese culture despite having lived in the United Provinces. Thus, slaves brought by the WIC from its colony in Brazil to its colony in North America would often have had Portuguese names.[15]

The names of Africans enslaved in New Netherland reveal as much about the early seventeenth-century context of European imperial ambitions and shifting colonial strengths as about the individuals themselves. For instance, seven of nine WIC slaves accused of murder in a 1641 court case had Spanish or Portuguese names. Unfortunately, it is impossible to determine where Africans in New Netherland received Portuguese, Spanish, and Christian names because the WIC obtained them from a wide range of sources. Portuguese, Spanish, or Christian names might have been given to them at almost any stage along the way to North America or in Africa itself. Not only did the Portuguese maintain a number of colonial outposts along the Atlantic coast of Africa, but Portuguese traders also lived in all of the major towns along the early seventeenth-century Luanda slave trade routes to the interior of central Africa.[16]

Moreover, traders involved in the African side of the early seventeenth-century slave trade sometimes kept large numbers of slaves, using them as a form of wealth and benefiting from their labor for a time before eventually selling them into the Atlantic market.[17] As a result, a number of slaves lived among Portuguese traders in Africa before making the forced migration to the Americas. The question is further complicated by the fact that people in parts of west central Africa had adopted Christianity, particularly in the kingdom of Kongo; thus European owners may not necessarily have given the Christian names to their African slaves.[18]

New Netherland slaves, particularly several who appeared in key court cases in the 1640s, may have been enslaved in Portuguese colonies before being acquired by the Dutch West India Company. If so, they may have been captured from Portuguese ships or colonies, or they may have come from regions in Africa with a strong Portuguese colonial and cultural presence.[19] Writing in the 1650s, for instance, Joannes de Laet estimated that WIC ships confiscated 2,356 slaves from enemy ships between 1623 and 1637. This number probably equaled or exceeded the number of slaves the company acquired through trade in that period.[20] Colonists and colonial officials in New Netherland preferred slaves who had already been "seasoned" in Brazil or the West Indies and did not seem to mind if a slave's earlier experience of bondage was under non-Dutch owners.[21] Until midcentury, many Africans came to New Netherland after having lived elsewhere in the European colonial Atlantic world.

Many enslaved Africans kept names that were not transformed into Dutch forms in New Netherland. As far as Dutch colonial officials were concerned, there was seldom any need to change enslaved people's names because they would not be fully assimilated into the free colonial community. Their names were one of several ways by which colonial officials set them apart from other people in the colony and indicated their place in the social order. This is not to say that non-Dutch names were unusual in New Netherland. New Amsterdam, in particular, was an international community with residents, traders, and seafarers from a wide range of cultures. Many people's names reflected their non-Dutch background, and many free people's non-Dutch names were not changed to Dutch forms (though some were modified).[22]

In other words, it was not that enslaved persons' names were the only indication of their unique status within the community but rather that names indicating Portuguese and African origins worked in combination with other symbols of marginality as marks of their low status, as did their skin color and brands on their bodies. The power of names as an indicator of low status is especially clear in cases in which enslaved Africans received names that identified them in relation to their physical characteristics or to others.

Several slaves were given the Dutch name of "Jan." For instance, Jan de Fort Orange and Jan Premero were both WIC slaves whose names appeared in a 1641 criminal court case.[23] Similarly, several slaves were named "Manuel." Three men who appeared in the same 1641 court case were owned by the WIC and were each named Manuel: Manuel de Gerrit de Reus, Manuel Minuit, and Manuel de Groote.[24] Two of these names are somewhat puzzling for slaves owned by the West India Company because they seem to indicate private rather than company ownership. The council records that list their names in the 1641 case clearly state, however, that all nine of the defendants were slaves of the WIC, so the names indicate either prior ownership or that the two men had been leased to private colonists.

Settlers who did not own slaves themselves were able to lease the labor of slaves owned by others.[25] Gerrit de Reus, for example, was one of the first Dutch farmers to settle on Manhattan and may have leased the labor of a West India Company slave named Manuel, perhaps on a long-term basis, as Manuel came to be known as Manuel de Gerrit de Reus. In addition, Manuel Minuit may have been owned at one time by Pieter Minuit, an early director general of the colony. Although Pieter Minuit had not been in New Netherland for several years and was dead in 1641, Manuel the slave continued to be identified with the former colony leader even though the West India Company claimed ownership of him.

Ultimately, no matter where the Africans had come from, once in New Netherland, colonial officials and colonists required them to work on behalf of others. The WIC used its slaves to build the fort on Manhattan, which was completed in 1635. African men who were in the colony before 1635 were put to work building a central symbol of the West India Company's claim to territory in North America. The company's slaves were typically made to labor on a variety of public works projects, including cutting timber for construction and firewood, splitting rails, clearing land, and burning lime, as well as on company-owned farms where they became agricultural workers.

We know about the kinds of early public works projects that enslaved African labor built on Manhattan because of a list drawn up in 1639. When Willem Kieft arrived in New Netherland to take up his post as the colony's director general, he asked for an accounting of the company's resources, including how they had been used during his predecessor's tenure. Company slaves were included as "company resources." Accordingly, Jacob Stoffelsen, overseer of the slaves, stated in a March 1639 deposition that slaves owned by the WIC had been employed in all of the aforementioned tasks.[26]

Slavery in New Netherland meant being forced to do unpaid work for others, but scholars are less certain about what it meant beyond this. In the nineteenth century, slavery in the United States almost uniformly denied enslaved persons any rights as human beings under the law, but early seventeenth-century slavery was neither as brutally restrictive (particularly in New Netherland) nor as clearly defined. In seventeenth-century New Netherland, enslaved Africans were permitted to marry, and some of those owned by the WIC had spouses and children.[27] Moreover, with the permission of their owners and of Dutch officials, African adults sometimes adopted orphaned or parentless African children.

Indeed, in many circumstances New Netherland colonial officials explicitly recognized slaves' family ties. In 1644, for instance, the Council for New Netherland accepted the need for enslaved men to support their wives and children as an appropriate argument in favor of the men's petition for manumission.[28] Those who petitioned set forth reasons that colonial officials evidently found persuasive: They had rendered many years of service; freedom either had been promised to them or was customary even when not explicitly promised; and they needed to do more work for themselves to support their families. Colonial officials evidently agreed and set them free.

In New Netherland, slaves had an array of rights beyond their ability to legitimate their family relationships under Dutch law, but it is difficult to determine the exact parameters of their rights in the seventeenth-century Dutch colony. Some evidence suggests that even company slaves were permitted to own certain kinds of property. Dutch court records, for example, reveal that Anthony Portugees, a WIC slave, sued a free New Netherland colonist in 1638 for damage done to his hog by the colonist's dog.[29]

Although scholars continue to disagree about the matter, evidence such as Anthony Portugees's lawsuit suggests that enslaved people in New Netherland may have had an unusually broad array of legal rights, although we know that, in other early seventeenth-century colonies, they also initially possessed far more privileges than did those at the end of the century. Some argue that slavery in New Netherland was more analogous to indentured servitude than to chattel slavery. Others disagree, maintaining instead that slavery was fundamentally different from other forms of servitude.

The disagreement endures partly because the surviving records are not nearly so extensive on this point as we would wish. As importantly, it persists because slaves in New Netherland were plainly able to exercise a number of important rights, many of which were seldom available to those in other colonies except during the earliest period of settlement, and their term of bondage seldom lasted for life. Apparently, various owners could impose significantly different circumstances on enslaved peoples. Morton Wagman, for instance, has argued that, as employees of the company, WIC-owned slaves had rights that were not extended to privately owned slaves in the colony.[30]

If enslaved people in New Netherland managed to form a real community or even effective periodic alliances, how was it possible for people thrown together in the harshest manner to forge bonds with others with whom they might not have anything else in common and who might not even speak the same language? As we shall see, Africans in New Netherland did manage to form a new and vibrant community and somehow managed to overcome differences of ethnicity, culture, and language in doing so. In part, the early dimensions of the Atlantic slave trade may have made such connections more possible than they might otherwise have been.

There is considerable evidence that most enslaved Africans sent to the Americas in the early seventeenth century came from the Angola region, including the kingdom of Kongo.[31] Moreover, several studies have demonstrated that Brazil received a majority of African slaves from Angola during that time, and, as we have seen, there is every reason to believe that the WIC obtained slaves for New Netherland via Brazil.[32]

John Thornton has suggested that the Angolan coast was one of three culturally distinct zones of Atlantic Africa from which slaves were sent to the Americas.[33] Sydney Mintz, Richard Price, and others take the position that most slaves came from different parts of the African continent, had diverse cultural traditions, and thus had little in common other than the experience of the Middle Passage. Thornton, however, argues persuasively that the Angolan coast was linguistically fairly homogeneous and that almost everyone in this large area spoke languages of the western Bantu subgroup.[34] He argues further that most people in the Angolan region in the late sixteenth and early seventeenth centuries spoke a form of either Kikongo or Kimbundu.

Citing evidence from early modern European observers, Thornton points out that Kikongo and Kimbundu were closely related, perhaps analogous to early modern Portuguese and Spanish. Speakers of these languages could communicate in a limited way and if necessary could learn one another's language fairly easily. Furthermore, those who lived in the remote interior of this region spoke an "Angolan" language (probably Kimbundu) that served as a lingua franca in more linguistically diverse areas.[35] Thornton acknowledges that the Angolan zone was quite diverse politically, and scholars have pointed to the wide range of political units in west central Africa as evidence that those who were enslaved from that region would have had little in common.

Thornton, however, has suggested that political rivalries in the seventeenth century operated mostly among elites rather than the ordinary people most likely to be sold as slaves. As a result, he argues that, before 1680, Africans in the Americas and the Caribbean had more common African linguistic and cultural ties than scholars previously believed were possible.[36] Most recently, Linda M. Heywood and Thornton have argued for the influence of what they call an "Atlantic Creole culture" in west central Africa and in other places throughout the Atlantic world where west central Africans were taken as slaves.[37]

Moreover, evidence from other American and Caribbean colonies demonstrates that national groups developed in many diaspora African communities, some of which devised more syncretic social structures, while others divided up along ethnic lines.[38] For example, Angolan slaves in the Brazilian maroon community of Palmares had their own leader, chosen from leaders of the larger, multiethnic community as a whole.[39] However, this was not a practice unique to runaway slave communities. Brazilian sources provide evidence of African ethnic organizations and brotherhoods in diaspora slave communities, as do sources from Mexico and other colonies.

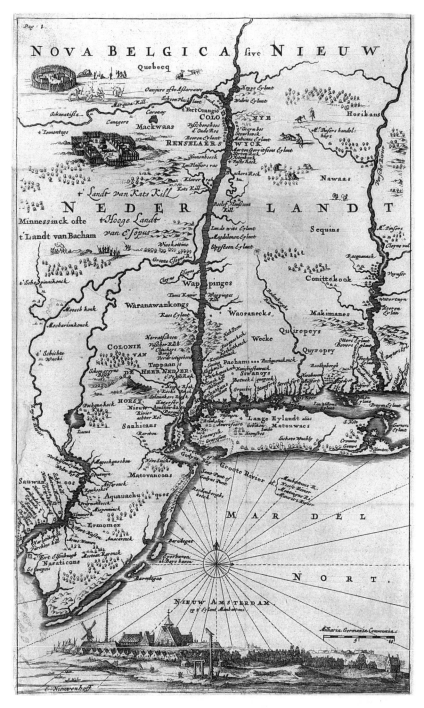

FIGURE 7. Adriaen van der Donck's map of New Netherland shows the Hudson River as the center of the colony and includes both the Connecticut and Delaware rivers as important parts of the colony. Van der Donck depicted many of the Indian nations

Significantly, for understanding the New Amsterdam African community, we have clear evidence of slave community structure in Brazil, where enslaved Africans came predominantly from west central Africa, just as most of those in New Netherland did. In Brazil, a distinct Kongo organization flourished in the early seventeenth century, and the Kongo nation there elected a king and queen from the early seventeenth century onward.[40] Examining sources from Brazil to Mexico, Thornton has argued that, despite the traumas of slavery, in most colonies one or more African nations or ethnic groups had enough members to create a diaspora community whose members were able to transmit, develop, and maintain the African culture they had brought with them. Particularly important for the analogous case of Africans in New Netherland, Thornton maintains further that, even when the numbers of people from one nation were small, new communities were nevertheless able to connect with others from the same vicinity in Africa.

In New Netherland most Africans either came from the Angola region of west central Africa or can be characterized as "Atlantic Creoles," people with considerable Atlantic and linguistic experience.[41] In either case, the preponderance of the evidence suggests that most Africans in New Netherland were from linguistically similar parts of west central Africa or had the experience of learning several languages or pidgins, including perhaps an Atlantic African pidgin. It is also important to consider other aspects of people's everyday lives in gauging the degree to which enslaved Africans managed to form alliances and build a community in New Netherland.

In New Amsterdam, living conditions were particularly important; slaves of the West India Company lived together in Manhattan. Despite the relative dearth of information on Africans in the Dutch colony, we know quite a lot. For example, we know that Africans who were owned by the WIC had at least some freedom of movement, could own at least small amounts of property, could sue in court, and spoke similar languages when they first arrived. We also know that most of them lived together in a neighborhood set in a marshy area in lower Manhattan.[42]

FIGURE 7. Continued
who lived in and near territory claimed by the Dutch, which illustrates how very vulnerable Dutch colonists were. This explains why, when crisis hit in the 1640s, Dutch officials were even more concerned about containing internal threats and found it necessary to have enslaved Africans help defend the colony from Native American attacks. The depiction of New Amsterdam at the bottom shows that the settlement was very much a town, with clusters of houses, including dwellings for enslaved Africans. Adriaen van der Donck, *Nova Belgica sive Nieuw Nederlandt*, Amsterdam, 1656. Courtesy of the John Carter Brown Library at Brown University.

Two criminal court cases from the 1640s reveal that enslaved Africans not only formed alliances with one another but also used those connections to limit the degree of Dutch colonial control over their lives. Indeed, their ability to shape the ways the Dutch judicial system could regulate crimes between diaspora Africans helped to create a crisis of Dutch authority in the 1640s, one that played out around the contours of a murder trial and a rape/sodomy trial. In these cases, Africans in New Netherland worked together to limit Dutch colonial and judicial power at a time when Dutch officials found themselves facing increasing challenges to their authority by Native Americans surrounding the colony and by enslaved Africans within it.

The 1640s began uneasily in New Netherland. Disturbed by continuing reports of the fallout of the English colonial war against the Pequots in New England, Dutch officials worried about rumors of alliances and external threats to the West India Company's colony. Beginning in 1641, when a WIC slave named Jan Premero was found dead, colony officials began to realize that intercultural alliances were also a matter of internal security. Over the course of five years, they faced signs that Africans within the settlement were prepared to work together in order to achieve their own ends and that their ability to maneuver as a group kept aspects of African life in New Netherland out of Dutch control. At the same time, New Netherland increasingly felt pressure from Native Americans around the colony.

Throughout the 1640s the choice Dutch officials faced became clear: They needed the cooperation of Africans in the colony—both free and enslaved—and they would have to make some concessions within the community if they were to be able to rely on Africans to help them with conflicts outside the settlement. Enslaved Africans owned by the company alone consisted of a hundred or so strong and able-bodied men. Faced with the prospect of an Indian war, New Netherland needed every man who could fight.

Two criminal court cases involving WIC slaves in the 1640s are particularly revealing of the ways in which company slaves formed an alliance and used it to limit the Dutch authorities' power over them. In the first case, nine African men owned by the WIC claimed that they acted together to kill another WIC slave and that they were equally responsible. No other African claimed to have knowledge of the murderer's identity. In the end, after the drawing of lots and a failed execution, the Dutch court pardoned all nine of the men. Three years later those same men went on to petition successfully for manumission.

Five years after the murder trial, African witnesses sought the intervention of Dutch officials to punish a man for raping a ten-year-old boy. As a result of testimony from African witnesses, the man was convicted of the capital crime of sodomy. Moreover, African witnesses helped to ensure a measure of leniency for the man's victim, who was also guilty of a capital offense under Dutch law.

The records of both trials are, of course, far more limited than we would wish. Written in Dutch, they follow certain prescribed legal formulas. As a result, we seldom hear from the Africans who were directly involved. Nonetheless, the two cases offer us an extraordinary glimpse of a different kind of early colonial alliance that played a significant role in the life of New Netherland.

The first case began (at least as a crime under Dutch law) with a murder. Jan Premero was murdered, and his body was found on January 6, 1641, in a wooded area of New Amsterdam, near the WIC's slave quarters.[43] Eleven days after Premero's death, the council in New Amsterdam charged Cleijn Antonio,[44] Paulo d'Angola, Gracia d'Angola,[45] Jan de Fort Orange, Manuel de Gerrit de Reus, Antonij Portugees, Manuel Minuit, Simon Conge, and Manuel de Groote with murder.[46]

All nine of the accused were WIC slaves. The court records state that all of these men confessed to killing Jan Premero and that their confessions were not elicited through torture or the use of shackles. However, New Netherland council officials were not satisfied with a group confession and pressed for more detailed information. The council persistently sought to determine which individual was responsible for the blow that finally caused Premero's death.

In the council's view, that person bore a greater responsibility than the others. Under Dutch law, the assumption was that Premero might have survived the beating he received up to the final blow. Despite pressure from council officials, the accused men maintained a single account of the events surrounding Premero's death. Under questioning, they insisted that none of them knew who had struck the mortal blow, that they had committed the murder together, and that they were equally guilty.

Murder was a capital crime in New Netherland, as it was in the United Provinces. Moreover, Dutch law and custom, as well as Dutch Calvinism, dictated that murder be punished by death in a public display of law and authority.[47] Accordingly, to resolve the case in a manner that would satisfy Dutch legal and cultural expectations while faced with the accused slaves' intransigence, the council ordered the men to draw lots: Only one of them would hang to death for the crime. Before the nine men did so, the council prayed that God would reveal the guilty individual in the choice of lots, and Manuel de Gerrit de Reus received the fatal one. He was then ordered to be held in prison until the next court day, when his sentence would be pronounced and carried out.

One week later, on January 24, 1641, the council met again and sentenced Manuel. They declared that the lot had fallen upon him "through the providence of God."[48] Because the council believed that God had intervened and pointed out the murderer, it stated that Manuel was accordingly barred from any exceptions or defenses in the case and sentenced him to be punished for Jan Premero's murder by hanging until dead. That same day Manuel de Gerrit de Reus was led to New Amsterdam's place of execution, where the executioner, who was also of African ancestry, proceeded to hang him. The records note explicitly that the unnamed executioner used two ropes or halters with which to hang Manuel, but both ropes broke under Manuel's weight.

At this the crowd called for mercy. When executions failed in early modern Europe, it was customary for the assembled community to ask criminal authorities to spare the condemned person. A failed execution was considered an act of God or at least to suggest that God had acted in the case. Thus, in New Amsterdam those who crowded around to see Manuel de Gerrit de Reus's hanging did what a Dutch crowd would have done in old Amsterdam. When they cried out for mercy, the Council of New Netherland granted their plea and pardoned Manuel. At the same time, the council pardoned the eight other enslaved men who had confessed to Premero's murder "on promise of good behavior and willing service."[49]

This brief outline of Jan Premero's death and the trial of nine other enslaved Africans for his murder summarizes almost all of the information that has survived about this crime. However, the limited court records provide us with additional insights into the crisis of colonial order that New Netherland faced in the 1640s and the ways in which alliances could take myriad forms in this period. In these cases we see a variety of perspectives on the situation in the colony.

From the perspective of the Dutch West India Company and its colonial officials, New Netherland was still maturing as a settlement. It faced constant danger from rival colonies and Native Americans. In that context, internal challenges to colonial authority, even from those with the least power, were taken particularly seriously as threats to social order and the company's interests. This was certainly the case in 1641. A Dutch-Algonquian war, which became known as Kieft's war, broke out only a few months after the conclusion of the Premero case. Director General Willem Kieft increasingly felt his authority challenged from all directions even before the beginning of the war. This sense of a new and fragile community at risk from internal and external challenges would persist throughout New Netherland's entire history as a colony.[50]

From the perspective of the enslaved Africans, New Netherland's most powerful expression of authority ironically also provided room for them to limit both the power of colonial officials and Dutch colonial intrusion into the internal boundaries of relations among Africans. From the viewpoint of historians interested in African diasporas and in slavery in North America, the 1640s cases provide important information about the lives of enslaved people in New Amsterdam, one of the earliest diaspora communities of Africans in North America about whom we have written documentation.

The 1641 murder of Jan Premero, the trial of his accused murderers, and the attempted execution of Manuel de Gerrit de Reus provide a window on competing cultural authorities and African cultural persistence in this early diaspora community, one that is often invisible in many other historical sources. Although the court records reveal that enslaved Africans were able to form their own alliances and maintain cultural boundaries between themselves and the dominant Dutch culture, their ability to do so was circumscribed by their status as slaves and by the colonial officials' efforts to control the colony's affairs.

Because New Netherland was a West India Company colony, its administrative structure was similar to that set up by the company for colonies throughout the Atlantic world. For instance, when the Council of New Netherland tried the nine men accused of murdering Jan Premero, it was functioning in two capacities. First, as the colony's executive council, it was authorized to determine colonial policy within WIC guidelines. It also functioned as a court of justice by holding court sessions once each week and passing judgment on all civil and criminal cases.[51]

The council was the highest authority in New Netherland for serious criminal matters throughout the colony,[52] and in 1641 it was still responsible for all policy and judicial matters in New Netherland, encompassing communities and territory from the Connecticut River to the Hudson River, Manhattan, and the Delaware River.[53] The council, whose composition was varied, met in New Amsterdam.

As the West India Company's highest-ranking official, the colony's director general was always a member of the council. Because he controlled two votes, he wielded twice the power of any other member. When Jan Premero died in the winter of 1641, the council probably consisted of only three men, with one serving as prosecutor and the other two adjudicating the case. As director general of New Netherland in 1641, Willem Kieft presided over the trial. In New Amsterdam, Cornelius vander Hoykins was both *fiscal* (prosecutor) and *schout* (the community's principal law enforcement officer) in this case.[54]

Like the director general, the fiscal was an appointed official of the West India Company. In addition to Kieft and vander Hoykins, Johannes de la Montagne was probably a member of the council in 1641.[55] Other men may also have been sitting on the council for the Premero trial; captains of West India Company ships were entitled to do so when they were in port.[56] It seems most likely, however, that only Kieft and de la Montagne heard the evidence that vander Hoykins presented and that they alone passed judgment in the case.

However, for the trial, sentencing, and punishment to go as the council planned in 1641, the accused men, the executioner, and the New Amsterdam community itself all needed to act according to the council's script. The executioner's role seems to have been particularly significant, yet it is one of the most oblique portions of the court records. The council records of the trial identified the executioner in the Premero case only as "a Negro"; he was not named.

Some modern interpreters have suggested that the public executioner or hangman in New Amsterdam was a slave named Pieter.[57] However, the evidence for this comes from 1662, twenty-one years after the slave murder trial of 1641.[58] In 1646 another African man named Jan de Neger agreed to serve as the executioner of a Dutch man named Wolf Nijssin in the private colony of Rensselaerswijck.[59] His role, however, seems to have been limited to the Nijssin case rather than to have been a continuing position.

The record of 1641 does not specify whether the executioner was a slave or a free black man, whether he was induced to take on the role only for this particular case, or whether he acted as executioner in New Amsterdam on an ongoing basis. In addition, the question of the executioner's status is not clear from the council references. Johannes Postma has suggested that the Dutch terms "negro," "neger," and "slave" were synonymous and were applied to slaves by early modern Dutch speakers, whereas "swarten" usually referred to free blacks.[60] Although Postma found evidence of these linguistic categories particularly in WIC colonial possessions in Africa, the New Netherland records do not indicate such a clear-cut distinction. "Negro" may have signified that an African was a slave, but it did not necessarily denote free or unfree status as consistently as Postma suggests was the case elsewhere.

Unfortunately, it is difficult to reach any conclusions about whether the man who executed Manuel de Gerrit de Reus's sentence was free or enslaved. The only information the council records provide is that he was a black man.[61] Jurisdictions in New Netherland typically used Africans as public executioners, which seems to have been a colonial modification of early modern Dutch judicial practice. Pieter Spierenburg, for instance, has written about the low status of executioners in the United Provinces, as well as fears of contamination popularly associated with them.[62] In New Netherland, where Africans occupied the lowest social level, the use of black executioners was a modification of existing Dutch punishment practices to conform to the colonial social order.[63]

Every step of the trial, sentence, execution, and pardon in the 1641 Premero case was imbued with ceremony and symbolism. In the United Provinces, as throughout other parts of Europe, public justice and the display of public order were profoundly ceremonial events. In Europe, early modern authorities found it important to reinforce and demonstrate their authority through public performances of their power in order to establish and enforce cultural boundaries.

Officials in European colonial possessions (and certainly West India Company officials in New Netherland) demonstrated repeatedly that colonial situations required extensive displays of colonial authority so as to maintain order in settings Europeans often feared would seduce colonial inhabitants into wildness and disorder. To have a kind of underground alliance of WIC slaves running throughout such displays was intensely unsettling to Dutch officials.[64]

In the Premero murder case, the Council for New Netherland demonstrated its authority by several performances of cultural boundaries, power, repression, and resistance. The surviving records tell us little about the first steps of the process, during which Premero's body was discovered and the *schout*, Cornelius vander Hoykins, settled on his suspects. The only reference to any part of the pretrial investigation is a formulaic reference to torture.

Arnold J. F. van Laer's translation states that "the defendants appeared in court and without torture or shackles voluntarily declared and confessed that they jointly committed the murder."[65] In the published translation the choice of English words suggests that the nine slaves confessed to Premero's murder without having been subjected to torture or questioned under inquisitorial duress. However, in the original manuscript the words are somewhat ambiguous and suggest a different meaning. The phrase that van Laer translated as "without torture or shackles" appears in the manuscript as "buiten pijne banden" or "outside torture and shackles"; it could also be translated literally as "outside pain and chains."[66]

Pieter Spierenburg's study of the criminal records of the city of Amsterdam includes a discussion of this formulaic pronouncement, which suggests the possibility that the nine men in this case may have been subjected to torture.[67] In Roman-Dutch law, judicial torture was covertly practiced because secrecy during the trial was a guiding principle of criminal procedure. The trial and the questioning of the accused were performances in which officials demonstrated their judicial power to the accused individuals rather than to the broader community, often in repressive, painful ways. The demonstration of colonial authority was particularly important when the accused were slaves because their alleged transgression represented an especially dangerous sign of resistance.

Although torture was not practiced in public spaces, Spierenburg points out that Dutch authorities made no secret of their use of it as an inquisitorial practice. On the contrary, public knowledge that judicial officials used the infliction of intense pain as a method of questioning only served to enhance their influence. As an example of Dutch court officials' open acknowledgment of this practice in criminal cases, Spierenburg states that "the sentences recited during an execution often began with the standard formula that the prisoner had confessed 'outside of pain and chains.'"[68]

Furthermore, this standard phrase did not necessarily mean that the defendant had not been tortured. It may have meant only that the accused individual had made or repeated a confession "voluntarily" after being tortured.[69] That is, the confession was spoken "outside" of—rather than during—torture.

Similarly, the court record for this 1641 New Netherland case may mean only that the accused men confessed "voluntarily" when they were not actually chained or being tortured.

Torture was indeed used in New Netherland, as well as in the United Provinces, so it is certainly possible that officials may have subjected the nine accused men to this practice in order to elicit their confession.[70] If so, the men's refusal to change their statement shows extraordinary unity. Ironically, however, the accused men had one limited but significant protection: their status as property. Because all of the men accused of killing Jan Premero were WIC slaves, the council members would have been well aware that causing serious damage to the men's bodies would bring a loss to the company.

For their part, the accused slaves' insistence that they were all equally guilty effectively limited the nature of the punishment the council could impose upon them. The group confession suggests that they had considered the unlikelihood that the council would subject all of them to extreme sanctions.[71] Their gamble proved to be correct. The council might have been willing to subject one or two company slaves to severe torture, but nine slaves represented a significant investment for the company.

We do not know for certain how many slaves the WIC owned in New Netherland. Most of them lived in New Amsterdam, and estimates range from twenty to thirty people in all. If the WIC had had thirty slaves in New Amsterdam, it would have lost almost one-third of its labor force. If it had owned a total of twenty slaves, however, its labor force would have been reduced almost by half. Either way, the loss of nine WIC slaves would have had a significant impact on company affairs in New Netherland.

The trial and execution of criminal sentences took place in various locations, and each was associated with different ceremonies intended to convey a number of symbolic messages. In the 1641 Premero case we see not only examples of the symbolism of Dutch colonial authority but also some of the ways in which Africans in the colony wove their own internal alliance throughout the fabric of the settlement. New Netherland's legal framework was modeled on the civic code of the city of Amsterdam. Colony officials replicated Dutch legal practice and established a weekly "day of justice."[72] The physical spaces used during the day of justice varied depending upon the intended audience. Although the trial itself was not a public event, it was a deliberate display of colonial authority performed with great care and ceremony. The fact that it was not open to the general public only emphasized the gravity of the sessions and the extensive range of the council's power.

The council's decision to have the nine convicted men draw lots was an unusual one. In seventeenth-century Roman-Dutch law, murder was punished by death. Simon van Leeuwen's *Commentaries on Roman-Dutch Law* considered the possibility of multiple assailants in a murder: "If death be caused in a fight in which several persons have engaged, and it is uncertain by whom the wound was inflicted, they will all be punished for the same, but with less than ordinary punishment of death, at discretion. . . . Except where they all went out deliberately for the purpose, and assailed the deceased, in which case they will all be punishable with death."[73]

The enslaved men's insistence that they committed the crime together and the absence of mitigating statements in the council record show that the council regarded this homicide as one in which the slaves deliberately set out to kill Jan Premero. Normally under Dutch law, all nine men should have received equal punishment (in this case, death). But in New Netherland, as in all other seventeenth-century American colonies, officials had to adapt to uniquely colonial circumstances. In this instance the confessed killers were also the property of the West India Company; thus, hanging all of them would create a significant economic loss for the company.

In this context, making the nine men draw lots accomplished several goals. It emphasized the council's arbitrary power and demonstrated that it could exercise complete control over the men's fates if it chose to do so. Perhaps more important, choosing lots supposedly drew God directly into the proceedings; in effect, the council turned over the decision to divine judgment. By creating the compromise solution of the lots, the council demonstrated its authority and simultaneously emphasized the divine basis for many of the colony's laws and social boundaries. The council's sentencing mechanism stressed that murder was a general crime against the laws of humankind, the laws and ordinances of the West India Company as the colony's supreme authority, and ultimately the laws of God.

It is also possible that the council chose the drawing of lots as a judicial ordeal that would be particularly appropriate for African defendants. Judicial ordeal was a common west central African practice. Moreover, the WIC had trading factories on the African coast, and a number of its New Netherland employees had previously served the company in Africa and would have known of some African punishments. Forms of divination and trial by ordeal were found in most Atlantic African societies.[74] Africans in New Netherland, then, would have understood drawing lots as such even if this specific practice was strange to them. Every successive step in the trial proceedings would have resonated with African traditions of subjecting accused criminals to a variety of ordeals. Thus, regardless of whether the council's choice of drawing lots grew out of Dutch officials' understanding of African traditions, the ritual operated on several levels of cultural meanings (whether or not they were shared meanings) for the council members, colonists, and the accused men.

For early modern Europeans, in Europe and in their American colonies, the punishment of criminals was designed to affect two different audiences. The first was the criminal, and the second was the community. Authorities expected people from all ranks of society to witness the execution of official justice and to draw moral and political lessons from the experience. For European officials, justice needed to create awe in those subjected to it, as well as in those who witnessed it.[75]

Colonial officials believed that public displays of their legal and cultural authority were necessary in order for them to maintain control in multicultural, polyglot communities.[76] Internal alliances, such as of Africans in New Netherland, that were confined to the colony but remained beyond the control of its officials posed a particularly thorny challenge to colonial control.

Furthermore, because New Netherland was a company colony, the interests of the West India Company were paramount in the formulation and implementation of policy. We have already seen this in several areas of the colony's administrative structure. In addition, long-term council members were officials of the West India Company.[77] They and all other company officials were expected to defend the WIC's interests. That explains why WIC ship's captains could be members of the council whenever they were in port in New Amsterdam. Because the company's interests would not be served by following the normal course of punishment for multiple murderers, the council kept its eye on the company's interests and created its innovative alternative.

The new solution enabled the council to create a public demonstration of its authority while preserving company property and protecting council members from criticism by inviting the hand of God to intervene in colony affairs. The council carefully recorded its new solution: "It is after mature deliberation resolved, inasmuch as the actual murderer can not be discovered, the defendants acknowledging only that they jointly committed the murder and that one is as guilty as another, to have them draw lots as to who shall be punished by hanging until death do ensue, praying Almighty God, creator of heaven and earth, to designate the culprit by lot."[78]

Manuel de Gerrit de Reus played a central role in the new strategy. Moreover, in his role we see not only the council's strategy but also signs of a vibrant African alliance within the colony. After Manuel drew the lot that singled him out, the council ordered that he be kept in prison until the next court day. Because New Amsterdam did not have a separate jail until it became a chartered municipality in the 1650s, in 1641 Manuel was likely held in a locked room in one of the company's buildings inside Fort Amsterdam.

The time lag between the day of the trial and the day of the execution was an important part of the overall ceremony of public order. The week during which Manuel was confined separated the trial, during which the council displayed its authority primarily to the accused slaves, from the execution, during which the council displayed its authority to the community. This delay allowed the

council to ensure that the execution would be carried out with careful attention paid to the event as a public display of order. It also gave New Amsterdam's
African community time to test the strengths of its bonds.

On January 24, 1641, the director general and the council formally pronounced the sentence in the case arising from the murder of Jan Premero.[79]
The formal sentence made it clear that the council regarded Premero's homicide as murder: "The ugly murderous deed is committed against the highest
majesty of God and his supreme rulers, whom he has deliberately robbed of
their servant, whose blood calls for vengeance before God."[80] It also made certain that everyone understood that the lot had fallen upon Manuel de Gerrit
de Reus "through the providence of God."[81] His guilt had not been determined
by human judges.

The judgment connected Premero's murder as an offense against God, the
West India Company, and the States General of the United Netherlands, and it
described the murder as a threat to public order in the colony. A crime of this
magnitude had to be punished because of its challenges to earthly and spiritual
authorities, and the record of the trial made this point explicitly: "All of which,"
the council declared, "can in no wise be tolerated or suffered in countries where
it is customary to maintain justice and should be punished as an example to
others."[82] Someone had to be punished; "therefore, we have condemned, as we
do hereby condemn, the aforesaid Manuel of Gerrit de Reus (insomuch as he
drew the lot) to be punished by hanging until death follows, as an example to
all such malefactors."[83]

The sentence was carried out the same day. Residents of the colony would
have learned in the week between the trial and Manuel's execution that the
event was going to take place. Mechanisms for public notice in New Amsterdam included circulating handbills, publicly posted notices, and proclamations
shouted by colonial messengers and accompanied by trumpets, drums, and
other symbols of the WIC's authority. Typically the council ordered the fort's
bell to be rung in such cases to summon the community to assemble at the
place of execution. At this point in the process, the display of public authority
was intended as much for the rest of the colony's inhabitants as for Manuel and
the remaining eight convicted men.

The council records state that Manuel stood on the ladder with "two good
ropes" around his neck and was pushed off the ladder by the executioner, "being
a Negro."[84] The symbolism of the executioner is important, but unfortunately it
remains oblique. If he were a slave of the West India Company, then the council
may have chosen him as a way to demonstrate that it possessed the power to
divide African solidarity even if it had not been able to separate the nine men
accused of murdering Premero. However, we cannot know for certain, but if
that was actually the council's intention, it failed. When the executioner pushed

Manuel off the ladder, both of the "good ropes" broke, "whereupon the inhabitants and bystanders called for mercy and very earnestly solicited the same."[85]

The council then used the failure of the ropes to its own and the company's advantage. The council, "having taken into consideration the request of the community, as also that the said Manuel had partly undergone his sentence, have graciously granted him his life and pardoned him and all other Negroes, on promise of good behavior and willing service."[86] Because Manuel had been chosen by lot, which was drawn after a formal prayer for God's assistance, the fact that the ropes broke was construed as a strong symbolic statement that he was not the man who had struck the fatal blow after all. As Calvinists, the council members would have believed that God intervenes in human affairs, but they also knew that God did not respond directly to every petition.

By pardoning Manuel publicly after he had been made to experience an attempted execution, the council could appear merciful and magnanimous. In pardoning Manuel and the other eight men, the council did not risk losing any of its public authority. The assembled spectators knew that in a similar situation they could not count on the ropes to break. Nonetheless, Africans in the colony must also have seen the pardon as a victory because in many ways the outcome of the trial acknowledged the strength of the alliance they had forged with one another. By sticking together, both the accused men and all of the other Africans owned by the WIC limited the array of choices open to Dutch authorities.

This was particularly significant in a murder case. The most serious crimes in New Netherland were those that somehow challenged Dutch or West India Company colonial authority. In the case of Jan Premero's murder, the breach of public law was doubly threatening because both the victim and the men who confessed to the murder were WIC property. From the company's perspective, failure both to make a public display of the accused slaves as criminals and to punish them would have been to allow the most dangerous kind of sedition to incubate.

The account of the council's search for Jan Premero's murderer is more than a story of Dutch colonial power. It is also the story of an intriguing intracolonial alliance of Africans that reached throughout the streets of New Amsterdam and underneath Dutch colonial structures. As sharply limited as the slaves' resistance was, these accused men managed to create cultural spaces within their community that New Netherland colonial officials could not penetrate. The men accused of murdering Premero were able to preserve their knowledge of the details of his death. It remained their secret, and there is no indication that Dutch officials ever learned the reason for the murder. It apparently was not a matter the Africans believed was within the purview of colonial authorities.[87] It illustrates that there was more than one kind of justice in New Amsterdam and more than one layer of cultural boundaries.

Africans, even when enslaved, could ally with one another for their own purposes. In 1641 the nine African men accused of killing Jan Premero ended up exercising more public power than the governing council was able to counter, despite its having the obvious tools and advantages of colonial and arbitrary control. The ways in which Africans in New Amsterdam pulled together to enforce their own moral boundaries become even clearer when we examine another criminal court case from the 1640s.

Five years later another enslaved African man stood before Dutch colonial officials accused of a serious crime. This time, however, the accusations did not come from the officials but arose from within the African community itself, which deliberately brought Dutch authorities into the matter. The incident happened in June of 1646. Several Africans in Manhattan went to Dutch officials and accused another enslaved African named Jan Creoli of raping a little boy named Manuel Congo. Dutch officials then took over the matter of punishment, but it is clear that the proceedings were initiated by Africans rather than Dutch officials, and several of the Africans were probably slaves of the West India Company.

The *fiscal* arrested Jan Creoli, placed him in confinement, and then questioned him in the boy's presence. As he faced Jan Creoli, the little boy told Dutch officials what had happened. The court record carefully states that Manuel Congo told his story without being threatened in any way, and significantly the records do not describe his statement primarily as the testimony of a victim but rather as a confession. This difference would prove quite important later in the proceedings. The record also notes explicitly that judicial torture was not used in questioning the child, and in that respect the procedure seems quite different from the one followed in the Jan Premero murder case. In 1646 the records state that Manuel Congo "without being threatened in any way confessed to the deed in the presence of the prisoner."[88]

The statement that a ten-year-old child who had been raped might "confess to the deed" seems startling to modern eyes, but it is highly significant for understanding Dutch authorities' actions. As far as New Netherland's officials were concerned, Manuel Congo was not just a victim but also a participant in the crime of sodomy despite his age and the fact that he had been raped. Dutch officials in New Netherland and in the United Provinces regarded sodomy as one of the worst social crimes possible, every bit as serious as murder.

Having heard the child's account, Dutch officials then turned their attention to his attacker. Jan Creoli later confessed to having raped young Manuel and also to having committed sodomy while in the West India Company's colony of Curaçao before coming to New Netherland.[89] The court record then cites biblical passages that describe sodomy as an abomination that God did not tolerate and that might bring forth God's wrath upon the entire community.

The council's language in describing the threat of divine displeasure for such a crime is even more explicit than its invocation of divine prohibition against killing, to which the council referred in the 1641 Premero case. Now, in 1646, the council provided an extensive account of biblical admonitions with regard to the threat that sodomy presented to society: "On account of which sins God Almighty overthrew Sodom and Gomorrah of the plain and exterminated the inhabitants from the earth (Genesis, ch. 19). See also God's covenant Leviticus, ch. 18, v. 22; and in the same chapter, v. 29 God says, 'For whosoever shall commit any of these abominations, even the souls that commit them shall be cut off from among their people.'"[90]

Having established biblical precedents for Dutch laws against sodomy, the council then invoked the name of God, solemnly stating that they did so in order to make certain they would render a just judgment. As in the Premero trial, the council first invoked God's role in the proceedings and then handed out its sentence. They condemned Jan Creoli to death for the rape of Manuel Congo and sentenced him to the kind of gruesome end reserved for the crime of sodomy.

In seventeenth-century Roman-Dutch law, murderers deserved a better execution than those found guilty of sodomy. The court specifically laid out the various steps involved in the punishment. First, Creoli was to be taken to Manhattan's place of justice, where Manuel de Gerrit de Reus had faced hanging five years before. There, he was to be strangled to death. Because his crime was regarded as particularly abhorrent, he would not be permitted to die by hanging, which was regarded as a more desirable execution.

However, Creoli's death was not the end of his sentence. The council wanted to make certain everyone understood that those who committed sodomy would have their very presence annihilated by colony authorities before God had a chance to wipe out the whole community and make it another Sodom and Gomorrah. The council decreed that, after Creoli had been strangled to death, his body would be burned to ashes.[91] The council was explicit about the symbolism of this punishment: "We condemn the said Jan Creoly, as we do hereby, to be brought to the place of justice to be strangled there to death and his body to be burned to ashes, as an example to others."[92] Creoli's crime and his presence on earth were to be eradicated, and that, indeed, is what happened to Jan Creoli on June 26, 1646.

Ordering all traces of Jan Creoli to be obliterated was not yet the end of the case, however. The council also turned its attention to ten-year-old Manuel Congo, Creoli's victim, and the problem of what to do about him. In passing sentence, the court noted that the crime, which it regarded primarily as sodomy rather than rape, was committed on Manuel Congo by force "as those who were present declared."[93] It also noted that Jan Creoli had confessed to having raped the boy and that he had "committed the crime by force and without the boy's consent."

Typically in a criminal case the court would then describe the crime for the official records and specify what the accused had done. In this case the court refused to describe the attack, explaining that a detailed account "in view of the abomination is not described here."[94] For the council this was not primarily a case about the abuse of a child or even a case of rape; it was first and foremost a case of sodomy. Dutch officials were unwavering in their conviction that sodomy was one of the most dangerous crimes possible.

Not only was sodomy a threat to the established social order—which in New Netherland was predominantly Dutch, Protestant, and Calvinist—and rape a terrible assault upon its victim, but sodomy also threatened the community's very existence. If it went unpunished, Calvinists believed that God might inflict a severe penalty on the entire community for having allowed such a sin in its midst. He might in fact eliminate the colony completely, as he had done with Sodom and Gomorrah.

The council specifically drew this connection: "For which reason such a man is not worthy to associate with mankind and the crime on account of its heinousness may not be tolerated or suffered, in order that the wrath of God may not descend upon us as it did upon Sodom."[95] The risk of divine retribution was just too great, and in the Indians the Dutch saw people all around them whom they feared God might use as agents of their destruction.

Indeed, from 1641, beginning several months after the Premero case, to 1645, New Netherland had fought a bloody war against neighboring Munsee Indians, with substantial loss of life among the colonists and an extraordinary number of deaths for the Munsee peoples in the greater Manhattan Rim area. The news that someone had committed sodomy in the colony reached Dutch officials only a few months after the end of one of the worst experiences in the colony's history. The terrible costs of the war had already made many officials and colonists wonder whether the colony had angered God.[96]

Now they had learned of behavior they knew would bring down divine wrath. Therefore, faced with Jan Creoli's rape of Manuel Congo in 1646, Dutch colonial officials were hyperaware that God might punish them further. As they looked around, the West India Company's officers saw a New Amsterdam that was besieged by murder, rape, and sodomy from within and by angry Algonquians who refused to pay colonial tribute from without.

Accordingly, to reach a decision in what it regarded as a serious matter in the context of this overall crisis, the court relied upon three sets of testimony. First, it had the statement of the attacker himself: Creoli confessed to having raped Manuel Congo and to having committed sodomy in another WIC colony before coming to Manhattan. Second, the court relied upon the declaration of the victim: Young Manuel Congo faced his attacker and testified that Creoli had raped him. However, the court did not rely on only those two sets of testimony. It also received information from witnesses who testified not only that Creoli had sodomized the little boy but also that the attack was a rape. Those witnesses were Africans, which again demonstrates the outlines of a resourceful African alliance within New Amsterdam.

The court record states at the outset that the case began when a number of blacks accused Jan Creoli of attacking Manuel Congo. Indeed, it begins by specifying that several Africans brought a complaint to the Dutch authorities. The charges originated, according to the transcript, because "Jan Creoly aforesaid is accused by some negroes of having committed sodomy by force with a boy of about ten years, named Manuel Congo, also a Negro."[97]

Without the intervention of African witnesses, who made a group decision to involve colonial authorities, Dutch officials would not have known about this crime. Although the approaches to the mechanisms of the Dutch judicial system in this case and the Premero case five years earlier were significantly different, both instances reveal that Africans in Manhattan formed alliances with one another in an effort to police their own community and to shape Dutch intervention into their internal affairs as much as possible.

In 1641 Africans successfully kept Dutch authorities from learning the details of Jan Premero's murder and thwarted colonial efforts to punish the murderer. In 1646 they made certain that Jan Creoli was prevented from ever attacking another child. In each case, however, Africans also had to contend with the reality that they were the least powerful people in the colony.

In 1646 Africans were able to deliver Creoli to the harsh penalty of Dutch punishment, but in doing so they also placed young Manuel Congo outside their protection. Because in Dutch eyes this was a case of sodomy rather than rape, the court dealt with Creoli first. In most modern jurisdictions, a child rape victim would be treated as the victim of a crime, but in early modern Dutch culture, sodomy was a far worse crime than rape and was always regarded as an offense involving two participants.

Even though Africans in New Amsterdam regarded Manuel as a victim and even though he was only ten years old, the boy was also punished.[98] In sentencing Manuel, the court first stated that the law dictated that a person with whom sodomy had been committed deserved to be put to death. However, in Manuel's case, the court considered his innocence and youth and ordered a more lenient sentence. It ordered a punishment that would take into account the fact that Manuel was attacked and that he was only ten.

The court ordered Manuel Congo to be taken to the place of justice and then to be tied to a post with wood piled around him, where he would be forced to watch Creoli's execution and be beaten with rods.[99] The fact that Dutch officials viewed this sentence as lenient tells us much about the degree to which they perceived sodomy as a dire threat to their community.

To Dutch eyes, the crimes of murder and sodomy seriously threatened their tenuous hold in North America. It is no accident that two cases in which we see Africans in Manhattan allying are incidents that involved these most dangerous of transgressions, which occurred at times of heightened Dutch fears of external, as well as internal, perils. Dutch colonial values were not the only ones of significance in either of these cases. In each one, we see the values of diaspora Africans and the larger Dutch colonial community at odds.

This is clearer in the Creoli trial, but it is also present in the Premero case. In the rape of Manuel Congo, it is significant that Dutch officials focused on the case primarily as sodomy, while the Africans who brought the incident to their attention seem to have considered it as child rape. Here we glimpse two very different sets of cultural standards and fears.

Yet in each one, Africans were able to accomplish important ends despite the very different expectations of Dutch officials. In the 1646 case, both Dutch authorities and Africans agreed that a specific behavior was a threat to the colony's well-being, but for different reasons. For the Calvinist Dutch, God's injunctions against sodomy were so severe that even the victim was tainted. But for the Africans who brought the complaint, the need to protect a child seems to have been paramount. Their chief concern seems to have been to protect the boy and to see that his attacker was punished as harshly as possible.

By 1646 Africans recognized that they needed to persuade Dutch authorities to do what they otherwise might have done themselves. The events of the 1641 Premero murder case had made it clear that Africans in Manhattan might face stern reprisals from Dutch authorities if they took the law into their own hands. It appears that many Africans in New Amsterdam wanted Jan Creoli to be punished and that they knew the Dutch court system would rigorously do so.

It is not apparent whether they realized that Manuel Congo would also be punished or whether they would have thought such punishment to be appropriate. Africans in New Amsterdam might well have been familiar with the severity of Dutch prohibitions against sodomy and may have feared more dramatic reprisals against the African community if Dutch officials were to learn of Manuel Congo's rape and then to discover that others had known about it and covered it up.

The Premero murder trial similarly illustrates the kinds of alliances Africans made in Manhattan in the first half of the seventeenth century. The case shows Africans standing together as the nine accused men refused to give the Dutch court the information it wanted and protected the identity of Premero's killer. Admittedly, nine people are not many, but the case shows us a larger unity of purpose. It is significant that not one of these men singled out any of the others, but it is even more noteworthy that no one else came forward to make an accusation.

The judicial process allowed ample time between the start of the Dutch investigation and the eventual attempted execution of Manuel de Gerrit de Reus for another member of New Amsterdam's African community to come forward, but no one did. The resounding silence suggests an agreement that unity was the best strategy for minimizing the severity of Dutch colonial power. It also indicates that Africans in New Amsterdam agreed about Premero's death and that no one was willing to single out anyone else for punishment. In contrast, the fact that five years later many Africans were willing to identify someone to Dutch officials for a different crime demonstrates that they were prepared to use the mechanisms of Dutch colonial authority when it suited them and that they did not protect one another from colonial punishment under all circumstances.

The two crimes were very different, and Africans responded accordingly. However, to understand the full dimensions of the threat that an intracolonial African alliance presented to New Netherland officials, we need to explore the Dutch-Algonquian war that engulfed the colony in the years between these two criminal cases. As we have seen, the men on the council possessed considerable institutional authority and held a great deal of power within the administrative structure of the West India Company's colony, yet they consistently faced challenges that were beyond the abilities of bureaucratic hierarchies to control.

They faced the reality that confronted seventeenth-century colony officials throughout North America, which was that conflict with other cultures and colonies was a constant threat. This was the reason the pursuit of alliances was an integral part of the fabric of seventeenth-century colonial life. Potential hostilities, especially the threat of open war, made people especially alert to signs of shifts in the web of alliances that encompassed eastern North America.

Furthermore, in the winter of 1641, when Dutch officials faced the unwavering position of an African alliance in New Amsterdam, it did so at a time of growing tension throughout the colony. Circumstances had become particularly tense as a result of a series of recent Dutch policy changes. Several modifications in WIC procedure made three years earlier had extraordinary consequences for everyone living in New Netherland. After 1638, the company's guidelines allowed more open participation in the fur trade and encouraged larger-scale European immigration.[100] In addition, the settlement came under new leadership when Willem Kieft arrived in 1638 to become the colony's new director general. Thus, the settlement faced significantly new regulations, an influx of fresh colonists, and a different colonial governor.

The colony's new leadership proved to be especially consequential. Director General Kieft sought to impose his personal authority and that of the West

India Company on colonists and neighboring native peoples alike, without taking either cultural differences or the unique circumstances of New Netherland into account. As he pushed for rapid expansion of colonial land holdings and settlements, his policies antagonized many of the Munsee-speaking peoples around the lower Hudson River.

Furthermore, his demand for a heavy tribute from Native Americans who lived near Fort Amsterdam generated great resistance beginning in late 1639. Munsee-Dutch friction continued to grow over the course of the next year, and almost no Native Americans paid the demanded tribute even though Dutch officials continued to insist on it. Even as he and his advisors pressed for unequivocal acknowledgments of their authority, Director General Kieft faced increasing evidence that his authority was being challenged from all corners.

After several incidents in which Raritan warriors either threatened Dutch traders or were accused of stealing farm animals, the council sent soldiers with orders to attack them, destroy their corn, and take prisoners unless the Raritans agreed to pay reparations for the missing Dutch livestock. When the Raritans refused, the Dutch troops attacked and killed many of the villagers, then captured and tortured the sachem's brother.[101] The troops' assault on the Raritan village led to growing, open hostility with the Raritans, whose warriors seized an opportunity to balance the situation by attacking colonial settlements on Staten Island in September of 1641.

That attack by the Raritans is often considered the start of what many historians call Kieft's Indian war. This series of bloody conflicts between Dutch colonists and troops and the Munsee peoples lasted until 1645. Some scholars estimate Munsee losses in 1643 and 1644 at around sixteen hundred dead, including all ages and genders.[102] Moreover, the war was so disastrous for the colony that Kieft's own advisory council (of which Isaac Allerton was a member) drew up a petition to the United Provinces' States General that requested that Kieft be recalled before he destroyed the colony.

Thus, when the council presided over the Premero murder trial in the winter of 1641, everyone in the colony was acutely aware that New Netherland and its colonial settlements were increasingly vulnerable and faced growing conflict with several Munsee groups. Moreover, the council was beginning to face increasing resistance within the colony itself. In that context, Willem Kieft and the council tried to force cooperation from the nine men accused of Premero's murder in a characteristically heavy-handed way.

Once again, the council tried to assert more authority than it could actually wield. While facing open hostility and defiance from Algonquians and increasing unrest from Europeans, the Council for New Netherland also discovered another alliance that was shaping the colony, a coalition of Africans within New Amsterdam.

7

Nations Intertwined

Alliances and the Susquehannocks' Geography of North America

Intercultural alliances had far-reaching impacts and shaped the lives of nearly everyone on the seventeenth-century Atlantic seaboard. We have seen the degree to which Europeans and Native Americans became linked from the earliest wave of European colonial ventures. These collaborative efforts look rather different when viewed primarily from the points of view of native peoples rather than from Europeans' perspectives. Indeed, when we try to understand the full extent of Native American influence and interests, the geography of eastern North America takes on significantly different dimensions. Nowhere is this clearer than in the mid-Atlantic region.

The mid-Atlantic area, which stretched from the northern limits of the Chesapeake Bay to Iroquoia and centered around the Delaware and Hudson River regions, at first appears to have been a bewildering array of cultures and alliances, each of which played a role in shaping events there. However, when we shift our focus to a region defined chiefly by Native American interests rather than colonial European ones, a clear pattern emerges out of the apparent confusion.

In the mid-Atlantic, events were regularly affected by the Indians' and the Europeans' constant efforts to build and benefit from intercultural connections. The pursuit of alliances in the mid-Atlantic came to a head in the 1650s, when the Susquehannocks' networks collided with Dutch colonial ambitions. The fallout eliminated one European nation from the imperial contest over North America and helped to weaken several other nations, including the Susquehannocks.

Moreover, the alliances and events that proved so important in the mid-Atlantic of the 1650s also illustrate that Native American disputes, coalitions, and decisions were frequently based as much on relationships with other Indian peoples as on interactions with colonial Europeans, even when they involved the latter. In their efforts to respond advantageously to changes precipitated by European colonization, Native Americans sometimes tried to turn European colonies into their own tributaries and subordinates, often as a way to improve their position in relation to other Indian nations.

In the 1650s the Susquehannocks were involved in virtually every important intergroup alliance in the region, either directly or indirectly (by trying to block others' alliances). After using their association with William Claiborne and his plantation to secure an increasingly large share of the fur trade in the Chesapeake Bay area, the Susquehannocks found a way to secure their route between the Chesapeake and Iroquoia by going through the modern Delaware River region, which was the Lenapes' homeland of Lenapehoking.

During the early seventeenth century, the two nations were frequently at odds; however, by 1650 the Susquehannocks and the Lenapes had joined in an alliance that was perhaps spurred by continuing wars between the Susquehannocks and the Five Nations Iroquois.[1] The Lenapes spoke Unami, an Algonquian language, and shared linguistic and kinship ties with Algonquian Munsee peoples who lived in the Manhattan area and had extensive, ongoing contacts with the Dutch around Fort Amsterdam.

In addition to being in conflict with the Lenapes in the early decades of the seventeenth century, the Susquehannocks frequently fought with an Iroquoian-speaking people named the Massawomecks. During the first few decades of the century the Massawomecks lived in the Chesapeake area and may well have dominated trade between the Chesapeake and the northern and inland peoples until the early 1630s. The escalating development of the Chesapeake fur trade after 1630, however, changed the patterns of economic interaction in the northern part of the bay area; the Massawomecks subsequently disappeared from the record, and the Susquehannocks began to figure in increasingly prominent ways.[2]

When we consider the people involved in the mid-Atlantic area, we face a particularly complicated picture, especially because territorial boundaries were quite unsettled in this region and rivalries were intense. This is as true when we focus on European activities in the area as when we consider Indians' actions; yet each emphasis shows us something rather different. A variety of peoples claimed all or part of the area ranging between the rivers now known as the Connecticut and the Delaware. This was true in the Chesapeake as well, but on the Delaware the competition involved a wider range of nations.

During much of the seventeenth century, this region was one of the most fiercely contested by European powers. For instance, the Dutch claimed it.

Colonists and colonial officials of the Dutch West India Company (WIC) regarded the company's colony of New Netherland as the region from the Versche Rivier (Fresh River) to the Noordt Rivier (North River) to the Zuydt Rivier (South River), with the fort and colonial town on Manhattan as the colony's center. Colonists and colonial officials alike recognized that many different Indian nations lived within the area who were not subject to the colony's authority. They also knew that small private colonies (patroonships) dotted the landscape on the Noordt and Zuydt rivers, autonomous enclaves surrounded by New Netherland itself and by Native American nations.

Furthermore, the English also claimed the region. The English Crown, as well as English colonists and colonial officials, called the Noordt Rivier of the Dutch the Hudson River; the Versche Rivier, the Connecticut River; and the Zuydt Rivier, the Delaware River.[3] English colonizers regarded these three waterways as vital to English colonial interests. From their perspective, the region belonged to English colonies—the southern portion to Virginia (or later to Maryland) and the Connecticut River valley to New England. Yet various English colonial interests were also rivals to territory in the mid-Atlantic, especially around the Delaware.

In early colonial North America the Delaware River valley was thus a hotly contested region, and its interwoven web of rivalries and alliances among European colonizers and Native Americans shifted frequently. Mapping this area and its peoples required continuous effort. The colonies of Virginia, New Netherland, New Sweden, Maryland, and New Haven each asserted claims to the region, and each jockeyed to push out its rivals' settlements. This was true even when the competitors were two different English colonies that owed loyalty to the same monarch, or to Parliament during the interregnum.

Furthermore, the rivalries in the Delaware River valley were more than just competing claims on paper. English, Dutch, and Swedish colonizing interests actually attempted to set up separate colonies on the Delaware. In the end, the only colonial settlements that lasted more than a few months were one that was first established by the Dutch in the late 1620s and a Swedish colony that was founded in 1638. Although New Sweden proved to be short lived, its colonists and officials claimed much of the Delaware and Schuylkill rivers.

The Swedes referred to the Dutch Zuydt Rivier and the English Delaware River as "our river," thereby acknowledging no one's claim but their own. New Sweden's colonists called the Algonquian Lenapes the "Renape," in their own way transcribing the liquid *l* of Unami languages. But New Sweden's colonists had other names for their Algonquian neighbors. Just as often, they referred to the Lenapes as "our river savages," thus trying with their language to assert a colonial control they never actually possessed in the realm of daily contact outside the written page.[4]

Other Indian nations in the region included the Iroquoian-speaking Susquehannocks. European colonists and traders in the mid-Atlantic paid careful attention to both the Lenapes and the Susquehannocks and worried about both groups' alliance networks. Both Swedish and Dutch colonists knew the Susquehannocks as the Minquas, but neither group was confident of its ability to dominate the Susquehannocks (quite the opposite, in fact). Although most of the Susquehannocks lived outside the formal boundaries claimed by New Netherland and New Sweden and outside the Lenapes' territory of Lenapehoking, they were regular travelers through all three areas.

As we have seen, by the early seventeenth century the Susquehannocks lived mainly in the Susquehanna Valley above the Chesapeake Bay, with a concentration of communities on the lower Susquehanna River not far from the mouth, as it enters the Chesapeake Bay. Portions of the Susquehannocks' territory lay within the claims of the English colonies of Virginia and Maryland, but in many ways the Susquehannocks were as much a part of New Netherland and New Sweden as they were of Virginia and Maryland.

They traded throughout parts of New Netherland, New Sweden, Lenapehoking, and Maryland and considered themselves fully within their rights to do so.[5] In addition, in a development that would prove especially significant by the mid-1650s, a small number of refugee Susquehannocks lived among Hackensack communities around Manhattan, within New Netherland.[6]

In many ways, however, the previous description of the mid-Atlantic presents a political and cultural geography of a region from Europeans' perspectives. When we consider the same area from native peoples' points of view, we see a very different American geography. For instance, one way to understand the impact of the European colonization of North America is to focus on Native Americans as clients of more powerful European colonizers. From this standpoint, it has made sense to focus on Europeans as allies whose presence brought disease and trade dependence to Native Americans, along with the benefits of such associations. Furthermore, there is no question that a large body of scholarship has demonstrated that the cost of European colonialism was extraordinarily high for Native Americans. As a result of the dramatic and unsettling changes brought by the Europeans' presence in North America, many Indians eventually became tributaries of European powers.

However, the first half of the seventeenth century tells a rather different tale for peoples living along the mid-Atlantic portion of the eastern seaboard, especially in Lenapehoking and New Netherland.[7] We have already seen that the balance of power often shifted during the first sixty years of the seventeenth century and that Europeans frequently found themselves in vulnerable positions. What becomes clear by examining the mid-Atlantic in the mid-seventeenth century is that Europeans and Native Americans sometimes reacted to European vulnerability by seeking protection from more powerful Indian nations. These were not alliances between equals. In the first half of the seventeenth century Europeans sometimes became clients of powerful Native American nations who acted as the European colonists' patrons.

Given much of what we know about later developments in which Native Americans steadily lost their lands and power to European colonial encroachment, it is startling to think of any European colony explicitly agreeing to become subordinate to a Native American nation. European settlements were certainly not uniformly weaker than their Indian neighbors, even in the mid-Atlantic. Complex alliance systems overlay Lenapehoking, New Netherland, and New Sweden and encompassed a range of partnerships and networks among Native Americans and Europeans.

Sometimes Europeans were allies of Native Americans, but they were also occasional clients of Native Americans. Conversely, Indians were at times clients of Europeans, but they were also sometimes allies of and even the dominant partners in their relationships with Europeans. Many people from a variety of Native American, European, and African cultures participated in intercultural alliances as a survival strategy in the midst of often-bewildering political and social changes. And they did so without necessarily giving up either their identities or their political autonomy.

A series of events that took place in the 1650s offers particularly clear examples of the extraordinarily wide range of intercultural alliances. North American partnerships could and sometimes did create chain reactions across hundreds of miles. Several events that took place in midcentury are especially revealing. Scholars have generally seen these events as separate and unrelated conflicts because most of those who have studied them have done so only from the perspective of the various European participants. However, when we reconsider these events from the standpoint of the Native Americans involved, it becomes clear that we must use a much broader framework in order to understand what happened and why people acted as they did.

Furthermore, these occurrences show us some of the ways that European colonists became caught up in Native Americans' alliance networks as subordinate players without truly understanding the full dimensions of Indians' actions. For if intercultural connections often succeeded because each party found something in the relationship that furthered its interests, rarely did either side fully comprehend its allies' motives or the cultural significance of the arrangement for the other party.

This lack of fundamental intercultural understanding mattered little when people entered into an association solely to facilitate limited trade or for a similarly narrow purpose. Yet, at times their inability to comprehend the cultural world of their neighbors and allies proved extremely dangerous. One thing that

Europeans frequently failed to grasp about their Indian allies was the full range of kinship ties and other connections that encompassed the native peoples' world. As a result, Europeans found themselves making decisions about allies, trade relations, and defense matters with a woefully incomplete picture of the context in which they lived.

Two events that shook the mid-Atlantic in the 1650s demonstrate some of the wide-ranging dimensions of the Susquehannocks' world and the Europeans' failure to be fully aware of them. The first is the Dutch and Indian conflict that began in the New Netherland Colony in the fall of 1655 and has come to be called the "peach war." This confrontation is usually explained as having been sparked by a single event: the murder of a Munsee woman by a Dutch colonist named Hendrick van Dyck (after he caught her stealing peaches from his orchard), which ignited long-smoldering intercultural tensions in the Manhattan area. The second event is the conquest of the New Sweden Colony by a military force from New Netherland, also in the early fall of 1655. This incident has generally been described as the final playing out of rivalries in the Delaware River region between the Dutch West India Company and Swedish colonizing interests. It is rarely considered in conjunction with the peach war in the Manhattan area.

Moreover, Native American–Dutch relationships have long occupied center stage in accounts of the peach war but have seldom received much attention from scholars seeking to explain Swedish-Dutch competition for the Delaware despite its central position in the fur trade. Although most modern scholars have seen the two events as unrelated, Swedish colonists claimed at the time that the two conflicts were indeed connected.

If we take the Swedish claims seriously, then we must reconsider these incidents from both Native American and European perspectives because Swedish settlers at the time understood that the Indians involved had their own goals and were not simply pawns of European interests. When we explore the two events from multiple points of view and give Native Americans' concerns full consideration, it becomes clear that the peach war should be interpreted in a larger context than scholars have previously understood.

This was not a conflict with roots only in New Netherland. Furthermore, the alliances that helped to shape the peach war and the Dutch-Swedish conflict reveal that patron-client relationships in the mid-Atlantic region were intercultural in the early and mid-seventeenth century and included complex new groupings and associations. A number of Indian nations cultivated Europeans as clients, while some Europeans cultivated Native Americans as trading partners.

However, the full dimensions of these intercultural alliances and patron-client relationships become apparent only if we follow the full range of such connections, even when they stretched beyond the regional divisions that often frame seventeenth-century colonial studies. Indeed, the Dutch conquest of New Sweden and the large-scale Indian invasion of Manhattan that launched the peach war had implications for people living as far away as Iroquoia to the north and the Chesapeake Bay to the south.[8]

As mentioned earlier, the Delaware River valley was a hotly contested region shaped by a web of rivalries and alliances among both European colonizers and Native Americans. The key partnerships in the Delaware are particularly confusing (as they were for those living there at the time) because they frequently shifted. Alliances need not last for decades in order to be important.

When English, Dutch, and Swedish colonizing interests were establishing their colonies along the Delaware River, they constantly had to find ways to deal with the Algonquian-speaking Lenapes and the Iroquoian-speaking Susquehannocks. In addition, although various settlements reached accommodation with the Lenapes and the Susquehannocks as separate groups, they also had to adjust to the fact that, by midcentury, the two Indian nations were generally peaceful allies but had ties that were quite far ranging.

In addition to their alliances and conflicts in the Chesapeake area, the Susquehannocks had close links with the Hurons, who had recently been defeated by the Five Nations Iroquois far to the north. The Five Nations' domination of the Hurons was not a distant issue for the Susquehannocks, who regarded it as a political and cultural matter that affected them directly. The Susquehannocks and the Hurons may have shared kinship ties; at a minimum, they had a close alliance. Like the Hurons, the Susquehannocks regarded the Haudenosaunee or Five Nations Iroquois as their enemies, and they considered the Five Nations' assault on the Hurons as a direct attack on themselves.[9] Presumably at least some of the Five Nations thought so too.

In addition to their ties to the Hurons, the Susquehannocks also had kinship ties and alliances closer to their main towns on the Susquehannock River. Small groups of refugee Susquehannocks, for instance, lived among various bands of Algonquian Munsees near Manhattan. In addition, the Susquehannocks' other Algonquian allies, the Lenapes, also had close connections and kinship ties with some of the lower Hudson River and Manhattan Rim Munsees. Furthermore, intercultural alliances and rivalries in Lenapehoking in the 1650s had roots in events twenty and thirty years earlier and in other regions ranging from Virginia to Iroquoia.

In the first decade of the seventeenth century Captain John Smith learned of the Susquehannocks as a powerful people who were actively trading in furs and European goods. Much taken with the possibilities of cultivating an alliance with the Susquehannocks, Smith used his descriptions of them in colonial promotional materials. Moreover, recent scholarship has confirmed his

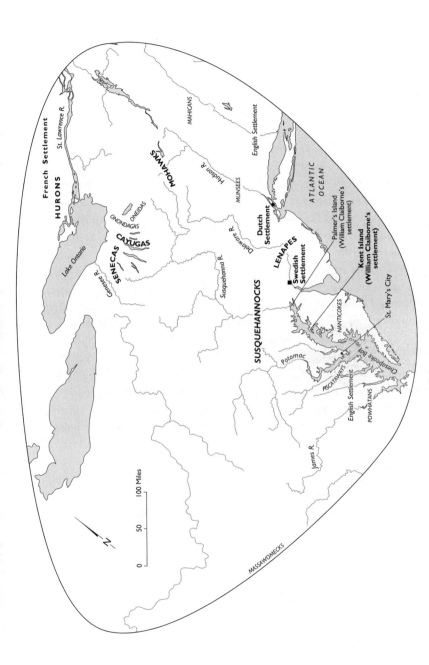

FIGURE 8. Map of eastern North America from a Susquehannock perspective. The Susquehannocks saw themselves as centrally important in their world—in this they were like everyone else. But they looked especially north and west for their most significant allies and enemies. The Senecas, Cayugas, Mohawks, and Massawomecks were particularly important rivals for much of this period. Further south and east, the Lenapes, New Sweden, and William Claiborne were particularly important allies and trading partners. Bill Nelson, 2008.

account and provided additional evidence of the growing importance of the Susquehannocks in the early seventeenth century. As we have seen, these Native Americans played a pivotal role in trade networks that extended from Iroquoia to the Chesapeake Bay.[10]

The Delaware and Susquehanna river valleys formed a crucial juncture in intercultural trade from the Chesapeake to Iroquoia. By securing an alliance with William Claiborne, the Susquehannocks were able to expand their power and control to a critical part of their trade networks stretching hundreds of miles, thereby at least partly rivaling the Five Nations' growing role in intercultural trade. In addition, as we have seen, the alliance gave Claiborne and his England-based partners greater access to better fur pelts in the 1630s.[11] As far as the Susquehannocks' new English allies were concerned, a collaborative effort with an important Indian nation such as the Susquehannocks would enable them to compete with French and Dutch merchants, who had already established trading connections with members of the Five Nations.

For their part, the partnership provided the Susquehannocks more access to European trade goods through those who shared common enemies; for instance, the Susquehannocks resented the fact that Dutch and French colonial traders favored other Native Americans in their trade. Many of the preferred trading partners of Dutch entrepreneurs were the Susquehannocks' enemies, and the Susquehannocks especially disliked the Dutch alliance with members of the Five Nations, or Haudenosaunee.

Although the London-Virginia-Susquehannock connection centered on the fur trade in the 1630s, its effect lasted for decades. In particular, the legacy of the earlier alliance had an impact on Susquehannocks' decisions and alliances into the 1650s. Therefore, to understand the connection between the Dutch conquest of New Sweden and the multination Indian attack on Manhattan in the fall of 1655, we need to examine both the historical links in the Susquehannocks' agreements and the connections they saw between past events and those of the 1650s and among the various peoples living in or near their sphere of influence.

The Anglo-Susquehannock alliance first described by Frederick Fausz was disrupted by rivalries between various English colonial interests in the late 1630s. When the dust settled on the inter-English conflicts and the new colony of Maryland claimed William Claiborne's Kent Island trading outpost, the Susquehannocks went looking for a new ally who could provide them with European goods. In a remarkably fortunate coincidence, at least as far as the Susquehannocks were concerned, the colony of New Sweden was founded right in the middle of Lenapehoking in 1638, just as Maryland's intervention had made the Susquehannock-Claiborne alliance untenable.

Officials in surrounding European colonies were dismayed. Neither New Netherland, Virginia, nor Maryland wanted yet another European power to gain a foothold near their claims. But from the Susquehannocks' perspective, the Swedes' arrival was ideal, and their reaction to the new European colony reveals much about the importance of intercultural alliances in the seventeenth century. The Susquehannocks began cultivating a partnership with Swedish colonial leaders soon after New Sweden was settled. Moreover, the new Susquehannock–New Sweden coalition was not one of equals. The Susquehannocks regarded themselves as the protectors of the New Sweden colonists and as the superior party in the alliance.[12] Accordingly, in the 1640s and 1650s, after their alliance with William Claiborne had been displaced by Maryland's opposition, the Susquehannocks turned instead to New Sweden. Throughout these two decades, the Susquehannocks cultivated the New Sweden colonists as clients or tributaries. Just as interestingly, both parties to the alliance well understood the nature of its distribution of power. New Sweden's colonial leaders accepted their position as clients of the mighty Susquehannocks.

The Susquehannocks' reaction to Maryland's challenge to Claiborne and his trade network explains much about their understanding of their obligations to their allies. Maryland officials realized that Claiborne had helped to create a lucrative trade through his ties with the Susquehannocks and soon understood that the Susquehannocks were a major military power in the region. Accordingly, Maryland officials tried to step in and take Claiborne's place in the old alliance, thinking that continuing the trade with Europeans would be the Susquehannocks' main interest. They seemed to assume that the Susquehannocks would care only about maintaining the flow of European items, not where they got their trade goods or what happened to their old trading partners. However, Maryland's colonists and officials soon learned that they had miscalculated. After Maryland pushed Claiborne out of his Kent and Palmer's islands trading bases, the new colony not only faced armed resistance from Claiborne but also found itself in a war with the Susquehannocks.

The Susquehannocks were not willing to substitute one European partner for another. Although trade was an important goal of their alliance with Claiborne, it was not the Susquehannocks' main objective. Beyond issues of power and dominance, alliances included obligations of generosity, reciprocity, and revenge for wrongs done to one's ally. When Maryland attacked Claiborne and his colonists, it unwittingly offended the Susquehannocks, who felt obliged to even the score on behalf of their ally, and this they did.

When Susquehannock warriors routed a force from Maryland in the winter of 1643, Maryland casualties included fifteen prisoners, whom the Susquehannocks refused to ransom and instead put to death after ritual torture. The Susquehannocks also captured two pieces of field artillery, thereby enhancing their ability to wage war against Europeans, as well as other Indian nations.[13] Moreover, the Susquehannocks' response was not confined to a handful of attacks. The colony of Maryland remained at war with them until 1652, when the two finally accepted the terms of a formal treaty.

Moreover, in the 1640s and 1650s the Susquehannocks were simultaneously maintaining far-flung networks of kinship, trade, and military ties, while also fighting enemies to their north and south. While battling their old nemesis, the Senecas, they also fought repeatedly with Maryland. Understanding the political landscape the Susquehannocks negotiated at midcentury shows us that events in the Delaware and Susquehannock valleys were connected to peoples and happenings far outside the area.

Seventeenth-century intercultural alliances were not contained by any one group's territorial or political claims. As a result, when we focus on only a single European colony or Indian nation, we rarely see the full dimensions of many intercultural alliances or the connections they created between colonies and native peoples.

Similarly, colonial events had ramifications that extended beyond North America and reached throughout the larger early modern Atlantic world. Events in Iroquoia and New France affected actions taken by the Dutch in the Hudson River valley and the Susquehannocks in the Chesapeake and Delaware regions. These were affected in turn by events in London and Jamestown. Moreover, incidents in the Baltic impinged on Dutch decisions to allow the Swedes to gain a foothold on the Delaware in 1638.

Examining the large-scale interconnections that influenced events in the early modern Atlantic world is crucial, but it sometimes skews our analysis too much in the direction of groups, especially of European communities and entities. For instance, descriptions of European colonial interests in Lenapehoking during the first half of the seventeenth century tend to focus on the claims of entire colonies, their home governments, and colonial sponsors. Analysis at that scale is important, but people's everyday experiences were less clear-cut than such an emphasis suggests. Networks of individual merchants, interpreters, and seafarers moved in and out of the region, participating in intercultural and intercolonial trade and making this a much less tidy map. These players navigated Swedish, Dutch, English, and Native American rivalries as they traveled throughout the regions and between Lenapehoking and other parts of the Atlantic world.

There is less evidence of the ways in which these participants negotiated Native American rivalries; however, some surviving evidence shows us how these European merchants and interpreters dealt with intercultural contacts in the seventeenth century. These individuals were skilled cultural mediators. In addition, some Native Americans also acted as cultural go-betweens by carrying messages from one colonial community to another. During the early phases of the Dutch military invasion of New Sweden in 1655, for instance, an Indian man relayed reports between the Dutch commander and New Sweden's governor.[14] Others played a more extensive role by acting as interpreters between colonists and other Indians.

Because so many aspects of their activities went undocumented in written records of the first half of the seventeenth century, it is difficult to understand both the extent to which European cultural brokers moved among Native American communities and the full role of Indian cultural mediators.[15] However, by carefully examining pieces of evidence that at first appear unrelated, we can often see beyond the minimal information available in the European records.

This is painstaking research, but it can sometimes open up startling new windows onto the past. In the case of the Dutch conquest of New Sweden and the "peach war," the experiences of Isaac Allerton suggest that the two incidents may have been related. They also show how a careful reconstruction of small events can illuminate larger issues and contexts.

Having left Plymouth Colony in the mid-1630s, Allerton had established a home and trading base in New Netherland by the 1640s. We do not know exactly when he first went to the Dutch colony, but he was well settled there by the late 1640s. From that time until his death, Allerton kept residences in both New Netherland and New Haven colonies and was active in trade with New Sweden. As the colonial American world expanded for European Protestants, Allerton followed the growth; indeed, in many ways he helped to create it.

In his later activities, as in his early years in Plymouth, Allerton was one of the boundary-crossing individuals who were so important in the early colonial period. Because he was an Englishman by birth, a prominent citizen of New Haven, and a founder of Plymouth Colony, he could identify himself as English when it was to his advantage to do so. However, because he had lived as a religious refugee in the United Provinces before emigrating to North America, he spoke Dutch. Moreover, as an influential member of the West India Company's New Netherland colony as well, he could also easily identify himself as Dutch.[16] He was justified in using either identity, and this flexibility proved to be extremely useful in the Delaware region.

While conducting trade with New Sweden, Allerton manipulated both identities to suit the circumstances. He and other traders, both Native American and European, quickly learned that, despite the challenges posed by political rivalries to those who wanted to trade in the Delaware region, it was worth the risk. The New Sweden colonists were chronically undersupplied, and New Sweden provided a captive market. By alternating his English and his Dutch identities, Allerton was able to survive the fluctuating tensions that sometimes made access to the region difficult.

To gain entry to waterways controlled by Dutch colonial authorities, Allerton emphasized his Dutch identity and New Amsterdam residence. However,

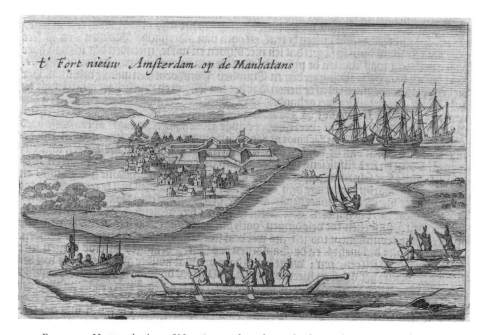

t' Fort nieuw Amsterdam op de Manhatans

FIGURE 9. Hartgers's view of New Amsterdam shows the fort and community and gives a sense of New Amsterdam as a vibrant center of intercultural trade. Several canoes of Native Americans paddle in the foreground, three European ships anchor offshore, and two smaller European vessels, such as Isaac Allerton frequently used, also navigate around the island. Hartgers's depiction was probably not based on eyewitness accounts. Nonetheless, its representation of ongoing intercultural contact is accurate. Joost Hartgers, "t' Fort nieuw Amsterdam op de Manhatans," in *Beschrivinghe van Virginia, Nieuw Nederlandt, Nieuw Engelandt*, Amsterdam, 1651. Courtesy of the John Carter Brown Library at Brown University.

because the Swedes saw the Dutch as their greatest threat and channeled their trade through English merchants, Allerton switched personas on the Delaware and presented himself as English to the Swedish governor and New Sweden colonists. In this manner he was able to take advantage of markets in both New Sweden and New Netherland. Native American traders also developed strategies to gain maximum advantage in both of those markets.

We know about boundary-crossing Europeans like Isaac Allerton because they regularly appeared in colonial records, often in colonial courts to finalize commercial agreements and in disputes arising from them. Native American boundary crossers also turn up in these records, though less frequently, and then they served more often as interpreters or spokespersons.[17] Moreover, the points of intersection between European traders like Allerton and Native American traders are even less clear because the details of those encounters

went largely unrecorded. Although they were part of the regular fabric of intercultural trade, they appeared in European records mostly when some part of
the relationship broke down. However, even the indirect references available to
us suggest that a careful search for evidence of the scope and impact of intercultural boundary crossing (and especially of trade and other alliances) may yield
surprisingly rich results.

One such document from New Netherland mentions Isaac Allerton in a
context that suggests that the peach war may not have been as distinct from the
Dutch conquest of New Sweden as scholars have thought. In 1655, while New
Netherland's director general, Petrus Stuyvesant, and a Dutch military force
were away from New Amsterdam on an expedition against New Sweden, a large
body of allied Munsee warriors attacked Manhattan. This assault has been
regarded as the start of the so-called peach war. The dispatch sent from New
Amsterdam colonists to Stuyvesant claimed in part that the Indians "forced
their way with intolerable insolence into the houses of citizens and showed
great insolence to Mr. Allerton."[18]

It seems significant that Allerton was singled out for insult. In 1655 Isaac
Allerton was sixty-nine years of age, fairly old by both European and Native
American standards. He was also an elder in the sense of being a prominent
community member whose advice and counsel carried weight. Native people
who had personal contact with Allerton or had dealings with New Amsterdam
and New Sweden would have known of Allerton's status within those European
settlements.

If we consider the possible reasons for choosing Allerton for a public demonstration of mockery, then we should also examine accounts from Dutch
observers who described the Indian warriors. Although historians have not
considered the two military expeditions as interrelated, some of those who
lived through them believed they were, and for many, the Indian warriors who
attacked Manhattan offered proof of this. A Dutch rumor spread from the
embattled New Netherland colonists to the Dutch troops on the Delaware and
claimed that a Susquehannock sachem had participated in the attacks on New
Netherland. In response, Stuyvesant and the Dutch soldiers on the Delaware
River accused New Sweden's governor of having instructed his colony's Susquehannock allies to attack New Amsterdam in order to create a diversion for the
Swedes.[19] The idea was that the invading Dutch force would have to return
to defend Manhattan, thereby allowing the Swedes to regroup and prepare a
better defense.

The Dutch rumor assumed that if Susquehannocks participated in the
fighting against New Netherland, then the Swedes must have been the guiding force behind it. It also presupposed that the Swedes were in control in the
Susquehannock–New Sweden alliance and that the Indians' actions must have

been the result of Swedish interests and were under Swedish control. However, one Swedish colonist took a different view.

Peter Lindeström, New Sweden's engineer and fortifications expert, later wrote about his experiences in North America. Lindeström used this incident to illustrate what he saw as the good qualities of Native Americans: "The savages . . . are a trustworthy and good-hearted folk, when they are not angered, and even brave-hearted [enough] to risk death for their good friends, to whom they have professed their friendship and faithfulness, as they did in the year 1655."[20] His description of the events of that September agreed with the Dutch rumor up to a point because he agreed that "when the Hollanders surprised us Swedes in New Sweden with hostility, then our river savages showed their friendship and faithfulness towards us."[21]

However, there was a key difference between the Dutch rumor and Lindeström's account. Lindeström claimed that he and other Swedish colonists had learned about the events in New Netherland only after the fact and was insistent on that point. In Lindeström's account of events, the Lenapes ("our river savages") played a key role because they had learned that the Dutch were planning to attack the Swedes: "Now this intention of the Hollanders was known to our river savages," he reported, "wherefore they betook themselves (unknown to us) and went to Manhattan City, in New Holland, to exact revenge on our behalf, doing great damage to the Hollander[s]."[22] Although denying responsibility for the Indians' attack, Lindeström could not keep from gloating over their success: "If the Hollanders in Manhattan City had not in a hurry sprung to arms and improved their fortifications, then the savages would have surprised them altogether and played master over the city."[23]

Lindeström further pointed out that the Dutch had accused the Swedes of provoking the Indians' attack on Manhattan, a charge that he took pains to point out was unjust. After describing the assault (with some relish) he wrote, "which [fact] the Holland General Steyvesandt [sic] severely flung at us, saying that we had incited these tyrannical and heathenish enemies against them, which we did not even know had taken place, before it was related to us and thrown at us."[24]

Which version, then, is accurate, or is neither one correct? Moreover, how does Isaac Allerton's experience connect with these rumors and conflicting accounts? The fact that Allerton was active in trade between New Netherland and New Sweden helps us understand why Indian warriors singled him out for public insults that deliberately mocked his power and status in the 1655 expedition against New Amsterdam. Understanding why Native American warriors ridiculed Allerton then helps us to comprehend the connections between the peach war and the Dutch conquest of New Sweden.[25]

If Indians from the region claimed by New Sweden or those who were allied with New Sweden had joined in the 1655 Manhattan attack as the Dutch rumor and Lindeström contended, they would have known that Allerton professed more than one loyalty. Allerton was often successful at maneuvering between different cultures or the competing interests of various groups. However, the controversy spreading through Lenapehoking provides a clear example that conflicts and colonial contests seldom had only two sides.

Moreover, when we begin to consider Native American perspectives, as well as competing European ones, we view an even more complicated picture. The conflict in Lenapehoking was clearly more than a Dutch and Swedish clash. It also involved many of their Native American allies, and the outcome had repercussions for English colonial plans. In this larger context, Allerton's political and cultural neutrality and personal power were insufficient to satisfy all of the participants. At least several of the Indians who invaded Manhattan and mocked Allerton had some degree of alliance with New Sweden. As importantly, they knew Allerton as someone who presented himself as a New Sweden ally, even as his layered and shifting alliances and attempts to move unscathed among all of the parties represented betrayal.

Let us consider the competing European accounts of the 1655 Native American attack on Manhattan. What can the Dutch and Swedish accounts tell us about whether Native Americans from southern Lenapehoking joined in the assault on Manhattan? The Dutch rumor claimed that a sachem of the Susquehannocks (or the Minquas, as the Dutch and Swedes called them) was involved in the attack on New Amsterdam. The Susquehannocks were closely allied with New Sweden, so if Susquehannock leaders and warriors joined with Algonquian Munsee warriors, this suggests a New Sweden connection. As mentioned earlier, Peter Lindeström described the warriors as "our river savages," which was how he referred to the Lenapes throughout his text.[26]

If some of New Sweden's Native American allies helped to attack Manhattan, were they Susquehannocks (as the Dutch claimed) or Lenapes (as the Swedes contended)? In either case, why would Susquehannock or Lenape warriors have decided to join with Munsee warriors, who were attacking the Dutch settlement in retaliation for the recent murder of a woman and over long-standing disagreements and tensions with the Dutch colony? The evidence suggests that aspects of both accounts (the Dutch accusation and Peter Lindeström's retroactive defense) explain much of what happened, but neither report gives us the whole picture. For that, we need to add the additional perspective of assuming that the Lenapes and the Susquehannocks had their own reasons for acting as they did. Additionally, to understand the Lenapes' and the Susquehannocks' points of view, we must reconsider alliances and events in Lenapehoking and stretching as far south as the Powhatans' territory of Tsenacommacah and as far north as Iroquoia.

The fact that New Sweden and the Susquehannocks established an important alliance soon after New Sweden was founded is a crucial piece of the puzzle. As part of their connection, the New Sweden colonists provided the Susquehannocks with guns, helped train them to use the weapons, and fought with them against militia from the neighboring English colony of Maryland.[27] The Swedes undertook these extraordinary measures on behalf of their Susquehannock allies because they depended on them heavily. New Sweden's colonists could offer the Susquehannocks guns and other European goods, and in turn the Susquehannocks provided the colony with a reliable source of high-quality furs. However, if that makes the alliance seem fairly evenly balanced, it is a misleading image. The Swedes were completely dependent upon continued good relations with the Susquehannocks and the Lenapes.[28] The colonists rarely received supplies from Sweden and had difficulty growing enough food. They survived by buying corn from the Lenapes during the entire span of the colony's history, but to do so, they found themselves in a tenuous situation.

In order to keep their alliance with both Indian nations, New Sweden needed access to the European goods that both the Susquehannocks and the Lenapes wanted. The long periods between the arrival of Swedish supply ships meant the colonists needed another source of provisions, so the Swedish colonists and colonial officials found more local ones. They bought European goods from English colonial merchants like Isaac Allerton and then resold them to the Susquehannocks for furs.

Thus the alliance between the Susquehannocks and New Sweden was not an equally balanced power relationship, and both groups knew it. As the superior party in the alliance, the Susquehannocks assumed the additional posture of being the Swedes' protectors. Swedish governor Johan Rising wrote his superiors that the Susquehannocks, or "Minquas . . . call themselves our protectors."[29] Although the Susquehannocks had suffered recent losses in battles with members of the Five Nations Iroquois, they were still known as powerful warriors, and their promises of protection carried considerable weight. Certainly they were far stronger militarily than the small colony of New Sweden, which never had more than four hundred colonists.[30]

However, Susquehannock losses to epidemic disease and in wars with the Five Nations affected their relationship with the Lenapes. Both groups had resolved their previous enmity and formed an alliance, which the Susquehannocks seem to have dominated for several years. Although scholars continue to disagree about which was the dominant partner, it seems clear that by 1650 the Lenapes were no longer clients of the Susquehannocks but had become equal participants.[31]

Moreover, they too seem to have been the dominant partner in their alliance with New Sweden. Not only did New Sweden's colonists depend upon the Lenapes for food, but the Lenapes also began to undercut the Swedes' role as brokers in the fur trade. In the same report in which he described the Susquehannocks as the colony's protectors, Governor Rising wrote that the Lenapes "threaten not only to kill our people in the land and ruin them, before we can become stronger and prevent such things, but also they threatened to destroy even the trade, both with the Minques [Susquehannocks] and the other savage nations, as well as with the Christians."[32]

His report continued by describing the situation as growing even worse because the Lenapes increasingly encroached on the Swedes' bartering. Governor Rising recognized that a flourishing trade was the lifeblood of the colony; without it, New Sweden's colonists had no chance. This made the Lenapes' actions particularly threatening because "they run to the Minques [Susquehannocks], and there they buy beavers and elk-skins, etc., for our goods."[33]

The Lenapes were effectively using New Sweden as a source of goods but then cutting the Swedes out of the region's larger trade networks by turning to both Susquehannock and Dutch markets. Rising lamented that, after buying Swedish merchandise and selling it to the Susquehannocks for furs, they "then proceed before our eyes to Manathas, where the traders can pay more for them than we do, because more ships, and more goods arrive there."[34]

If the Swedes were acutely aware of their isolation and weakness, their native neighbors and allies were, too. Rising pointed out that, although the Lenapes had the power to destroy New Sweden, they did not do so: "Yet we associate with them to a certain extent, and they are fond of us, because we do not do them any harm or act hostile toward them. Otherwise, they would indeed ruin our cattle, yes probably the people on the land."[35] Accordingly, New Sweden became a client colony of the Susquehannocks and the Lenapes as an act of survival, and these intercultural patron-and-client relationships became entangled with events at Manhattan in the fall of 1655.

In 1655, when the Dutch force sailed into the Delaware, New Netherland not only absorbed New Sweden but also became enmeshed in the shifting alliances and enmities of Lenape, Susquehannock, and Haudenosaunee (Five Nations) peoples. The evidence suggests that Lenape and Susquehannock warriors joined in the attack on Manhattan. Some small groups of Susquehannock refugees already lived among the Munsee Indians near Manhattan and had kinship ties with New Sweden's Susquehannock patrons.[36]

Moreover, the Lenapes had close links with the Minisinks and other Munsees who lived near Manhattan. Thus, it would not have been surprising for either group to form short-term alliances with Manhattan-area Algonquians against the Dutch. Furthermore, the Susquehannocks, who regarded themselves as the Swedes' protectors, had previously retaliated against the rivals of their European clients, as when they fought against Maryland in retaliation for Maryland's actions against William Claiborne and their other Virginia trading partners.

Accordingly, the defense of their client colony might have been reason enough for Susquehannock warriors to attack Manhattan, but shifting alliances and enmities between different Indian nations provide another explanation for their participation. The Dutch were allies of the Haudenosaunee. The Susquehannocks resented the Dutch for channeling their trade through the Mohawks and other peoples of the Five Nations. Perhaps more important, the Susquehannocks regarded some of the Five Nations as among their paramount enemies. Indeed, in the 1640s and 1650s they were engaged in almost constant conflict with the Senecas. The Susquehannocks and the Five Nations (or at least the Mohawks and the Senecas) regarded one another as competitors in the fur trade. The Susquehannocks, for instance, had attempted to develop more of a trade with Dutch merchants since the 1620s. However, by the 1640s and 1650s the Mohawks had instead become the primary suppliers of furs to Dutch traders.[37]

In their continuing effort to expand their alliance and trade networks, the Susquehannocks tried to enlist the Hurons to join with them in seeking a trade treaty with the Five Nations Iroquois in the late 1640s. The Susquehannocks wanted a multilateral agreement in which each party would refrain from interfering in the others' trade activities.[38] However, the alliance was never formed. Instead, the Susquehannocks and their allies suffered great losses in wars with the Iroquois.

While seeking control of the fur trade, the Iroquois had fought against the Hurons in the late 1640s and early 1650s and defeated them decisively in 1652.[39] In addition, archaeological evidence suggests that the Susquehannocks suffered a devastating loss in battle with the Iroquois in 1652, during which the Iroquois took five to six hundred Susquehannock prisoners.[40] From the Susquehannocks' perspective, New Netherland appeared to be a client colony of Iroquoia. The Five Nations increasingly controlled (or tried to control) trade routes to the Dutch and were steadily and successfully attacking their rivals, the Susquehannocks and their Huron allies.

While the Dutch feared that the Swedes were behind the assault in order to divert Dutch attention and allow the Swedes to regroup, their fear was focused on the wrong powers. By attacking New Amsterdam, Susquehannock warriors could exact revenge for the Dutch strike against their New Sweden clients or tributaries in a manner consistent with traditional Native American practice. An offensive move against the Dutch had the added value of enabling the Susquehannocks to strike a blow against an important Iroquois client and thus exact revenge on the Iroquois as well. The onslaught at Fort Amsterdam included mockery directed at prominent citizens like Isaac Allerton and symbolic displays of power in the form of house invasions.

New Netherland's conquest of New Sweden, although also violent in parts, was similarly a symbolic statement of power that humiliated the relatively defenseless Swedish colonial officials.[41] Thus, public insult at Manhattan appropriately turned the tables on Dutch colonial control and satisfied different needs of the various nations the warriors represented. Furthermore, Susquehannock participants had the additional advantage of sending an indirect but unmistakable message to the Five Nations Iroquois without having to attack them directly. A strike at a Five Nations client was a blow at the Five Nations themselves and reprisal for the Dutch move against the Susquehannocks' client.

Accordingly, the Dutch conquest of New Sweden and the Native American attack on Manhattan in 1655 were different aspects of the same event. Moreover, the interplay of intercultural alliances in the Delaware and Hudson valleys during the early and mid-seventeenth century provides a fascinating glimpse of a range of ways in which Europeans and Native Americans experimented with colonialism during the early colonial era. When they mapped one another, they tried to place one another into their own grids of meanings. Additionally, they sought to do so by seeing other cultures as their inferiors whenever the balance of power allowed them to do so. In the seventeenth century, Indians and Europeans frequently believed themselves justified in evaluating one another as subordinate groups. Power shifted so quickly and so often that each group found moments when its members believed they could control their world and their neighbors.

We do not usually see that native peoples might have tried to turn the tables on Europeans and treat the interlopers as colonized groups because we know that Indian peoples never succeeded in dominating Europeans as thoroughly as Europeans ultimately controlled them. Yet, interpretations that assume overwhelming European supremacy for the early colonial period can be too heavily influenced by the outcome of much later events.

Those who lived in the early and mid-seventeenth century did not know how things would turn out in the long run. They could not know, for example, that the Susquehannocks would eventually disappear as a separate nation, that European colonies would survive these early, uncertain years, or that, when they did take permanent hold, encroaching European colonists would increasingly stop at nothing to obtain Indian lands. In this early period, power shifted quickly and frequently; alliances were intercultural, and European colonies could become clients of Indians, just as some Native Americans became clients and tributaries of European colonies.

Finally, events on the Delaware and Hudson rivers in the 1650s show the crucial importance of including Native American perspectives in our analysis of the colonial past because, when we do so, even the most traditionally European incidents take on a different meaning. However, we cannot see the full dimensions of the networks and alliances that shaped people's lives if we fail to recognize that people living in North America in the seventeenth century were connected to others in distant communities.

Epilogue

Captain Claiborne's Lost Isle

During the first half of the seventeenth century many alliances stretched hundreds of miles, far beyond any one group's territory or colony. Even when these connections were more narrowly contained, they were regularly directed at threats from outside the region. This book has taken a broad view in order to capture the full dimension of these collaborative efforts. By doing so, it becomes clear that intercultural partnerships shaped eastern North America from Iroquoia to the Chesapeake Bay and entangled everyone who was living there in one way or another. Actions and alliances in one region had an extremely important ripple effect on people in far distant places. Even when the connection was not direct, people were almost always linked to someone who did have an explicit relationship to the event or cooperative effort.

Intercultural alliances continued to shape the last century of the colonial period, but by the 1670s they had shifted west, north, and south. On the eastern seaboard intercultural partnerships and understandings became overwhelmed by escalating cycles of conflict and repeated Native American losses. But throughout the first half of the seventeenth century, people worked assiduously to create intercultural connections, sometimes with spectacular failure but occasionally with extraordinary success. For a new generation of Europeans on North America's eastern seaboard, however, the 1670s brought an end to the assumption that intercultural associations were either desirable or necessary.

The spread of epidemic disease, the dramatic increase in European populations in North America, and the shifts in political power on the East Coast all combined to end the era of widespread intercultural cooperation. Of course, these arrangements did not end entirely, but by the 1670s the shifting balance of power between colonists and Native Americans made possible the scene in which Isaac Allerton's son was able to fight against the Susquehannocks in ways his father's generation was not. It brought about the moment when the Susquehannocks found themselves besieged by an angry militia from Virginia and Maryland because of actions undertaken by other Indian peoples. Yet, as dramatically as the world of North America in 1676 had altered in the past thirty to forty years, some older colonists refused to recognize the enormity of the changes that had swept in. Isaac Allerton died at the end of the 1650s, before the remarkable transformation in North America. William Claiborne was still alive in the 1670s, though he could not stop looking to the past and thinking about what might have been.

In March of 1676/77, less than two years after Allerton Jr. and John Washington's siege of the Susquehannock fort, William Claiborne made one last attempt to have his former lands restored to him. Claiborne petitioned Charles II

FIGURE 10. Although William Claiborne continued to try to regain Kent Island after being driven out by Maryland, he never succeeded. This early map of Maryland explicitly shows Kent Island as part of Lord Baltimore's colony. George Alsop, *A Land-skip of the Province of Maryland or the Lord Baltimors Plantation neere Virginia*, London, 1638. Courtesy of the John Carter Brown Library at Brown University.

to ask for the return of Kent Island.[1] After almost forty years, he was still chafing at what he saw as the injustice of Lord Baltimore's unchecked expansion into Claiborne's legitimately acquired territory.

Claiborne asked Charles II to restore his fortune and make good the "ten thousand pounds sterling in Goods Catle Servants & many Plantations" that he had lost when Lord Baltimore forced him off of Kent Island.[2] And he wanted his island back as well. However, even William Claiborne seems to have recognized some of the changes in the North American political landscape; he did not propose to rekindle his old relationship with the Susquehannocks or recapture his former role in the fur trade. Too much had changed, and Claiborne recognized that much, even if he could not see that he would never regain his lost isle.

Claiborne supported his petition first by appealing to old loyalties. Reminding Charles II that Claiborne had been a loyal servant and official of the king's father and grandfather both before and during the English civil war, he titled his petition "the Humble Petition of Coll: Wm: Claiborne a Poor Old servant of your Majesty's father & Grandfather."[3] But whereas in those early years Claiborne had embraced the potential advantages of forming intercultural alliances, by 1677 he had long since given up on the idea. His petition now stressed that the demonstration of his loyalty had included many years "being most spent in his Discoveries & warrs against the Indians as Chiefe Commander."[4]

The petition would remain one of William Claiborne's great, unfulfilled hopes. He never got Kent or Palmer's islands back. The world of his old age had changed irrevocably from the one he had helped to shape in his youth. The day when any Europeans within their reach had to supplicate or make peace with the Susquehannocks had passed. The days when two small islands in the Chesapeake Bay could serve as linchpins in a web of intercultural alliances as far north as Iroquoia were over.

Notes

PROLOGUE

1. The commission to Colonel Washington and Major Allerton from Governor Berkeley and his council is reprinted in *William and Mary Quarterly*, 1st ser., 4 (1895): 86.

2. For the letter from Colonel John Washington and Major Isaac Allerton Jr. to Maryland's governor Charles Calvert and his council see "Proceedings of the Council of Maryland, 1671–1675," in *Archives of Maryland, Proceedings of the Council of Maryland 1671–1681*, ed. William Hand Browne (Baltimore: Maryland Historical Society, 1896), 48–49.

3. For some of the depositions attesting to Allerton Jr.'s and Washington's conduct in the affair of the murdered Susquehannocks see Lyon Tyler, "Col. John Washington. Further Details of His Life from the Records of Westmoreland Co. Virginia," *William and Mary Quarterly*, 1st ser., 2 (1893): 38–43. The depositions all contend that a Maryland officer named Major Truman ordered the execution of the Susquehannock leaders and that he had them put to death without Washington's or Allerton's support.

INTRODUCTION

1. Captain John Smith, *A Map of Virginia: With a description of the Countrey, the Commodities, People, Government and Religion* (London, 1612).

2. See, for example, *The History of Cartography*, vol. 2, bk. 3, *Cartography in the Traditional African, American, Arctic, Australian, and Pacific Societies*, ed. David Woodward and G. Malcolm Lewis (University of Chicago Press, 1998).

3. See, for example, ibid., vol. 1 and vol. 2, bk. 3.

4. For related works that emphasize the connections between mapping and culture and between mapping and ethnography see Richard Helgerson, *Forms of Nationhood:*

The Elizabethan Writing of England (Chicago: University of Chicago Press, 1992); Richard Helgerson, "The Land Speaks: Cartography, Chorography, and Subversion in Renaissance England," *Representations* 16 (1986): 50–85; Laura Hostetler, *Qing Colonial Enterprise: Ethnography and Cartography in Early Modern China* (Chicago: University of Chicago Press, 2001); Lesley B. Cormack, *Charting an Empire: Geography at the English Universities, 1580–1620* (Chicago: University of Chicago Press, 1997).

5. For a similar emphasis on the degree to which colonial cultures were the product of shared cultural creation and contestation see Lauren Benton, *Law and Colonial Cultures: Legal Regimes in World History, 1400–1900* (New York: Cambridge University Press, 2002).

6. William Starna has characterized the Iroquois League as "a system of periodic alliances," and his understanding of the nature of the ties that bound the Haudenosaunee together has informed my interpretation of a wide variety of intercultural connections in this period. Not everything included in this book was part of a "system," but everyone experimented with "periodic alliances."

7. Much of James Axtell's important work has demonstrated both the continuing vitality of native cultures and the great cost to them of European colonization. See, for example, James Axtell: *The European and the Indian: Essays in the Ethnohistory of Colonial North America* (New York: Oxford University Press, 1981); *The Invasion Within: The Contest of Cultures in Colonial North America* (New York: Oxford University Press, 1985); *After Columbus: Essays in the Ethnohistory of Colonial North America* (New York: Oxford University Press, 1988); and *Beyond 1492: Encounters in Colonial North America* (New York: Oxford University Press, 1992). For other scholars who have demonstrated the continuing power and influence of Indian peoples see Karen Ordahl Kupperman, *Indians and English: Facing Off in Early America* (Ithaca, N.Y.: Cornell University Press, 2000); José António Brandão, *"Your Fyre Shall Burn No More": Iroquois Policy toward New France and Its Native Allies to 1701* (Lincoln: University of Nebraska Press, 1997); Michael Leroy Oberg, *Dominion and Civility: English Imperialism and Native America, 1585–1685* (Ithaca, N.Y.: Cornell University Press, 1999).

8. Many groups did indeed incorporate components of other societies such as language and material culture, but in the first half of the seventeenth century most groups limited and controlled their absorption of foreign elements. The major exceptions to this generalization include Christianized communities of Native Americans, such as the Hurons in New France and the Algonquian Praying Indians in New England.

9. For thoughtful discussions of African identities in the colonial period see Linda M. Heywood and John K. Thornton, *Central Africans, Atlantic Creoles, and the Making of the Foundation of the Americas, 1585–1660* (New York: Cambridge University Press, 2007); Ira Berlin, *Many Thousands Gone: The First Two Centuries of Slavery in North America* (Cambridge, Mass.: Belknap Press of Harvard University Press, 1998); and Michael Angelo Gomez, *Exchanging Our Country Marks: The Transformation of African Identities in the Colonial and Antebellum South* (Chapel Hill: University of North Carolina Press, 1998).

CHAPTER 1: MAPPING THE PEOPLES OF THE WORLD

1. Recently the work of a number of scholars has brought the importance of maps and mapping into the forefront of early modern and colonial North American history.

Scholars such as Svetlana Alpers, J. B. Harley, and Richard Helgerson have demonstrated that early modern Europeans began thinking more extensively about space in the context of political and cultural relationships, even as changes in print and cartographic technologies greatly increased their familiarity with maps and mapping concepts. Moreover, G. Malcolm Lewis, Barbara Mundy, and others have demonstrated that Native Americans had their own well-established mapping traditions.

2. P. D. A. Harvey, *Maps in Tudor England* (Chicago: University of Chicago Press, 1993), 6–8, 17, 25, 64.

3. *Euclides Elements of Geometry: The first VI Books: In a compendious form contracted and Demonstrated by Captain Thomas Rudd* (London, 1651), E4 verso.

4. Ibid.

5. Ibid.

6. Ibid.

7. See also *The Complete Works of Captain John Smith (1580–1631)*, ed. Philip L. Barbour (Chapel Hill: Published for the Institute of Early American History and Culture, Williamsburg, Va., by the University of North Carolina Press, 1986), vol. 1, 388.

8. Thomas Blundeville, *A Briefe Description of Universal Mappes and Cardes, and of Their Vse, and Also the Vse of Ptholemey his Tables* (London, 1589), A2 verso.

9. Ibid.

10. Harvey, *Maps in Tudor England*, 64.

11. Robert Kayll, *The Trades Increase* (London, 1615), 34.

12. Ibid.

13. Significantly, Diggs used the language of navigation and cartography to drive his point home: "I obserue such inclination, such a secret variation in the Compasse of that Pamphletors discourse, as makes me very iealous, for all his faire conclusion that hee framed his Almanacke for the Meridian of Toledo rather than our Ilands good fortune." Diggs, *Defence of Trade*, 4–5. Diggs's accusation that Kayll had "framed his Almanacke for the Meridian of Toledo" rather pointedly accuses the author of putting out Spanish propaganda in the guise of concern for English national interests. Diggs suspected the pamphlet of being not only pro-Spanish but also part of a Spanish plot to undermine English society.

14. In his epistle to the reader, Roberts confessed, rather like many a current scholar, that he had been forced to modify his topic: "But after long and tedious inquisition, I found that the further I sailed in this Ocean, the vaster were my desires, and the fewer were my furtherances to my wished Port; so that perceiving the Worke thus to increase upon me, beyond my expectation and first purpose, I was constrained (with the wind-scanted Seaman) to cast about againe, and limit my selfe to a narrower scantling." Lewes Roberts, *The Marchants Mapp of Commerce; wherein the vniversall manner and matter of trade, is compendiously handled* (London, 1638), A4 recto.

15. For instance, Roberts described himself as a sailor whose careful navigation allowed him to bring a valuable map home to fellow travelers:

I have at last by due sounding of the Channell, safely sailed over the Ocean aforementioned, and brought my Barke to an Anchor in her desired Harbour, and I hope so well observed the depths, shoulds, rocks and sands thereof, that he that navigates after me, and by this my Mapp, shall bee secured from all dangers, and thereby bring his accompts to that wished Port, that may prove both to his owne profit and Commoditie.

Roberts, *Marchants Mapp of Commerce*, unnumbered page following A4.

16. Greg Dening has written about the early modern Europeans' intermixture of technical and cultural interest in navigation: "Navigation was the medium of progressive and current science. It gave cultural focus to the science of angles, circles, and time. Its problems opened up the principal mathematical issues of the day." Greg Dening, *Performances* (Chicago: University of Chicago Press, 1996), 216.

17. In one such example, Michael Lok prefaced his 1625 *Historie of the West Indies* by comparing his book to a small vessel at the mercy of the ocean while in search of a safe harbor. See Michael Lok, *Historie of the West Indies* (London, 1625), B.

18. Greville's report on trade in the East contributed to the formation of the East India Company. On his role in public affairs, see Fulke Greville, *The Remains: Being Poems of Monarchy and Religion*, ed. G. A. Wilkes (New York: Oxford University Press, 1965), 1–19.

For the passage on maps and laws, see Fulke Greville, Lord Brooke, "A Treatise of Monarchy, of Lawes," section vii, stanza 246, in Greville, *Remains*, 96.

19. See, for instance, Keith Wrightson, *English Society 1580–1680* (New Brunswick, N.J.: Rutgers University Press, 1982); Karen Ordahl Kupperman, *Settling with the Indians: The Meeting of English and Indian Cultures in America, 1580–1640* (Totowa, N.J.: Rowman and Littlefield, 1980), 141–43, 147. For an extremely important recent study on the effects of the English civil war and interregnum on England's American colonies, see Carla Gardina Pestana, *The English Atlantic in an Age of Revolution, 1640–1661* (Cambridge, Mass.: Harvard University Press, 2007).

20. See, for example, Karen Ordahl Kupperman, "Introduction: The Changing Definition of America," in *America in European Consciousness 1493–1750*, ed. Karen Ordahl Kupperman (Chapel Hill: Published for the Institute of Early American History and Culture, Williamsburg, Va., by the University of North Carolina Press, 1995), 22.

21. Samvel Purchas, *Purchas his Pilgrimage. or Relations of the World and the Religions Observed in All Ages and Places discouered, from the Creation unto this Present*, 3d ed. (London, 1617), bk. 1, ch. 2, 15.

22. George Hakewill, *An Apologie or Declaration of the Power and Providence of God in the Government of the World* (Oxford, 1630), 42.

23. Purchas, *Purchas his Pilgrimage*, 33.

24. Thomas Fuller, *The Sermons of Mr. Henry Smith* (London, 1675), B verso. AAS Mather Library, shelf 21, no. 639.

25. One writer lamented the death of protestant kings, "according to whom we steered and governed our ships in the vast ocean of this troublesome world"; another recommended saving praises for the dead and not prematurely using them on the living: "Therefore in the mean while, best for her to Feare the Lord, and so be praise-worthy, than to be praised for the present. . . . It is safest praising Her as a Master of a ship is . . . when she is safely arriued in the Hauen, past all danger of shipwracke." See Frederike Schloer, *The Death of the Two Reknowned Kings* (London, 1633), 14, for the first quotation and Hanniball Gamon, *The Praise of a Godly Woman* (London, 1627), 22, for the second.

26. "Among other rare inventions," Hakewill wrote, "that of the Marriners Compasse is most worthy of admiration." He continued: "By meanes of it, was Navigation perfected, the liues and goods of many thousands haue bin, and daily are preserved: It findes out a way thorow the vast Ocean, in the greatest storms and darkest nights, where

is neither path to follow, nor inhabitant or passenger to inquire; It points out the way to the skilfull Marriner when all other helpes faile him." George Hakewill, *An Apologie or Declaration of the Power and Providence of God in the Government of the World* (Oxford, 1630), 281–82.

27. See also James Horn, *Adapting to a New World: English Society in the Seventeenth-Century Chesapeake* (Chapel Hill: University of North Carolina Press, 1994).

28. The quotation continues: "Like a ship tossed in tempests in the deepe waters, often covered with the lofty waves, up and downe, and often sunke under water in all mens eyes." Finiens Canus Vove, *Zions Ioy in Her King, Coming in his Glory* (London, 1643), 3.

29. He extended his metaphor considerably:

> The instruments we have for discovery are but few, yet sure and trusty, our Compasse, and Crosse staffe or Jacobs staffe. . . . Our Jacobs staffe is the observation of the high and great workes of God, daily appearing in the world; and from thence we will see what we can finde out of Christs coming . . . to fill our Sayles with a prosperous gale of his Spirit; to sit at the sterne and direct our course by our sure tried Compassee unto the wished haven.

Ibid. "Jacob's staff" was a commonly used mariner's term for the cross-staff.

30. William Teelinck, "Pavls Complaint against His Natvrall Corrvption" (London, 1621), 47–48. "Many a man goeth vnder the curse of God because of his sinnes, and neuer thinkes of his deliuerance, passing along as it were, with an easie gale in a smooth Sea, without any perturbation at all."

31. John Spencer, *A Discourse concerning Vulgar Prophecies* (London, 1665), A3 recto. Similarly, in *The Sovles Conflict with it selfe*, Richard Sibbs wrote that "the soule cannot but bee disquited when it knowes not what to cleave unto, like a ship tossed with contrary windes." Richard Sibbs, *The Sovles Conflict with it selfe*, 2d ed. (London, 1636), 34.

32. Robert Mandevill, *Timothies Taske or A Christian Sea-Card* (Oxford, 1619).

33. Mandevill continued with his theme: "Timothie as Pilot keepes the sterne. Tradition is the rock which he must shun. The place of arriuall is the promised Land, that coelestiall Canaan which is aboue. His exchange there the richest for commodity, & rarest for perpetuity, euen the saluation of himselfe, & those that saile with him." Ibid., 63.

34. Purchas, *Purchas his Pilgrimage*, bk. 9, ch. 15, 1102. By contrast, he had lamented earlier: "We may here deplore of the vnhappy sight of Armenia, which though it repeopled the world, yet is it least beholding to her viperous off-spring, a Map of the worlds miseries, through so many ages." Ibid., bk. 4, ch. 1, 388.

35. Daniel Dike, *Certaine Comfortable Sermons Vpon the CXXIV. Psalme* (London, 1617), 39–40. Almost thirty years later Simeon Ash preached to the House of Lords and used a similar metaphor, with the added twist of Christ as a self-interested ship's master. "This is the language of our Lord," Ash told the peers, "Sions deliverance is salvation to me, the support of a sinking Church, is the upholding of me. Should the Church suffer shipwrack in the stormie Seas of this troublesome world, Iesus Christ, the owner, the Master thereof, would judge himselfe a great looser, therefore for his own sake, he will secure and save her." Simeon Ash, "The Church Sinking, Saved by Christ. Set out in a Sermon Preached from Isai. lxiii 24 before the Right Honourable the House of Lords, in the Abby-Church at Westminster, on Wednesday, Febr. 26, 1644, being the day of the Monthly publike Fast," 2.

36. William Goode, "The Discoverie of a Publiqve Spirit: Presented in a Sermon before the Honourable House of Commons at Margarets Westminster, at their Publique Fast, March 26, 1645."

37. The Council for New England, records 1622–1623. AAS manuscript collections, Council Room, 64.

38. Ferdinando Gorges, "A Briefe narration of the Originall Undertakings of the Advancement of Plantations into the parts of America" (1658), in *America Painted to the Life* (London, 1659), 4.

39. Ibid.

40. Ibid.

41. Ibid.

42. Ibid, 4–5.

43. "Notes in writing besides more ptiuie by mouth that were giuen by a Genteman, Anno, 1580 to M. Arthure Pette and to M. Charles Iackman, sent by the marchants of the Muscouie companie for the discouerie of the northeast strayte, not altogether unfit for some other enterprises of discouerie, hereafter to bee taken in hande," in Richard Hakluyt, *Divers voyages touching the discouerie of America, and the Ilands adiacent vnto the same, ande first of all by our Englismen, and afterwards by the Frenchmen and Britons: And certaine notes of aduertisements for observations, necessarie for such as shall heereafter make the like attempt, With two mappes annexed hereunto for the plainer understanding of the whole matter.* "Imprinted at London for Thomas Woodcock, dwelling in paules Church-yard, at the signe of the black beare" (Readex Microprint, 1966), no page numbers.

44. George Hakewill, *An Apologie or Declaration of the Power and Providence of God in the Government of the World* (Oxford, 1630), 281–82. Hakewill went on to make the argument that navigation was enabling God to bring all nations together into a single commonwealth. According to Hakewill, all of the developments in navigation were for the purpose of expanding Christendom. Nonetheless, what is most interesting for our purposes is his assumption that ethnographic observation, "their severall formes of government and religion observed," and navigation were integrally linked.

45. William Bourne, *A booke called the Treasure for traueilers, deuided into fiue Bookes or partes, contaynyng very necessary matters, for all sortes of Trauailers, eyther by Sea or by Lande* (London, 1578), preface to the reader, no page numbers.

46. Ibid.

47. In early modern trade and many related colonial enterprises, the English aristocracy in general was much more active than other European nobles; similarly, elite English women were unusually prominent in such undertakings. One example of an upper-class English woman as patron of books that publicized colonial ventures and navigational knowledge is Lady Frances, Duchess of Richmond and Lennox, who provided liberal patronage for the 1624 printing of Captain John Smith's *Generall Historie of Virginia, New-England, and the Summer Isles* (London, 1624). See *Captain John Smith's Circular or Prospectus of His Generall Historie of Virginia, New-England, and the Summer Isles* (Cambridge, 1914).

48. John Smith, *An Accidence or Path-way to experience* (London, 1626), dedicatory epistle to Sir Robert Heath. Robert Manwarying also addressed himself to the maritime education of upper-status Englishmen. In describing the information his dictionary offered, he used analogies drawn from upper-status English life:

This booke shall make a man understand what other men say, and speake properly himselfe; which how convenient, comely, and necessary a thing it is, allmen (of sence) doe know. Should not man be Leashed (being a hunting or hawking) if he should cry Hey, -Ret, to the Hownds, and hooke againe to the Spaniels: Or were it not ridiculous for a man (speaking of the wars) to call a trench a Ditch: Or (at Sea) the Star-boord, and Lar-boord, the right and left of a Ship, and yet they doe simply the same, and both dogs and men will understand them alike.

Manwaryng, *The Seaman's Dictionary* (London, 1644), A2 verso.

49. This expedition never actually took place. It was supposed to leave between June 1582 and March 1583, under the command of Sir William Stanley, Richard Bingham, and Martin Frobisher. On their return they would have been required to furnish the information gathered on the basis of these instructions. See *New American World*, vol. 3, *English Plans for North America. The Roanoke Voyages. New England Ventures*, ed. David B. Quinn, with the assistance of Alison M. Quinn and Susan Hillier (London: Arno Press, 1979), 239. Although the expedition did not actually occur and Thomas Bavin made no observations, I have included his instructions in this discussion. The directives to Bavin are one of the best examples of a widespread kind of colonial planning and instruction in the late sixteenth and early seventeenth centuries, though few samples have survived intact.

50. Bavin's instructions included notes for a second person who would act as observer. Paul Hulton argues that these two roles were basically the same ones filled by Thomas Harriot and John White on the Roanoke expedition three years later. Paul Hulton, *America 1585: The Complete Drawings of John White* (Chapel Hill: University of North Carolina Press, 1984).

51. Quoted in ibid., 9. The original is in the British Library, Department of Manuscripts, add. ms. 38823, 1–8. Printed in full in Quinn et al., *New American World*, vol. 2, 238–45. See also David B. Quinn, "European Perceptions of American Ecology, 1492–1612," in *Visions of America since 1492*, ed. Deborah L. Madsen (New York: St. Martin's Press, 1994), 3–22.

52. Ibid.

53. Thomas Palmer, *An Essay of the Means how to make our Trauailes, into forraine Coutnries, the more profitable and honourable* (London, 1606), 20.

54. Willem Lodewijcksz, *Teerste Boek, Historie van Indien* (Amsterdam, 1617).

55. See Elizabeth L. Eisenstein, *The Printing Revolution in Early Modern Europe* (New York: Cambridge University Press, 1983).

56. One of the most important ways that Blaeu ensured that his charts and maps were updated with the very latest knowledge, drawn directly from experience, was to confer with seafarers themselves. In his address to the reader, he acknowledged "the aide and furtherance of manie expert and skilfull Sailers, Pilots, and Masters." Willem Jansz Blaeu, *The Light of Navigation* (Amsterdam, 1612), with an introduction by R. A. Skelton, *Theatrum Orbis Terrarum*, 1st ser., vol. 6 (New York: World Publishing, 1964), vii. On the location of the Blaeu family shop see *A Catalogue by Joan Blaeu*, a facsimile with accompanying text by Ir. C. Koeman (Amsterdam, N. Israel, 1967), 5.

Although Blaeu's work was among the most accurate and prized in Europe, he was not the only one to seek the most up-to-date information from the men who had directly experienced it. Dudley Diggs assured his readers that "it may please you then to know, that the substance of this which you haue read, was taken out of Custome-bookes, out of the East-India Companies bookes, out of Grocers, Warehouse-keepers, Marchants bookes, and conference with men of best experience." Diggs, *Defence of Trade*. Johannes de Laet used an extensive array of published narratives about the New World in compiling his own description of it, but he also consulted the journals of shipmasters and pilots in order to get the latest information: "Beneffens verscheyden gheschreven Journalen van verscheyden Schippers ende Stier-lieden/welcker namen wy hier ende daer in onse Beschrijvingeh hebben uytghedruckt." Ioannes de Laet, *Nieuwe Wereldt Ofte Beschrijvinghe van West-Indien* (Leyden, 1625).

57. Willem Blaeu, *The Light of Navigation: Wherein Are Declared and Lively Pourtrayed, all the Coasts and Havens, of the West, North and East Seas. Collected Partly Out of the Books of the principall Authors which have written of Navigation (as Lucas Iohnson Waghenaer and divers others) partly also out of manie other expert Seafaring Mens writings and verball declarations: corrected from manie faults, and inlarged with manie newe Descriptions and Cardes. Divided into two Books. Heerunto Are Added (Beside an Institution in the Art of Navigation) newe Tables of the Declination of the Sonne, according to Tycho Brahes Observations, applied to the Meridian of Amsterdam. Together with newe Tables and Instructions to teach men the right use of the North-Starre, and other firme starres, profitable for all Seafaring men*. William Iohnson (Amsterdam, 1612), "An Introduction for the understanding of the Celestiall Sphere, Chap. XXV. Of the Sea-cardes," no page number.

58. Ibid.

59. Ibid.

60. The quotation continues: "And dealing in tyme he shall obteine it, wherby he shall know your Carde." Blaeu, *Light of Navigation*, "Chap. XXI. What is necessarie for a Seafaring man or Pilot further to know, together with an instruction to all young Seafaring men, that desire to be good Pilots," no page number.

61. Blaeu was quite open about his assumption that guessing was an important navigational skill:

> You must likewise take heed to your steering, to see how much you must winde on either side in your Carde. And further when you finde a good & sure height, by your Cross-staffee or Astrolabium, that will give you a good securitie of your right gessing, so that your compassing agreeth also with it, and then you shall certainley see in your Carde how all pointes and Countries lye from you, but if your gessing and your height agree not together, then you must warily correct your gessing according to your height, and see as near as you can whether you saile either to litle or to much in your gessing, and all this must be done with good skill and understanding in your Carde, and when you come to the place where you wil seeke for Land, then without doubt you shall land in such a place as your Instrument & good gessing showe you.

Ibid., no page number.

62. Ibid.

63. Ibid. Blaeu made the point several times that reproducing and representing direct experience was a sure path to knowledge:

> To that end when you sayle out of any river or haven, you must reckon everie course along the reach from tonne to tonne, or from beacon to beacon, which you must

keepe well and perfectly and write it in a booke, and some times drawe the situation in manner of a Carde, and when you begin to leave the Land, then you must take good heede, of the Capes, Points, Towres, and other markes, and how the mouth of the Haven reacheth into the Sea, what deapth is at the enterance of the Haven, and how deepe it is both within and without, cast out your lead often tymes, and let it not rest when you are in the Haven nor in the Streame, whereby in sayling out and into the river, you shall know what countries are flattes, or shoring that you may beware of them, & when you are coming without the Land, then you must earnestly marke what hilles or downes lie there aboutes, what churches, towers, casterls, or other markes stand upon them, and those you must note and counterfeit with a péne upon severall strokes of the compasse, as they change their forme of standings by sayling along by them, oftentymes using the lead, all which being perfectly noted, it will be a great help unto you to know the said Landes, when you come thither again.

64. *The Oxford English Dictionary* lists numerous definitions of counterfeit, some of which clearly indicate falseness and an intention to deceive. Other meanings, however, are consistent with the one used here, which denotes a representation of an object at one remove. Definitions include the following: "A.1. made in imitation of that which is genuine; imitated, forged. 2. Made to a pattern; fashioned, wrought. 4. Represented by a picture or image. B.5. Imitated or represented in a picture or image … portrayed. C.3. An imitation or representation in painting, sculpture, etc.; an image, likeness, portrait."

Definitions of the verb *to counterfeit* similarly include meanings that indicate falseness and an intent to deceive. However, they too list now-obsolete meanings that did not imply deception, merely imitation. For instance, "1. to make an imitation of, imitate (with intent to deceive) 2. to make (anything) in fraudulent imitation of something else; to make or devise (something spurious) and pass it off as genuine; to forge 7. to take, receive, or have the appearance of; to 'imitate,' be an imitation of, simulate, resemble, be like (without implying deceit.) 8c. to make an imitation or copy of (a thing) 9. to represent by a picture, statue, or the like; to depict, delineate, portray. Also said of the picture, etc." *Oxford English Dictionary*, 2d ed., prepared by J. A. Simpson and E. S. C. Weiner, vol. 3 cham-creeky (Oxford, UK: Clarendon Press, 1989), 1027–28.

Similarly, the authoritative Dutch dictionary, *Woordenboek der Nederlandsche Taal*, defines *konterfeiten* (obsolete spelling, *conterfeiten*) as "to portray, depict, create an image of something," as well as "to create imitations with an intention to deceive." Definitions for konterfeiten as implying deception include "1a. met betrekking tot personene of hum uitingen of handelingen: nadoen, nabootsen. b. Met betrekking tot zaken: namaken, vervalschen." However, definitions of konterfeiten as creating an image, representation, or portrait include the following: "2. afbeelden, uitbeelden, portretteeren." Moreover, *konterfeytsel* is defined as an image, representation, or portrait: "Konterfeitsel, afbeelding, portret." See *Woordenboek der Nederlandsche Taal*, Zevende Deel. Drie en dertigste Aflevering. Kloekmodedig-Kloot. Bewerkt door Dr. J. Heinsius (Leiden, the Netherlands: Martinus Nijhoff, 1936), 5312–14.

65. Thomas Palmer, *An Essay of the Means how to make our Trauailes, into forraine countries, the more profitable and honourable* (London, 1606), 20.

66. See, for example, John Nicholl, *An Houre Glass of Indian Newes* (London, 1607), B1 recto, and Silvester Jourdain, *Plaine description of the Barmvdas* (London, 1613), A4 recto.

67. See the facsimile reproduced in Hulton, *America 1585*, 39.

68. For an interesting cultural interpretation of Saxton's maps of England see Richard Helgerson, "The Land Speaks: Cartography, Chorography, and Subversion in Renaissance England," *Representations* 16 (1986): 50–85, and Richard Helgerson, *Forms of Nationhood: The Elizabethan Writing of England* (Chicago: University of Chicago Press, 1992).

69. Modern scholars have regarded these maps as remarkably accurate. See, for example, David B. Quinn, "European Perceptions of American Ecology, 1492–1612," in Madsen, ed., *Visions of America since 1492*, 12.

70. David B. Quinn, "Introduction," in *The English New England Voyages 1602–1608*, ed. David B. Quinn and Alison M. Quinn (London: Hakluyt Society, 1983), 9.

71. Samuel Purchas, the great compiler of colonial materials and travel narratives, is known to have destroyed many sources that he was given to read before 1625. See, for example, "Introduction," in ibid., 2.

72. Paul Hulton, "Introduction," in Thomas Harriot, *A Briefe and True Report of the New Found Land of Virginia*. This is the complete 1590 edition with the twenty-eight engravings by Theodor de Bry based on the drawings of John White and other illustrations (New York: Dover, 1972).

73. See, for example, *The New World: The First Pictures of America Made by John White and Jacques le Moyne and Engraved by Theodore de Bry with Contemporary Narratives of the Huguenot Settlement in Florida, 1562–1565 and the Virginia Colony, 1585–1590*, ed. and annotated by Stefan Lorant (New York: Duell, Sloan, and Pearce, 1946). See also Paul Hulton and David B. Quinn, *The American Drawings of John White*, 2 vols. (Chapel Hill: University of North Carolina Press, 1964).

74. The Drake manuscript has been published in a facsimile edition as *Histoire naturelle des Indes: The Drake Manuscript in the Pierpont Morgan Library*, preface by Charles E. Pierce Jr.; foreword by Patrick O'Brian; introduction by Verlyn Klinkenborg; trans. Ruth S. Kraemer (New York: Norton, 1996). The Drake manuscript was not known to scholars until the Pierpont Morgan Library received it as a bequest in 1983.

75. See Barbara Mundy, *The Mapping of New Spain: Indigenous Cartography and the Maps of the Relaciones Geográficas* (Chicago: University of Chicago Press, 1996), 13.

76. Hulton, "Introduction," in Harriot, *Briefe and True Report*, xiv.

77. Other artists who worked for Johan Maurits in Brazil included Georg Markgraf, Zacharias Wagner, and Caspar Schmalkalden. See R. Joppien, "The Dutch Vision of Brazil: Johan Maurits and His artists," in *Johan Maurits van Nassau-Siegen 1604–1679: A Humanist Prince in Europe and Brazil: Essays on the Occasion of the Tercentenary of His Death*, ed. E. van den Boogaart in collaboration with H. R. Hoetink and P. J. P. Whitehead (The Hague: Johan Maurits van Nassau Stichting, 1979), 297–376.

78. Lodewijcksz, *Teerste Boeck*, Bij recto, C recto, D recto, G recto.

79. *Documents relative to the Colonial History of the State of New-York*, ed. E. B. O'Callaghan (Albany, N.Y.: Weed, Parsons, 1856), vol. 1, 262.

80. Greg Dening, "The Theatricality of History Making and the Paradoxes of Acting," in Dening, *Performances*, 108–109.

81. Robert Stafforde, *A Geographicall and Anthologicall description* (London, 1618), 7–67.

82. Ibid., 7.

83. Ibid., 21, 37–38.

84. Harriot, *Briefe and True Report of the New Found Land of Virginia*, 268.

85. Ibid.

86. Ibid.

87. Stafforde, *Geographicall and Anthologicall description*, 29.

88. Laura Hostetler has made a similar argument for early modern China; see *Qing Colonial Enterprise: Ethnography and Cartography in Early Modern China* (Chicago: University of Chicago Press, 2001).

89. Edward Herbert, *The Autobiography of Edward, Lord Herbert of Cherbury*; with introduction, notes, appendices, and a continuation of the life, by Sidney Lee, 2d ed., rev. (New York: Dutton, 1906), 27. See also Lesley B. Cormack, *Charting an Empire: Geography at the English Universities, 1580–1620* (Chicago: University of Chicago Press, 1997).

90. David Harris Sacks has argued that the "body politic" was a central social metaphor for sixteenth-century Bristolians. David Harris Sacks, *The Widening Gate: Bristol and the Atlantic Economy, 1450–1700* (Berkeley: University of California Press, 1991), 192. I suggest that the "body politic" was a central social metaphor for early modern English people generally familiar throughout Europe.

For instance, in *The Defence of Trade*, Dudley Diggs compared England's polity with Powhatan's political organization in Virginia: "As wee are the Bodies of our King, and of our Countrie (though in truth their greatest treasure, witness a •Pohatan, or a P Virginia, without them yet.) This necessarie relatiue of Soueraigntie. Liuing bodies, vnimploi'd are nothing. • A poore naked King of P The goodliest Countrie in the world, were it well inhabited." Diggs, *Defence of Trade*, 32.

91. Joyce Chaplin has noted that Smith probably misunderstood a number of aspects of his contact with the Susquehannocks. She points out that Smith's depiction of the Susquehannock warrior shows him balancing a bow and a pipe, which probably symbolized the offer of an alliance as an alternative to war. See Joyce E. Chaplin, *Subject Matter: Technology, the Body, and Science on the Anglo-American Frontier, 1500–1676* (Cambridge, Mass.: Harvard University Press, 2001), 108.

92. Karen Ordahl Kupperman, ed., *Captain John Smith: A Select Edition of His Writings* (Chapel Hill: Published for the Institute of Early American History and Culture by the University of North Carolina Press, 1988), 98.

93. Smith may well have been wrong about the source of the Susquehannocks' trade goods, but the important point here is that he believed them to have an established trading relationship with the French. For more on this topic see ch. 5, this volume.

94. Both images were adapted from John White's Roanoke drawings; thus each was much more symbolic than representative.

95. These warrior marks were most likely produced by scarification.

96. For additional discussion of this issue see Kupperman, *Settling with the Indians*, 37–39.

CHAPTER 2: LAYING THE GROUNDWORK FOR ALLIANCES

1. French explorer Jacques Cartier sought alliances with some Indian nations in the 1530s, and French, English, Dutch, and Swedish colonial expeditions in the following hundred years similarly tried to learn as much as possible about existing Native American alliances and to participate in them in the most advantageous ways possible.

2. The record shows that a number of Europeans made preemptive strikes against various Indian nations after 1610 and in some cases long afterward. However, they were not as widely used as a preliminary course of action after the first decade of the seventeenth century.

3. For a discussion of English colonists' expectation of treachery and betrayal see Karen Ordahl Kupperman, "English Perceptions of Treachery, 1583–1640: The Case of the American 'Savages,'" *Historical Journal* 20 (1977): 263–87.

4. For a modern analysis of this incident see Karen Ordahl Kupperman, *Roanoke: The Abandoned Colony* (Totowa, N.J.: Rowman Allanheld, 1984). Kupperman points out that the soldiers exacerbated tensions between colonists and Indians because they employed harsh strategies they had learned in European wars.

5. See "Anonymous Journal of the 1585 Virginia Voyage," in *The First Colonists: Documents on the Planting of the First English Settlements in North America 1584–1590*, ed. David B. Quinn and Alison M. Quinn (Raleigh: N.C. Division of Archives and History, 1985), 18. The anonymous author describes one tilt boat, two ship's boats, and a new pinnace and mentions at least forty men who went on the expedition, but his actual account suggests there were more than that.

6. Ibid.

7. Lee Miller has suggested that the silver cup was probably a silver communion chalice, and so its theft was an assault on not only English property but also English Christianity. Lee Miller, *Roanoke: Solving the Mystery of the Lost Colony* (New York: Arcade, 2001).

8. My description is based on a literal reading of a journal that reported the events. However, Quinn and Quinn wrote that Grenville took the remaining boats and continued exploring, while Amadas returned to Aquascococke with his boat. Quinn and Quinn, "Anonymous Journal," 140n5.

9. Ibid., 18.

10. The text is as follows: "not receiving it according to his promise." Ibid.

11. Ibid.

12. Thomas Parramore has offered the intriguing argument that the colonists did not migrate to the Chesapeake Bay but instead journeyed west to the land of other native allies. See Thomas C. Parramore, with Peter C. Stewart and Tommy L. Bogger, *Norfolk: The First Four Centuries* (Charlottesville: University Press of Virginia, 1994), ch. 1, and Thomas C. Parramore, "The 'Lost Colony' Found: A Documentary Perspective," *North Carolina Historical Review* 78 (2001): 67–83. I thank Karen Ordahl Kupperman for directing me to Parramore's work. Lee Miller has also argued that the Lost Colonists went west; see Miller, *Roanoke*. My point here applies to either scenario. Whether they traveled north or west, the Roanoke colonists depended completely on their connections with Indian nations and on the choices they made as to which ones would be their allies.

13. See *The English New England Voyages, 1602–1608*, ed. David B. Quinn and Alison M. Quinn (London: Hakluyt Society, 1983), ser. 2, vol. 161, 231. Quinn notes that Waymouth wanted the opportunity to lead an expedition in search of a northwest passage but also suggests that he may have been responding to reports in 1602 that the Roanoke colonists were still alive.

14. Ibid., 233.

15. Ibid., 234.

16. Ibid., 234–35.

17. Charles M. Hudson, *Knights of Spain, Warriors of the Sun: Hernando de Soto and the South's Ancient Chiefdoms* (Athens: University of Georgia Press, 1997).

18. Quinn and Quinn, *English New England Voyages*, 221. If Indians really did fear one dog as much as twenty of the men, this made the mastiffs an extremely effective weapon. There were only forty-two men on the trip, so Pring was claiming that the Indians were more wary of the two dogs than of the entire human crew.

19. Ibid., 221n4.

20. Ibid., 221.

21. Later colonies also continued to incorporate mastiffs and other dogs (at least in their planning). The *Mayflower's* passenger manifest lists two dogs aboard ship for the Plymouth colonists: one mastiff and one spaniel. The mastiff would presumably have been for defense, war, and perhaps hunting people, while the spaniel would have been for hunting animals.

22. See David B. Quinn's introduction to Thomas Canner's account of the voyage in *New American World: A Documentary History of North America to 1612*, vol. 5, *The Extension of Settlement in Florida, Virginia, and the Spanish Southwest*, ed. David B. Quinn, with the assistance of Alison M. Quinn and Susan Hillier (New York: Arno, 1979), 163.

23. "Thomas Canner's Account of Bartholomew Gilbert's Voyage in Search of Chesapeake Bay," in ibid., 164.

24. Ibid., 166.

25. Ibid.

26. George Percy, "A Discourse of the Plantation of the Southern Colonie in Virginia," in ibid., 268. Percy's account was published by Samuel Purchas in *Purchas his Pilgrimes*, vol. 4 (1625). Purchas likely published only selections from a longer document, but David B. Quinn has argued that Purchas does not seem to have altered the portion he published in any other way. See ibid., 266.

27. Ibid., 268.

28. Ibid., 268–69.

29. Ibid., 269.

30. Jacques Cartier kidnapped at least two Indian men and took them back to France for the winter. There they learned some French and later returned to act as local pilots of Cartier's ships on his second voyage. See Peter Cook, "Kings, Captains, and Kin: French Views of Native American Political Cultures in the Sixteenth and Seventeenth Centuries," in Peter C. Mancall, ed., *The Atlantic World and Virginia, 1550–1624* (Chapel Hill: Published for the Omohundro Institute of Early American History and Culture, Williamsburg, Va., by the University of North Carolina Press, 2007), 319–20. For a discussion of the experiences of numerous kidnapped Americans see Alden T. Vaughan, *Transatlantic Encounters: American Indians in Britain, 1500–1776* (New York: Cambridge University Press, 2006).

31. Harlow had been a Sagadahoc colonist. See Philip L. Barbour, *The Complete Works of Captain John Smith*, vol. 1 (Chapel Hill: Published for the Institute of Early American History and Culture, Williamsburg, Va., by the University of North Carolina Press, 1986), 293. In 1658 Gorges called him Captain Henry Harley, or Captain Harles. Epenow had been seized by a London ship, whose captain first tried to sell him and twenty-nine others as slaves in Spain. However, the Spanish were not buying American

slaves. Epenow then ended up as a living exhibit of wonder in London for a time before Harlow took him to Gorges.

32. Thomas Shepard, *The Clear Sun-Shine of the Gospel Breaking Forth upon the Indians in New-England, or, an Historical Narration of God's Wonderful Workings upon Sundry of the Indians, both Chief Governors and Common People* (London: Cotes for John Bellamy, 1648), includes a description of the difficulties that John Eliot and other ministers encountered in trying to use one Algonquian dialect with a different people who sometimes lived relatively close by. In a description of a 1647 visit to Cape Cod by Thomas Shepard, John Eliot, and other puritans, Shepard noted:

> We first found these Indians (not very farre from ours) to understand (but with much difficulty) the usual language of those in our parts, partly in regard of the different dialect which generally varies in 40 or 60 miles, and partly and especially in regard of their not being accustomed unto sacred language about the holy things of God, wherein Mr. Eliot excels any other of the English that in the Indian language about common matters excel him: I say therefore although they did with much difficulty understand him, yet they did understand him, although by many circumlocutions and variations of speech and the help of one or two interpreters which were then present.

33. Council for New England, *A briefe Relation of the Discovery and Plantation of New England* (London, 1622), B3 recto.

34. Ibid.

35. Gorges, "A Briefe narration of the Originall Undertakings of the Advancement of Plantations into the parts of America" (1658), in *America Painted to the Life* (London, 1659), 15, AAS. Recalling events of earlier years, Gorges wrote this book when he was about seventy years old. His grandson had the book published.

36. Council for New England, *Briefe Relation*, B3 verso.

37. Gorges, "Briefe narration," 20. Gorges commissioned Captain Dermer to explore New England in 1619, and Dermer was engaged in that venture until he died in Virginia in 1621. This event probably took place around 1620.

38. Ibid.

39. Ibid.

40. Gorges clearly suggests that the Council for New England or some of its members were aware of the Tarrantine war (1607–1615), especially of its latter phase, when the Mi'kmaqs moved against the Penobscot sachem Bashabes. See Gorges, "Briefe narration," 17.

41. Ibid, 4.

42. Ibid.

43. Ibid., 4–5.

44. Jogues was in New Amsterdam awaiting passage back to France after his captivity among the Mohawks. See *Narratives of New Netherland, 1609–1664*, ed. J. Franklin Jameson, with three maps and facsimile (New York: Charles Scribner's Sons, 1909), 259. I thank Charles T. Gehring for bringing this passage to my attention.

45. See, for example, Lois M. Feister, "Linguistic Communication between the Dutch and Indians in New Netherland 1609–1664," *Ethnohistory* 20 (1973): 25–38; Ives Goddard, "The Ethnohistorical Implications of Early Delaware Linguistic Materials," *Man in the Northeast* 1 (1971): 14–26; J. Dyneley Prince, "An Ancient New Jersey Indian

Jargon," *American Anthropologist* 14 (1912): 508–24; Richard Rhodes, "Algonquian Trade Languages," in *Papers of the Thirteenth Algonquian Conference*, ed. William Cowan (Ottawa: Carleton University, 1982), 1–10.

46. "Letter of Reverend Jonas Michaelius, 1628," in *Narratives of New Netherland, 1609–1664*, ed. Jameson, 126.

47. Ibid.

48. Ibid., 127.

49. Ibid.

50. Ibid.

51. Ibid. Michaelius had previously served in West Africa, and he owned Angolan slaves in New Netherland.

52. I use the term "pagans" here as early modern Christian Europeans used it—to refer to non-Christians. I do not intend any pejorative meaning.

53. "Letter of Reverend Jonas Michaelius," 127.

54. Ibid.

55. Ibid. Ashdod was an ancient city between the modern towns of Gaza and Jaffa. Throughout its history it was frequently conquered by new invaders but retained a position as a trade outpost. Both elements of its history suggest that people would have spoken many languages there, as well as some kind of a trade language.

56. Ibid.

57. Ibid.

58. Ibid., 128.

59. Ibid.

60. Ibid.

61. Ibid.

62. Ibid.

63. Ibid., 129.

64. The quotation continues:

> Although it would be attended with some expense, we ought, by means of presents and promises, to obtain the children, with the gratitude and consent of the parents, in order to place them under the instruction of some experienced, and godly schoolmaster, where they may be instructed not only to speak, read, and write in our language, but also especially in the fundamentals of our Christian religion; and where, besides, they will see nothing but good examples of virtuous living; but they must sometimes speak their native tongue among themselves in order not to forget it, as being evidently a principal means of spreading the knowledge of religion through the whole nation. (Ibid.)

CHAPTER 3: "YOU CALLED HIM FATHER"

1. *Captain John Smith: A Select Edition of His Writings*, ed. Karen Ordahl Kupperman (Chapel Hill: Published for the Institute of Early American History and Culture by the University of North Carolina Press, 1988), 72.

2. Ibid.

3. Ibid.

4. Ibid.

5. Ibid.

6. Ibid.

7. Ibid.

8. See, for instance, Helen Rountree, "Who Were the Powhatans, and Did They Have a Unified 'Foreign Policy'?" in *Powhatan Foreign Relations, 1500–1722,* ed. Helen Rountree (Charlottesville: University Press of Virginia, 1993), 1–4.

9. Ibid., 5–7.

10. Wayne E. Clark and Helen C. Rountree, "The Powhatans and the Maryland Mainland," in Rountree, ed., *Powhatan Foreign Relations,* 131–32.

11. For instance, Pocahontas was visiting Potawomeck when the English captured her in 1613. For a discussion of the significance of this information with respect to Powhatan foreign relations see ibid.

12. Helen Rountree, "Summary and Implications," in *Powhatan Foreign Relations,* 207–10.

13. The identity and location of the Massawomecks have remained a mystery to scholars. Much of the scholarship that focuses on these issues is summarized in James F. Pendergast, *The Massawomeck: Raiders and Traders into the Chesapeake Bay in the Seventeenth Century,* vol. 81, part 2 (Philadelphia: American Philosophical Society, 1991).

14. See Helen C. Rountree, *The Powhatan Indians of Virginia: Their Traditional Culture* (Norman: University of Oklahoma Press, 1989), 91.

15. There is a great deal of scholarly literature on Pocahontas, and popular treatments of her life and importance are even more numerous. See, for example, Kathleen Brown, *Good Wives, Nasty Wenches, and Anxious Patriarchs: Gender, Race, and Power in Colonial Virginia* (Chapel Hill: Published for the Institute of Early American History and Culture by the University of North Carolina Press, 1998); Susana Dillon, *Mujeres que hicieron America: Biográficas transgresoras* (Buenos Aires: Editorial Catari, 1992), 75–79; Karen Ordahl Kupperman, *Indians and English: Facing Off in Early America* (Ithaca, N.Y.: Cornell University Press, 2000); Leo Lemay, *Did Pocahontas Save John Smith?* (Athens: University of Georgia Press, 1992); Daniel Richter, *Facing East from Indian Country* (Cambridge, Mass.: Harvard University Press, 2001); Helen C. Rountree, *Pocahontas's People: The Powhatan Indians of Virginia through Four Centuries* (Norman: University of Oklahoma Press, 1990); Robert S. Tilton, *Pocahontas: The Evolution of an American Narrative* (New York: Cambridge University Press, 1994).

16. See, for instance, Karen Ordahl Kupperman, *Roanoke: The Abandoned Colony* (New York: Barnes & Noble, 1993); Karen Ordahl Kupperman, *Settling with the Indians: The Meeting of English and Indian Cultures* (Totowa, N.J.: Rowman and Littlefield, 1980); Kupperman, *Indians and English.*

17. Ian Steele, for instance, has written that Powhatan was confident that he and his warriors could control or ultimately destroy the group of barely more than a hundred Englishmen who arrived on the James River in 1607. See Ian K. Steele, *Warpaths: Invasions of North America* (New York: Oxford University Press, 1994), 39. Other scholars have made the same point about Powhatan's assessment of his strength relative to the Virginian colony. See, for example, Christian F. Feest, "Virginia Algonquians," in *The Handbook of North American Indians,* vol. 15, *Northeast,* ed. Bruce Trigger (Washington, D.C.: Smithsonian Institution Press, 1978), 253–70; Rountree, *Pocahontas's People,* 20–24.

18. See Captain John Smith, *The Generall Historie of Virginia, New-England, and the Summer Isles*, bk. 4 of *The Complete Works of Captain John Smith (1580–1631) in Three Volumes*, ed. Philip L. Barbour, vol. 2 (Chapel Hill: Published for the Institute of Early American History and Culture by the University of North Carolina Press, 1986), 261.

19. My analysis of the respective roles of fathers and maternal uncles draws on studies of other matrilineal Algonquians. The evidence for Powhatan child-rearing practices is not as extensive; however, the predominance of the evidence strongly suggests that the Powhatans, like many other Eastern Woodlands Americans, were matrilineal. Thus, I have based this argument on that assumption and by analogy with other Indian nations. In doing so, I am adopting the same methodological approach used by Frederic Gleach in his study of early Powhatan-English contact; see Frederic W. Gleach, *Powhatan's World and Colonial Virginia: A Conflict of Cultures* (Lincoln: University of Nebraska Press, 1997), 31–35.

For a discussion of the evidence in favor of an interpretation of Powhatan descent as matrilineal see Rountree, *Pocahontas's People*, 8–10, and Rountree, *Powhatan Indians of Virginia*, 88–96.

20. Gleach has argued persuasively that Wahunsonacock was an especially powerful leader because he possessed extraordinary spiritual, as well as political, power. See Gleach, *Powhatan's World and Colonial Virginia*, 31–35.

21. On one occasion Wahunsonacock sent Pocahontas with a messenger named Rawhunt to negotiate the release of several Powhatan men held hostage at Jamestown. See Captain John Smith, *A True Relation of Such Occurrences and Accidents of Noate as Hath Hapned in Virginia*, in *Complete Works of Captain John Smith*, vol. 1, 93.

22. Helen Rountree has argued that English and Powhatan cultures were similar in the low status of girls, noting that both lived in a "world in which prepubescent girls had little real power." See Rountree, *Pocahontas's People*, 39–40. I agree with Rountree's assessment. Indeed, the fact that young girls lacked real power in English culture enabled Pocahontas to enjoy extensive access to the English community at Jamestown. That this also served Wahunsonacock's purposes as a leader demonstrates his creativity in dealing with the English settlement.

23. Smith made this statement in his 1617 letter to Queen Anne during Pocahontas's visit to England. See Smith, *Generall Historie*, bk. 4, 259.

24. Some scholars refer to the ongoing violence between Powhatans and English during the 1610s as the first Anglo-Powhatan war. Initially, by putting the Powhatans' political and military objectives on the same footing as the Europeans', this terminology provided a useful balance to older views of Indian attacks as massacres of innocent colonists or as random, senseless violence by uncivilized peoples. However, Gleach has argued that this term unintentionally privileges European cultural perspectives and that the European notion of a war is an inaccurate concept for the relationship between Powhatans and English from the Powhatans' perspectives, even during violent confrontations. For a discussion of this point and Gleach's theory of a Powhatan aesthetic of war see Gleach, *Powhatan's World and Colonial Virginia*, 4–6, 43–54.

25. For this reason, some scholars question whether the event actually happened. Rountree, for instance, has suggested that Smith fabricated the story as part of his efforts to take advantage of Pocahontas's celebrity in London. See Rountree, *Pocahontas's People*, 38–39.

26. Helen Rountree disputes the adoption theory on the grounds that too little is known about specifically Powhatan adoption rituals and that Smith's account of his attempted, or mock, execution is not consistent with the status with which he would have been received. See Rountree, *Powhatan Indians of Virginia*, 121.

Several other scholars such as Philip Barbour and J. Frederick Fausz have argued that the event did occur but that Smith mistook an adoption ceremony for an aborted execution. Frederic W. Gleach has reconsidered the earlier arguments of Barbour and Fausz, along with Rountree's critique. Setting earlier interpretations against evidence about adoption rituals of other Eastern Woodlands peoples, Gleach makes a very persuasive case for the Powhatan ceremony as one that adopted Smith and the entire English colony into the Powhatan world. See Gleach, *Powhatan's World and Colonial Virginia*, 116–122. For a recent discussion of Wahunsonacock's attempt to incorporate the Jamestown settlers as a subsidiary people and of his offer of kinship to Smith see James Horn, "Imperfect Understandings: Rumor, Knowledge, and Uncertainty in Early Virginia," in Peter C. Mancall, ed., *The Atlantic World and Virginia, 1550–1624* (Chapel Hill: Published for the Omohundro Institute of Early American History and Culture, Williamsburg, Va., by the University of North Carolina Press, 2007), 526.

27. Smith described this event only in *The Generall Historie of Virginia, New-England, and the Summer Isles*, first published in 1624, long after the events he reported in it. Moreover, it was published not only after Pocahontas and Wahunsonacock had died but also after the 1622 Powhatan attack on the Virginia colonists, which marked the definitive end of the alliance. See Smith, *Generall Historie*, bk. 3, 151–52.

28. For a similar interpretation of Wahunsonacock's efforts to incorporate Smith and the Jamestown English see Margaret Holmes Williamson, "Pocahontas and Captain John Smith: Examining a Historical Myth," *History and Anthropology* 5 (1992): 365–402.

29. A similar transition was part of the Powhatan coming-of-age ceremony for boys, called the Huskanaw. During the Huskanaw, boys who had reached puberty were taken from their families and placed under the care of a spiritual leader, who guided them through a series of arduous initiation rituals in which their boyhood identities "died." Afterward, the young men returned to the community with new adult identities. See, for example, Rountree, "Who Were the Powhatans?" 5; Clark and Rountree, "Powhatans and the Maryland Mainland," 120.

30. James Horn has made a similar point. See James Horn, *A Land as God Made It: Jamestown and the Birth of America* (New York: Basic Books, 2005).

31. Smith, *Generall Historie*, bk. 3, 183.

32. Ibid., 184.

33. Ibid.

34. Gregory Waselkov has argued that the mantle in the Ashmolean is the one Powhatan gave to Smith and that it represents a map of Powhatan's paramount chiefdom. See Gregory A. Waselkov, "Indian Maps of the Colonial Southeast," in *Powhatan's Mantle: Indians in the Colonial Southeast*, ed. Peter H. Wood, Gregory A. Waselkov, and M. Thomas Hatley (Lincoln: University of Nebraska Press, 1989), 292–334.

35. The many accounts of Wahunsonacock's majestic and dignified demeanor are consistent not only with his position as paramount chief but also with Frederic Gleach's argument that Wahunsonacock was particularly powerful because he possessed the

qualities of a revered military and political leader, as well as a great spiritual leader. Gleach, *Powhatan's World and Colonial Virginia*, 31–35.

36. Smith, *Generall Historie*, bk. 3, 184.

37. Indeed, in the days before the ritual crowning, when Wahunsonacock told Smith that he would not travel to Jamestown and that Newport, as an emissary of King James, must journey to see Wahunsonacock in his own territory, Wahunsonacock also told Smith that he was greatly mistaken about the geography of Tsenacommacah. Smith added, "whereupon he began to draw plots upon the ground (according to his discourse) of all those Regions." See ibid., 183.

38. Ibid., 243–44.

39. See, for instance, Stephen R. Potter's discussion of the Virginia Company's directives to the colonists in Stephen R. Potter, "Early English Effects on Virginia Algonquian Exchange and Tribute in the Tidewater Potomac," in *Powhatan's Mantle*, ed. Waselkov, Wood, and Hatley, 158.

40. Potter notes that the Patawomekes played a crucial role in trade networks that ran through the Chesapeake region and that some scholars have interpreted their name as meaning "trading center." See ibid. and Philip L. Barbour, "The Earliest Reconnaissance of the Chesapeake Bay Area," *Virginia Magazine of History and Biography* 79(3) (1971): 240.

41. Ralph Hamor's description of Pocahontas's kidnapping suggests that the Patawomekes controlled a great portion of regional trade and may have held regular trading sessions that, to the colonists, resembled English market days. Ralph Hamor, *A True Discourse of the Present Estate of Virginia* (London, 1615), 4.

42. See Smith, *Generall Historie*, bk. 3, 245.

43. On Dale's marriage proposal see Rountree, *Pocahontas's People*, 60.

44. Smith also reported that, "Arriving at Plimoth, according to his [Uttamatomakin's] directions, he got a long sticke, whereon by notches hee did thinke to have kept the number of all the men hee could see, but he was quickly wearie of that taske." Smith, *Generall Historie*, bk. 3, 261.

45. Ibid.

CHAPTER 4: ALLIANCE MAKING AND THE STRUGGLE FOR THE SOUL OF PLYMOUTH COLONY

1. Bradford's history has been published in several versions. Throughout this chapter I rely on Samuel Eliot Morison's edition. See William Bradford, *Of Plymouth Plantation 1620–1647*, ed. Samuel Eliot Morison (New York: Knopf, 1987).

2. Ibid., 86.

3. I have traced Allerton's residency and property ownership through town and colony court records, church membership lists, and the probate recording of his will. He lived in the colonies of Plymouth, Massachusetts Bay, New Netherland, and New Haven. In each of those colonies and in Virginia he owned property. His trading network included Plymouth, Massachusetts Bay, New Netherland, New Haven, New Sweden, Virginia, Barbados, Curaçao, and England. He held office in Plymouth and New Netherland.

4. Ira Berlin has demonstrated that a significant number of mostly mixed-race peoples relied quite successfully on similarly flexible identities and strategies. Dubbed "Atlantic

Creoles" by Berlin, these people played a vitally important role in the early Atlantic world. Ira Berlin, "From Creole to African: Atlantic Creoles and the Origins of African-American Society in Mainland North America," *William and Mary Quarterly*, 3d. ser., 53 (1996): 251–88; Ira Berlin, *Many Thousands Gone: The First Two Centuries of Slavery in North America* (Cambridge, Mass.: Belknap Press of Harvard University Press, 1998).

5. For instance, Charles M. Andrews mentions many of Allerton's transcolonial ventures but does not connect them because, after Allerton left Plymouth, he became peripheral to Andrews's main narrative. See Andrews, *The Colonial Period of American History*, 4 vols. (New Haven, Conn.: Yale University Press, 1934–1938), vol. 1, 274, 285, 286, 288–89, 294, 318, 345, 404; vol. 2, 154n, 174n, 175. Allerton did not spend enough time in Massachusetts Bay to warrant sustained attention by Bernard Bailyn in *The New England Merchants in the Seventeenth Century* (Cambridge, Mass.: Harvard University Press, 1955); Isabel Calder, in her history of New Haven Colony, devoted some attention to Allerton, but because she was focusing on the fortunes of one colony, Allerton was not central to the account. Calder, *The New Haven Colony* (New Haven, Conn.: Yale University Press, 1934). David Hackett Fischer has conflated Allerton's activities with those of his son and described the two as one person because Allerton senior's wide-ranging commercial and cultural connections and identifications did not fit clearly within a more circumscribed story and because, in such an account, it is extremely difficult to uncover enough information about people like Allerton. See Fischer, *Albion's Seed: Four British Folkways in America* (New York: Oxford University Press, 1989), 218–19n11.

6. Stephen Innes, *Creating the Commonwealth: The Economic Culture of Puritan New England* (New York: Norton, 1995); John Frederick Martin, *Profits in the Wilderness: Entrepreneurship and the Founding of New England Towns in the Seventeenth Century* (Chapel Hill: Published for the Institute of Early American History and Culture, Williamsburg, Va., by the University of North Carolina Press, 1991); Mark A. Peterson, *The Price of Redemption: The Spiritual Economy of Puritan New England* (Stanford, Calif.: Stanford University Press, 1997).

7. I estimate Allerton's age would have been twenty-two in 1608 because he gave a deposition in 1639 in which he stated that his age was "about 53 yeares." If Allerton were fifty-three in 1639, then he would have been born in 1586. See *Notebook Kept by Thomas Lechford, Esq., Lawyer, in Boston, Massachusetts Bay, from June 27, 1638, to July 29, 1641, Archaeologia Americana, Transactions and Collections of the American Antiquarian Society*, vol. 7 (Cambridge, Mass., 1885), 189.

See also Walter S. Allerton, *A History of the Allerton Family in the United States, 1585–1885, and a Genealogy of the Descendants of Isaac Allerton, "Mayflower Pilgrim," Plymouth Massachusetts, 1620* (Chicago: Samuel Waters Allerton, 1900); Charles Edward Banks, *The English Ancestry and Homes of the Pilgrim Fathers, Who Came to Plymouth on the "Mayflower" in 1620, the "Fortune" in 1621, and the "Anne" and the "Little James" in 1623* (New York, 1929); Eugene Aubrey Stratton, *Plymouth Colony: Its History and People, 1620–1691* (Salt Lake City: Ancestry Publishing, 1986), 234. Stratton is the most accurate secondary source for biographical information about Isaac Allerton.

8. Stratton, *Plymouth Colony*, provides biographical details of Isaac and Mary Allerton's children, Bartholomew, Remember, and Mary. Other genealogists have argued that the couple had another daughter, Sarah. However, Stratton maintains that Sarah was

the daughter of Isaac and his second wife, Fear Brewster, and was born in Plymouth Colony; see 233–35. Another child died in Leiden and was buried in St. Pieters; see Henry Martyn Dexter and Morton Dexter, *The England and Holland of the Pilgrims* (New York, 1905), 583.

9. For a discussion of Allerton's work in Leiden see Stratton, *Plymouth Colony*, 18–19, 30. For the assertion that Allerton learned Dutch while living in Leiden see Walter S. Allerton, *A History of the Allerton Family in the United States, 1585 to 1885, and a Genealogy of the Descendants of Isaac Allerton*, 508–52, and Lora Altine Woodbury Underhill, *Descendants of Edward Small of New England and the Allied Families with Tracings of English Ancestry* (Boston and New York: Houghton Mifflin, 1934).

Wherever he learned it, colonial records clearly indicate that Allerton knew Dutch when he lived in North America. A number report him acting as an interpreter between English and Dutch colonists and for the tribunals of various colonies. For example, in 1658 in New Amsterdam Allerton translated for the burgomasters [chief magistrates of a town] and *schepens* [alderpersons] in a dispute over a seaman's wages. "Robert Passele, pltf. v/s Skipper Igsiter, deft., demands payment of eight months wages @ fl.18. per month earned from deft. As a seaman. Deft requests Mr. Allerton as interpreter, who appears in Court." *Records of New Amsterdam, 1653 to 1679*, vol. 2, *Burgomaster and Schepens*, 381. In early 1654 and 1655 he testified as a witness on behalf of "Lawranc Corneliusson, a Dutchman," before the New Haven Court of Magistrates, *New Haven Colony Records*, vol. 2, 126.

For Allerton's participation in the planning stages of the migration to North America see the June 10, 1620, letter of Samuel Fuller, Edward Winslow, William Bradford, and Isaac Allerton to John Carver and Robert Cushman in Bradford, *Of Plymouth Plantation*, appendix III, "Correspondence of June 1620 between the Leyden Committee and their Agents in London, on the Agreement with the Adventurers," 360–61.

10. For instance, Thomas Palmer wrote that many travelers were other than they pretended to be. Many, he warned, were secretly intelligencers, or spies. Thomas Palmer, *An Essay of the Means how to make our Travailes, into forraine Countries, the more profitable and honourable* (London, 1606).

Some dissimulation was considered excusable, as, for instance, when someone publicly professed one faith because of political pressure and persecution while secretly adhering to another. See, for example, Edward Brerewood, *Enquiries Touching the Diversity of Languages, and Religions through the cheife parts of the world* (London, 1614), ¶¶ verso.

See also Perez Zagorin, *Ways of Lying: Dissimulation, Persecution, and Conformity in Early Modern Europe* (Cambridge, Mass.: Harvard University Press, 1990). See also Stephen Greenblatt, *Renaissance Self-fashioning: From More to Shakespeare* (Chicago: University of Chicago Press, 2005); and Greenblatt, *Sir Walter Ralegh: The Renaissance Man and His Roles* (New Haven, Conn.: Yale University Press, 1973).

11. William Castell, *A Short Discoverie of the Coasts and Continent of America* (London, 1644), bk. 2, 53. Castell suggested that accounts of Spanish success in converting Indians to Roman Catholicism were exaggerated in order to persuade English Protestants to stay away from potentially lucrative colonial regions.

12. See, for example, Norbert Elias, *The History of Manners*, trans. Edmund Jephcott. Vol. 1 of *The Civilizing Process* (New York: Pantheon, 1982). See also *A Cultural History*

of Gesture, ed. Jan Bremmer and Herman Roodenburg (Ithaca, N.Y.: Cornell University Press, 1992); Zagorin, *Ways of Lying*.

13. In 1621 the Plymouth colonists reported to their supporters in England and the United Provinces that they had selected Allerton as assistant to the new governor, William Bradford. In his account of these years, Bradford wrote that the two men "by renewed election every year, continued sundry years together." Bradford, *Of Plymouth Plantation*, 86. Allerton began working as factor between the colonists and the London merchants who supported them when he and Edward Winslow went to England in 1624; see ibid., 174–75. See also *Governor William Bradford's Letter Book* (Boston, 1906), 9.

14. In 1626 Allerton negotiated a debt purchase agreement with the London merchants who had backed the colony. He carried the agreement back to Plymouth for the other colonists to consider; they agreed to its terms in 1627. See Bradford, *Of Plymouth Plantation*, 182–83; George D. Langdon Jr., *Pilgrim Colony: A History of New Plymouth, 1620–1691* (New Haven, Conn.: Yale University Press, 1966); Charles M. Andrews, *The Colonial Period of American History*, vol. 1, *The Settlements*, 284–85; and Stratton, *Plymouth Colony*, 27–28, 32, 44. Stratton provides a good, succinct explanation of Plymouth's debt purchase. For a fuller treatment see Ruth A. McIntyre, *Debts Hopeful and Desperate: Financing the Plymouth Colony* (Plymouth, Mass.: Plimouth Plantation, 1963). For a list of the colonists who agreed to purchase the debts see Bradford, *Of Plymouth Plantation*, 197. For a list that was apparently compiled later see *Plymouth Colony Records, Court Orders*, vol. 2, *1641–1651*, 177.

On Allerton's success in acquiring a patent for land along the Kennebec in 1628 see Bradford, *Of Plymouth Plantation*, 193, 200, and Stratton, *Plymouth Colony*, 44. The patent and the charter were vitally important because the Plymouth settlement was outside the boundaries of its Virginia Company patent and its next patent, issued in 1621 by the Council for New England, was for only seven years; in addition, the group wanted authority to expand northward to gain better access to furs. The original patent is referred to as the Peirce patent for the named grantee; see, for example, Bradford, *Of Plymouth Plantation*, 93.

15. Stratton has described Allerton as a kind of "'minister of Foreign Affairs and Trade,'" which is one of the best descriptions of his role as Plymouth's London agent. See Stratton, *Plymouth Colony*, 44.

16. On the importance of kinship ties in early colonial trade networks see David Cressy, *Coming Over: Migration and Communication between England and New England in the Seventeenth Century* (New York: Cambridge University Press, 1987), and Oliver A. Rink, *Holland on the Hudson: An Economic and Social History of Dutch New York* (Ithaca, N.Y.: Cornell University Press, 1989).

When Allerton's youngest son, Isaac Allerton Jr., reached adulthood, he participated in trade for a brief time, assisting his father and using his father's networks to establish his own standing. However, this was a short phase of his life. Apparently wanting to set his son up as a landed gentleman, the elder Allerton purchased land in Virginia's Northern Neck in 1650. The younger Allerton did indeed become a Virginia gentleman, attaining the rank of colonel in the militia and serving in the House of Burgesses and as a justice of the peace. Allerton senior also included his brother-in-law, Jonathan Brewster, in his trade network at times, but most of it depended upon nonkinship connections.

17. Wampanoag is the name now used by modern descendants of the Pokanokets. See Kathleen J. Bragdon, *Native People of Southern New England, 1500–1650* (Norman: University of Oklahoma Press, 1996), 21.

18. *Mourt's Relation: A Journal of the Pilgrims at Plymouth*, introduction by Dwight B. Heath (Boston: Applewood, 1986), 58. *Mourt's Relation* is thought to be a compilation of entries from the journals of Edward Winslow and William Bradford.

19. Allerton's negotiations for the Kennebec patent and a new royal charter for the colony brought him into contact with court circles. The Kennebec patent became known as the Bradford patent because William Bradford was the named grantee. The other colonist was Edward Winslow.

20. For an overview of the history of Morton's colony see Andrews, *Colonial Period of American History*, vol. 1, 332–34.

21. Bradford recorded his version of these events. See *Of Plymouth Plantation*, 205–208.

22. Ibid., 205.

23. Ibid., 216.

24. Ibid.

25. See Cynthia J. Van Zandt, "The Dutch Connection: Isaac Allerton and the Dynamics of English Cultural Anxiety in the Gouden Eeuw," in *Connecting Cultures: The Netherlands in Five Centuries of Transatlantic Exchange*, ed. Rosemarijn Hoefte and Johanna C. Kardux. European Contributions to American Studies, gen. ed. Rob Kroes (Amsterdam: VU University Press, 1994), 51–76.

26. See ibid., 66–67.

27. *Governor Bradford's Letter Book*, 34–35.

28. Ibid.

29. On wampum's transition from an object of spiritual power used in rituals to a medium of exchange see Lynn Ceci, "Native Wampum as a Peripheral Resource in the Seventeenth-century World System," in *The Pequots in Southern New England: The Fall and Rise of an American Indian Nation*, ed. Laurence M. Hauptman and James D. Wherry (Norman: University of Oklahoma Press, 1990), 48, 63.

30. Bradford, *Of Plymouth Plantation*, 203.

31. Ibid. "Fort Orania" was Bradford's spelling for the New Netherland Fort Oranje, now Albany.

32. Ibid.

33. Ibid., 193, 200. See also Stratton, *Plymouth Colony*, 44.

34. Charles M. Andrews placed the site of the Penobscot post at present-day Castine; *Colonial Period of American History*, vol. 1, *Settlements*, 288.

35. Bradford, *Of Plymouth Plantation*, 219.

36. Ibid.

37. According to Bradford, in 1631 "Ashley likewise was taken in a trap . . . for trading powder and shot with the Indians; and was seized upon by some in authority"; ibid., 232–33.

38. Morton also wrote and published the satirical *New English Canaan*, in which he set forth his version of life among the puritans of New England, including the separatists of Plymouth.

39. Andrews remains the best survey of the various colonial projects that competed during the early seventeenth century; *Colonial Period of American History*, vol. 1,

Settlements, 413. He provides very useful background on the struggle between Gorges and the Massachusetts Bay factions at 400–429. See also *Winthrop's Journal*, vol. 1, 127, 129.

40. Winslow took over Allerton's role as Plymouth's factor in the 1630s, after the most explosive round of differences turned into open conflict.

41. Morton was a lawyer and a member of Clifford's Inn. See Andrews, *Colonial Period of American History*, vol. 1, 332.

42. Ibid., 420–21.

43. The letter is dated the "1 of the 5th mo. 1637," *The Winthrop Papers*, ed. Allyn Bailey Forbes (Boston: Massachusetts Historical Society, 1943), vol. 3, 437.

44. Ibid.

45. Ibid. Isaac Allerton was Winslow's neighbor in Plymouth. A scheme of the "meer-steads & garden plotes of [those] which came first layed out 1620" shows Francis Cooke had the plot between "Mr. Isaak Allerton" and "Edward Winslow" on the south side of the street. See *Records of the colony of New Plymouth, in New England. Printed by order of the legislature of the commonwealth of Massachusetts*, vol. 12, ed. David Pusifer, *Plymouth Colony Deeds 1620–1651 and Indian Records* (Boston: W. White, 1861), 3. I thank Ian Aebel for his assistance with this reference.

46. *Winthrop Papers*, vol. 4, 304.

47. Ibid.

48. Ibid.

49. Allerton, for instance, was a respected member of the New Haven church. He and his wife had prominent seats in the New Haven town meetinghouse. See Franklin Bowditch Dexter, ed., *New Haven Town Records, 1649–1662*, New Haven Colony Historical Society, Ancient Town Records, vol. 1 (New Haven, Conn., 1917), 270–73.

50. "Richard Iles of Charlestown in New England, Carpenter," sought Allerton's help to recover his servant on Mar. 19, 1638/1639. See *Notebook Kept by Thomas Lechford*, 270–73.

51. "Peter Garland of New England, Mariner," appointed Allerton his attorney to recover a debt from Thomas Beech; ibid., 35–36.

52. James Perry, *The Formation of a Society on Virginia's Eastern Shore, 1615–1655* (Chapel Hill, University of North Carolina Press, published for the Institute of Early American History and Culture, 1988), 148, emphasizes this shift in colonial trade patterns and its effect on Virginia's eastern shore. In *New England Merchants* Bailyn makes a similar point on the effect of the English civil war on New England's trade. The activities of people like Allerton demonstrate that the change affected an entire economic system.

53. Bradford, *Of Plymouth Plantation*, 347.

54. For examples of references to "Mr. Allerton" see Bradford, *Of Plymouth Plantation*; Charles Jeremy Hoadly, ed., *Records of the Colony and Plantation of New Haven from 1638–1649* (Hartford, Conn.: Case, Tiffany and Company, 1857), vol. 1, 116, 304, 309; *New Haven Town Records, 1649–1662*, 145–46; *New York Historical Manuscripts, Dutch*, vols. GG, HH, and II, land papers (Dutch period), trans. and ed. Charles T. Gehring (Baltimore, 1981), 30, 35; John Romeyn Brodhead, *Documents relative to the Colonial Period of the State of New-York; Procured in Holland, England, and France*, ed. Edmund Bailey O'Callaghan (Albany, 1856), vol. 12, trans. B. Fernow, 63, 98, 120 (hereafter cited as *NYCD*); Nathaniel Bradstreet Shurteff, ed., *Plymouth Colony Records*, vol. 1, 20, 21, 32–33;

Records of the Court of Assistants of the Colony of the Massachusetts Bay 1630–1692, vol. 2 (Boston, 1904), 46.

55. Allerton was in New Amsterdam by 1639 at the latest and probably was there as many as four years earlier. In 1639, for example, New Netherland director general Willem Kieft offered to trade corn or money to Allerton for tobacco. See Edmund Bailey O'Callaghan, *Calendar of Dutch Historical Manuscripts in the Office of the Secretary of State, Albany, New York 1630–1664* (1856; repr., Ridgewood, N.J.: Gregg, 1968), vol. 1, 5.

It is not clear when Allerton first went to New Haven to live. He evidently had a presence there by at least 1642 because he sold the yacht *Hope* to Govert Loockermans in New Amsterdam, reserving the right of a return trip to Rodeberch, the Dutch name for New Haven. See John H. Innes, *New Amsterdam and Its People: Studies, Social and Topographical, of the Town under Dutch and Early English Rule* (Port Washington, N.Y.: Friedman, 1969), vol. 2, 335. Allerton was probably attracted to New Haven's large harbor and location near New Amsterdam. In addition, New Haven was an especially suitable home for a merchant because it was founded by a group of London merchants who, as puritans, had left England for North America.

56. See, for example, Paul Otto, *The Dutch-Munsee Encounter in America: The Struggle for Sovereignty in the Hudson Valley* (New York: Berghahn, 2006), and Donna Merwick, *The Shame and the Sorrow: Dutch-Amerindian Encounters in New Netherland* (Philadelphia: University of Pennsylvania Press, 2006).

57. *NYCD*, vol. 1, 192–93, for the "Certificate of the Election of the Eight Men." Allerton's signature appears on the various petitions from the Eight Men; see also 139–40, 209–13. Forty-six men constituted the "Commonality of the Manhattans," who gave their consent to the creation of the Eight Men; see 191–92. This conflict has become known as Governor Kieft's Indian war because Kieft's unchecked antagonism provoked open hostilities with the Munsees.

58. Thomas Hall was another English merchant who lived and traded in New Amsterdam and became one of the Eight. See *NYCD*, vol. 1, 191–92.

59. Allerton and Captain John Underhill appeared before a general court at New Haven to request troops for New Netherland on Oct. 27, 1643. See Hoadly, ed., *Records of the Colony and Plantation*, vol. 1, 116.

60. *Proceedings of the Massachusetts Historical Society*, vol. 84 (Boston: Massachusetts Historical Society, 1973), 105–109. For an introduction to the letters and a discussion of the context in which they were written see Jon Butler, "Two 1642 Letters from Virginia Puritans," *Massachusetts Historical Society Proceedings* 84 (1974): 99–109. The first letter was "To the Pastors and Elders of Christs Church in New England and the Rest of the Faithfull," from "Richard Bennet," "Dan Gaking" (perhaps Daniel Gookin), and "John Hyll &c. to the number of 71," 105–106. The second letter was "To the Reverend Mr John Davenport Pastor of the Church of Christ at Quilopyacke, Present These: In New England," from "William Durand" in Norfolk, Va., 107, 109. Quilopyacke was a variation on Quinnipiac, the Algonquian name initially adopted by the New Haven colonists.

61. *Winthrop's Journal*, vol. 2, 94.

62. Ibid.

63. Ibid.

64. O'Callaghan, *Calendar of Dutch Historical Manuscripts*, vol. 2, 31; vol. 4, 96–105. See also *The Records of New Amsterdam from 1653 to 1674 Anno Domini*, ed. Berthold

Fernow, *Vol. I: Minutes of the Court of Burgomasters and Schepens 1653–1655* (New York: Knickerbocker Press, 1897), 226.

65. O'Callaghan, *Calendar of Dutch Historical Manuscripts*, vol. 4, 86.

66. Ibid. Allerton was on the receiving end of a smuggling venture more than once, and there is no record that he suffered for it. For example, proceedings were brought "against Thomas Hall, on a charge of smuggling a quantity of malt to Isaac Allerton" in New Netherland, Sept. 8, 1654; ibid., vol. 5, council minutes, 141.

67. The Eight sent petitions in 1643 as the Indian crisis escalated. See O'Callaghan, ed., *NYCD*, vol. 1, 190–91, 209–13; see also *NYCD*, vol. 12, *Documents relating to the History and Settlements of the Towns along the Hudson and Mohawk Rivers (with the Exception of Albany), from 1630–1684*, 16; O'Callaghan, *Calendar of Dutch Historical Manuscripts*, 87.

68. *Winthrop Papers*, vol. 4, 507–508.

69. In 1644 Allerton was one of several merchants who sold tobacco to New Sweden governor Printz to resupply the *Swan* for its return trip to Sweden; see Amandus Johnson, *Swedish Settlements on the Delaware; their history and relation to the Indians, Dutch, and English, 1638–1664, with an account of the South, the New Sweden, and the American Companies, and the efforts of Sweden to regain the colony* (New York: University of Pennsylvania, D. Appleton & co, 1911), vol. 1, 316–18. Allerton sold 11,346 pounds of tobacco at five stivers/pound. On this trip he arrived too late; other merchants had brought too much tobacco for the market, and Allerton was forced to reduce his prices from seven stivers/pound. He did, however, sell a much larger quantity than other merchants who received a higher price.

70. By 1643 Allerton had a trade relationship with Thomas Bushrode of Kichatagn in Virginia. "Phillip White of New England Mariner Anthony Hodgkins of Virginia Inholder and George Roome of Reade Island in New England Seaman" entered into an agreement with Bushrode to pay Allerton "one Thousand pounds weight of good and well conditioned Porke at the Manhawtus." Susie Ames, ed., *County Court Records of Accomack-Northampton, Virginia 1640–1645* (Charlottesville: University Press of Virginia, 1973), 379.

71. In addition to trading in Virginia, Allerton bought land in Northumberland county in 1650. He may well have been intending to set his son up as a landed gentleman; see note 16, this chapter. See also, for example, a complaint of the Machoatick Indians about Allerton's plantation in *William and Mary Quarterly* 1st ser. 8 (1899/1900): 24.

72. See, for example, Johnson, *Swedish Settlements on the Delaware*, vol. 1, 339–40. Virginia trader Edmund Scarburgh was one of the merchants stopped by Stuyvesant; see Perry, *Formation of a Society*; Suzy Ames, *Studies of the Virginia Eastern Shore in the Seventeenth Century* (New York: Russell and Russell, 1940).

73. Johnson, *Swedish Settlements on the Delaware*, vol. 1, 437.

74. Innes, *History of New Amsterdam*, vol. 1, 42.

75. O'Callaghan, *Calendar of Dutch Historical Manuscripts*, 57.

76. Allerton evidently provided detailed information about the size and strength of the naval force but did not confirm whether New Netherland was its target. The council minutes of May 30, 1654, state the following:

> Rumors have been circulating for several days, which were confirmed in detail last evening by Dr. Isaacq [*sic*] Allerton, that 10 or 12 days ago six ships arrived at Boston

from Old England, namely, two merchantmen and four capital ships of the parliament or the present government of England, having on board Colonel Sussex, Captain Leverdt and Captain Huk, and a certain number of soldiers aboard each ship. also some munitions of war and engineering equipment. However, he, Allerton, declared not to know whether they were to be used against us or against the French, because the instructions had not yet been opened and were not to be opened until ten days after their arrival in Boston.

See *Council Minutes, 1652–1654, New York Historical Manuscripts: Dutch*, vol. 5, trans. and ed. Charles T. Gehring (Baltimore: Genealogical Publishing, 1983), 138. See also O'Callaghan, *Calendar of Dutch Historical Manuscripts*, 137. The meaning of "Dr." in relation to Allerton is not clear. I have seen no other reference to him as "Dr."

77. Stellan Dahlgren and Hans Norman, *The Rise and Fall of New Sweden: Governor Johan Rising's Journal 1654–1655 in Its Historical Context* (Uppsala: Uppsala University Press, 1988), 179.

78. Ibid., 31, 179, 185–87; Johnson, *Swedish Settlements on the Delaware*, vol. 2, 515–16, 579. New Haven officials gave Allerton a letter for delivery to Governor Rising in the fall of 1654.

79. Johnson, *Swedish Settlements on the Delaware*, vol. 2, 579.

80. Ibid.

81. Dahlgren and Norman, *Rise and Fall of New Sweden*, 183. Stuyvesant's question illustrates the uncertainty he felt with so many English residents of the colony. More important, it demonstrates his trust in Allerton because Allerton was free to go and to return without penalty.

82. John Davenport to John Winthrop Jr., in Isabel Calder, ed., *The Letters of John Davenport, Puritan Divine* (New Haven, Conn.: Published for the First Church of Christ in New Haven by Yale University Press, 1934), 125.

83. For an account of the disappearance and rediscovery of Bradford's manuscript see Samuel Eliot Morison's introduction to *Of Plymouth Plantation*, xxvii–xl.

84. See Bradford, *Of Plymouth Plantation*, 202, 216–18, 232; McIntyre, *Debts Hopeful and Desperate*, 52–60.

CHAPTER 5: CAPTAIN CLAIBORNE'S ALLIANCE

1. For a detailed examination of early trade in Virginia see Susan E. Hillier, "The Trade of the Virginia Colony, 1606 to 1660," PhD diss., University of Liverpool, 1971. For a discussion of the importance of the fur trade in Virginia through the 1630s see p. 290. For a more recent exploration of Virginia's extensive intercolonial ties, with sensitive attention to intercultural dimensions of intercolonial trade, see April Lee Hatfield, *Atlantic Virginia: Intercolonial Relations in the Seventeenth Century* (Philadelphia: University of Pennsylvania Press, 2004).

2. See, for instance, Bernard Bailyn, *The New England Merchants in the Seventeenth Century* (Cambridge, Mass.: Harvard University Press, 1955); Allen W. Trelease, *Indian Affairs in Colonial New York: The Seventeenth Century* (Lincoln: University of Nebraska Press, 1997); José António Brandão, *"Your Fyre Shall Burn No More": Iroquois Policy*

toward New France and Its Native Allies to 1701 (Lincoln: University of Nebraska Press, 1997).

3. This chapter owes a great deal to the pioneering studies of Francis Jennings and J. Frederick Fausz. In the 1960s Jennings insisted that the history of European colonies in seventeenth-century North America could not be fully understood without knowledge of the Susquehannocks. See Francis Jennings, "Glory, Death, and Transfiguration: The Susquehannock Indians in the Seventeenth Century," *Proceedings of the American Philosophical Society* 112 (1968): 15–53.

Fausz first wrote extensively on the Susquehannocks' trade relationship with William Claiborne and the London trading firm of William Cloberry. Moreover, his work also emphasized the importance of intercultural alliances in the seventeenth-century Chesapeake. See J. Frederick Fausz, "Present at the 'Creation': The Chesapeake World That Greeted the Maryland Colonists," *Maryland Historical Magazine* 79 (1984): 7–20; J. Frederick Fausz, "Merging and Emerging Worlds: Anglo-Indian Interest Groups and the Development of the Seventeenth-century Chesapeake," in *Colonial Chesapeake Society*, ed. Lois Green Carr, Philip D. Morgan, and Jean B. Russo (Chapel Hill: Published for the Institute of Early American History and Culture, Williamsburg, Va., by the University of North Carolina Press, 1988), 47–98.

4. James Rice has suggested that the Susquehannocks and the Tockwoghs both wanted the English as allies in these early meetings. James D. Rice, "Escape from Tsenacommacah: Chesapeake Algonquians and the Powhatan Menace," in *The Atlantic World and Virginia, 1550–1624*, ed. Peter C. Mancall (Chapel Hill: Published for the Omohundro Institute of Early American History and Culture, Williamsburg, Va., by the University of North Carolina Press, 2007), 117.

5. For a good chronological description of Susquehannock-English contacts from the early seventeenth century to the 1630s see Fausz, "Present at the 'Creation.'"

6. See Brandão, *"Your Fyre Shall Burn No More."*

7. The Susquehannocks appear in seventeenth-century records under various names. I have chosen to use "Susquehannock" throughout this book because it is the name by which historians best know the nation. However, although seventeenth-century English colonists used the name "Susquehannock," it does not appear to have been the Susquehannocks' own name for themselves. No one yet knows for certain what they called themselves.

A 1661 treaty between the Susquehannocks and Maryland Colony also mentions the Kaiquariegehaga, which Francis Jennings has suggested may have been a variant of Atrakwaeronnon, as a member of the united nations of the Susquehannocks. In the eighteenth century, English colonists knew the descendants of the Susquehannocks as the Conestogas, a name derived from an Iroquois name for the Susquehannocks.

The Huron name for the Susquehannocks was Andaste, and it may well be that the Susquehannocks called themselves by that or a related name. Because of their close relationship with the Hurons, many seventeenth-century French observers also called the Susquehannocks the Andaste, or the Andastoerrhonon. Some French sources also used the name Akhrakuaeronon, though Francis Jennings has noted that the significance of this term is unclear.

The Dutch and Swedes called the Susquehannocks the Minquas or Minquaas. Minquaa was almost certainly derived from an Algonquian word, as there are no bilabials in Iroquois languages.

For a fuller discussion of these terms and their appearance in seventeenth-century sources see Francis Jennings, "Susquehannock," in *The Handbook of North American Indians*, vol. 15, *Northeast* (Washington, D.C.: Smithsonian Institution Press, 1978), 367.

8. See Jennings, "Glory, Death, and Transfiguration," 16.

9. Ibid., 16–17.

10. For a discussion of the importance of the Susquehanna, Juniata, and Ohio river routes in the seventeenth century see Jennings, "Susquehannock," 364; Jennings, "Glory, Death, and Transfiguration," 17–18; Cynthia J. Van Zandt, "Negotiating Settlement: Colonialism, Cultural Exchange, and Conflict in Early Colonial Atlantic North America, 1580–1660," PhD diss., University of Connecticut, 1998, 247.

Contemporaries described the importance of this route. The best seventeenth-century depiction of it is that of Augustine Herrmans, who explained it in 1670; however, it was clearly a significant route before 1670. Governor Johan Printz of New Sweden wrote of establishing dealings with Indians who plied their trade in beaver furs along this corridor. See Albert Cook Myers, ed., *Narratives of Early Pennsylvania, West New Jersey, and Delaware 1630–1707* (1912; New York, Barnes and Noble Books, 1967), 103–104n2. The assessment that the southern part of the Susquehanna River gave the Susquehannocks a secure location from which to wage war on their paramount enemies is my own interpretation of the evidence.

11. See Samuel de Champlain, *Works*, ed. H. P. Biggar (Toronto: Champlain Society, 1922–1933), vol. 3, 54–55; Charles A. Hanna, *The Wilderness Trail* (New York, 1911), vol. 1, 27–28.

12. Champlain, *Works*, 54–55; Hanna, *Wilderness Trail*, vol. 1, 27–28.

13. See Trelease, *Indian Affairs in Colonial New York*, 33–34.

14. The surviving accounts of the three Dutch traders and their capture by Susquehannocks do not provide the names of the other two men. Only Kleynties was identified and then only by his surname.

15. See Champlain, *Works*, vol. 3, 54–55; John Romeyn Brodhead, *Documents relative to the Colonial Period of the State of New-York; Procured in Holland, England, and France*, ed. Edmund Bailey O'Callaghan (Albany, 1856), vol. 1, 14; see also Trelease, *Indian Affairs in Colonial New York*, 33–34; Hanna, *Wilderness Trail*, vol. 1, 28.

16. Champlain, *Works*, vol. 3, 54–55.

17. Kleynties and the other two captives were ransomed in 1616 by Dutch trader Captain Cornelis Hendricksen. Hendricksen was exploring the Delaware River and its tributaries and trading with the Indians he met along the way when he learned of the Susquehannocks' Dutch captives and successfully ransomed them. Trelease cites Brodhead (see note 15, this chapter), vol. 1, 14, in *Indian Affairs in Colonial New York*, 33–34; Alexander C. Flick, *The History of the State of New York* (New York: Columbia University Press, 1933), vol. 1, 167; John Romeyn Brodhead, *History of the State of New York* (New York: Harper Brothers, 1853–1871), vol. 1, 78–79.

18. Allen Trelease carefully considered the possibility of a Mohawk-Dutch alliance before the 1640s but rejected it as unsupported by the evidence. Trelease, *Indian Affairs in Colonial New York*, 34. Trelease argues convincingly that the Algonquian Mahicans were more closely allied with the Dutch in these early years.

19. Champlain, *Works*, vol. 3, 54–55.

20. Reuben Gold Thwaites, ed., *The Jesuit Relations and Allied Documents: Travels and Explorations of the Jesuit Missionaries in New France 1610–1791* (Cleveland: Burrows Bros., 1896–1901), vol. 33.

21. Champlain, *Works*, vol. 3, 54–55. I have followed the lead of Charles A. Hanna in inserting bracketed identifications into the quotation from Champlain. See Hanna, *Wilderness Trail*, vol. 1, 28.

22. On Claiborne as surveyor for the Virginia Colony see Charles M. Andrews, *The Colonial Period of American History* (New Haven: Yale University Press, 1934), vol. 1, 132; Erich Isaac, "Kent Island, Part I: The Period of Settlement," in *Maryland Historical Magazine* 52 (1957): 95.

23. Isaac, "Kent Island," 96.

24. William Hand Browne, ed., *Archives of Maryland, Proceedings of the Council of Maryland 1667–1687/8* (Baltimore: Maryland Historical Society, 1887), vol. 5, 158.

25. I am indebted to the work of Erich Isaac for this account of Claiborne's move into the intercultural fur trade in the 1620s. Isaac has provided a detailed reconstruction of the creation of Claiborne's Kent and Palmer's island bases in "Kent Island," 93–119.

26. Trading licenses in Virginia's early years were quite clearly bounded. They were issued for a limited period of time, usually a single trading season, which lasted a few months, and frequently specified both a region and particular Indian nations with whom one was permitted to barter.

27. See, for example, Isaac, "Kent Island," 98. Although Claiborne owned the Accomack property, at least as far as the colony of Virginia was concerned, he had not yet done anything with it.

28. This was the same Isaack de Rasière who later visited and sold wampum to Plymouth Colony. See chapter 4.

29. See Oliver A. Rink, *Holland on the Hudson: An Economic and Social History of Dutch New York* (Ithaca, N.Y.: Cornell University Press, 1986), 81–87.

30. "Letter from Isaack de Rasière to the Directors of the Amsterdam Chamber of the West India Company, Fort Amsterdam on Manhattan Island, September 23, 1626," in *Documents relating to New Netherland, 1624–1626*, trans. and ed. A. J. F. van Laer (San Marino, Calif.: Henry E. Huntington Library and Art Gallery, 1924), 187. See also Rink, *Holland on the Hudson*, 85. The similarities between the early history of Jamestown and New Netherland are remarkable. The problems and resentment of Verhulst and the uneasy fit between the company's instructions and the realities of life in North America were quite similar to the difficulties in Jamestown during its first years.

31. "Letter from Isaack de Rasière," 192. In the same passage de Rasière complained that "Your Honors, by granting the assistant-commissary, Gerrit Fongersz, a vote in the Council, put him above me." The issue was one of effective leadership, as well as status and hierarchy.

32. Ibid.

33. The Dutch text reads as follows: "Also de Minquaes om de Zuyt met haer dertigen off veertighen sterck hier hebben gheweest ende hebben vrientschap aen ons versocht." I have quoted van Laer's English translation of this passage in the main body of this chapter immediately preceding note number 32 on p. 128.

34. "Letter from Isaack de Rasière," 192.

35. Ibid.

36. Ibid., 196.

37. Ibid.

38. Ibid., 196–97.

39. See, for example, Isaac, "Kent Island," 98.

40. See, for example, ibid., 100.

41. Henry Fleet reported that he returned to the Potomac in October 1631 to trade and discovered that "by reason of my absence, the Indians had not preserved their beaver, but burned it, as the custom is." He went on to describe how he tried to regularize the trade by persuading them to save the furs until the following spring: "Whereupon I endeavoured to alter that custom, and to preserve it [the furs] for me against the next Spring, promising to come there with commodities in exchange by the first of April." See Capt. Henry Fleet, "A Brief Journal of a Voyage in the Barque 'Virginia' to Virginia and Other Parts of the Continent of America," *Northern Neck of Virginia Historical Magazine* 6 (1956): 479.

42. William Waller Hening, *The Statutes at Large; Being a Collection of All the Laws of Virginia, from the First Session of the Legislature, in the Year 1619*, vol. 1 (1823; Charlottesville: Published for the Jamestown Foundation of the Commonwealth of Virginia by the University Press of Virginia, 1969), 140–41. The following March, the House of Burgesses insisted that the war with the Algonquians continue and that colonists carry on with all of the expeditions it had mandated the past October. That meant that colonists had to initiate strikes against the Pamunkeys and other neighboring Algonquian nations again that month, in March, and once more in July. See Hening, *Statutes at Large*, vol. 1, 153.

43. Beverley Fleet, *Virginia Colonial Abstracts*, vol. 17 (Baltimore: Genealogical Publishing, 1961), 35, and Isaac, "Kent Island," 94.

44. Hillier, "The Trade of the Virginia Colony," 351.

45. Fleet, *Virginia Colonial Abstracts*, 35–36. See also "*Claiborne vs. Cloberry et al.* in the High Court of Admiralty," *Maryland Historical Magazine* 26 (1931): 381–404.

46. See, for example, Thomas E. Davidson, "Relations between the Powhatans and the Eastern Shore," in *Powhatan Foreign Relations, 1500–1722*, ed. Helen Rountree (Charlottesville: University Press of Virginia, 1993), 151.

CHAPTER 6: ALLIANCES OF NECESSITY

1. Much of the material in this chapter focuses on Africans who were held as slaves by the Dutch West India Company. When not using individual names, I alternate among the terms "slaves," "enslaved people," and "Africans." No single term adequately conveys the fullest sense of either the humanity of enslaved people or what it meant that Dutch officials regarded them as property. Accordingly, I use the term "slave" when examining a case from the perspective of Dutch colonists and colonial officials and "enslaved men" when writing from the perspective of Africans themselves. Most frequently I use the term "enslaved Africans" to emphasize the importance of the condition of bondage but with the designation of African as a cultural and ethnic descriptor (analogous to Dutch or European in that sense). This reinforces the understanding of Africans as migrants to North America with the crucial reminder that most of these migrations were involuntary.

2. In New Netherland, WIC officials actively considered using enslaved Africans as militia to help defend the colony as late as 1658. During the Esopus war, Director General

Petrus Stuyvesant sent to Curaçao for supplies and for Africans whom he might use either as laborers or soldiers. In his search for more fighting men, Stuyvesant also sent requests to Virginia to negotiate a defensive alliance between the two colonies against the Esopus threat and to ask for additional soldiers. See, for example, Allen W. Trelease, *Indian Affairs in Colonial New York: The Seventeenth Century* (Ithaca, N.Y.: Cornell University Press, 1960), 156, and O'Callaghan, *NYCD* (see ch. 4, note 54), vol. 13, 138–47, 163.

3. A great deal of recent scholarship has shown that slavery before the end of the seventeenth century was quite different from that in the eighteenth and nineteenth centuries. Much research has also begun to make it clear that regional differences were as important in shaping people's various experiences as changes over time. See, for instance, Ira Berlin, *Many Thousands Gone: The First Two Centuries of Slavery in North America* (Cambridge, Mass.: Harvard University Press, 1999); Ira Berlin, "Time, Space, and the Evolution of Afro-American Slavery in British Mainland North America," *American Historical Review* 84 (1980): 44–78; T. H. Breen and Stephen Innes, *"Myne Owne Ground": Race and Freedom on Virginia's Eastern Shore, 1640–1676* (New York: Oxford University Press, 1980); Kathleen Brown, *Good Wives, Nasty Wenches, and Anxious Patriarchs: Gender, Race, and Power in Colonial Virginia* (Chapel Hill: Published for the Institute of Early American History and Culture by the University of North Carolina Press, 1996). A recent reexamination of slavery in New Netherland suggests that the fact that most slaves in New Netherland were from west central Africa and therefore likely Christians may have contributed to their somewhat more flexible status. See Linda M. Heywood and John K. Thornton, *Central Africans, Atlantic Creoles, and the Making of the Foundation of the Americas, 1585–1660* (New York: Cambridge University Press, 2007), 299.

4. For a study of the history of Africans in New Amsterdam and New York see Thelma Wills Foote, *Black and White Manhattan: The History of Racial Formation in Colonial New York City* (New York: Oxford University Press, 2004).

5. Although Heywood and Thornton have persuasively argued that most Africans in Dutch and English colonies in the first half of the seventeenth century were from west central Africa, they discuss people as having been taken from several different regions within that broad area. See Heywood and Thornton, *Central Africans*, 38, 41, 48.

6. Johannes Menne Postma, *The Dutch in the Atlantic Slave Trade, 1600–1815* (New York: Cambridge University Press, 1990), 106, discusses the limited written evidence on trade routes and markets in the African interior and the resulting limitations on determining the origin of many African slaves.

7. For the effect of the decline of the Kongo state after the mid-sixteenth century and its impact on the supply of slaves for the Atlantic slave trade see Postma, *Dutch in the Atlantic Slave Trade*, 101; John Kelly Thornton, *Africa and Africans in the Making of the Atlantic World, 1400–1680* (New York: Cambridge University Press, 1992).

8. Heywood and Thornton point out that 90 percent of slaves listed by Johannes de Laet as having been carried on WIC ships from 1624 to 1636 were from Angola. Heywood and Thornton, *Central Africans*, 41.

9. On branding and the Dutch West India Company see Postma, *Dutch in the Atlantic Slave Trade*, 237.

10. Ibid.

11. John Thornton has argued that in the sixteenth and seventeenth centuries the Angolan coast was one of three culturally distinct zones in Atlantic Africa and that it was

linguistically quite homogeneous, with most people speaking languages of the western Bantu subgroup. Thornton, *Africa and Africans*, 190–91. See also Heywood and Thornton's argument about Atlantic Creole culture in *Central Africans*.

12. In a discussion of factors that led to the expansion of the Dutch West India Company's participation in the Atlantic slave trade, Johannes Postma states that colonists in Dutch Brazil (New Holland) were accustomed to acquiring Bantu-speaking slaves through the Angolan ports of west central Africa. See Postma, *Dutch in the Atlantic Slave Trade*, 18.

13. Heywood and Thornton, *Central Africans*, 8.

14. On Dutch participation in the Atlantic slave trade see Postma, *Dutch in the Atlantic Slave Trade*; Ernst van den Boogaart and Pieter C. Emmer, "The Dutch Participation in the Atlantic Slave Trade, 1596–1650," in *The Uncommon Market: Essays in the Economic History of the Atlantic Slave Trade*, ed. Henry A. Gemery and Jan S. Hogendorn (New York: Academic Press, 1979), 353–75.

15. See Postma, *Dutch in the Atlantic Slave Trade*, 19.

16. See Anne Hilton, *The Kingdom of Kongo* (New York: Oxford University Press, 1985), 77.

17. See Thornton, *Africa and Africans*, 107–108.

18. Ibid., 254–55. Also see Hilton, *Kingdom of Kongo*, 90–103, for a somewhat different interpretation of Christianity in Kongo. See also Heywood and Thornton, *Central Africans*.

19. Richard Ligon described slaves in Barbados who had lived among the Portuguese and who were skilled in European fencing. However, he offered no explanation of how or why those men had ended up there as English slaves. Ligon lived in Barbados from September 1647 until sometime in 1650; see Richard Ligon, *A Trve & Exact History of the Island of Barbados* (London, 1657), 52. John Thornton discusses the role of Portuguese settlers from São Tomé who became a favored community in Kongo and later in Ndongo; see Thornton, *Africa and Africans*, 61.

20. De Laet included this estimate of slaves captured by WIC ships in a compendium of the various categories of goods taken by WIC ships engaged in privateering, along with an assessment of the total value of each type of merchandise at market (e.g., "Lijste Ende Estimatie Vande Goederen Die Inde Voorgaende Ghenomen Schepen by De Compagnie Zijn Bekommen, Ende Hier Te Lande In-Gebracht Ende Verkocht, Ofte Elders In Hare Conquesten Verbesight"). De Laet wrote that the 2,356 captured Africans were sold for an average of 250 gulden each for a total of 589,000 gulden: "2356 Negros, by de onse ghebeneficeert* (*Gewonnen) die maer reeckene teghen 250 gulden yeder neger, hoewel vele ongelijck meer zijn verkocht."

De Laet made no distinction between human and other kinds of cargo other than profit gained for the company. Other goods included on his list were tobacco, indigo, and cotton. Joannes de Laet, *Iaerlyck Verhael van de Verrichtingen der Geotroyeerde West-Indische Compagnie in derthien Boecken. Vierde Deel Boek VI–XIII* (1634–1636). Uitgegeven Door S. P. l'Honoré Naber en J. C. M. Warnsinck (1644; repr., The Hague, 1937), 287. See also Postma, *Dutch in the Atlantic Slave Trade*, 13.

21. See Edgar J. McManus, *A History of Negro Slavery in New York*, foreword by Richard B. Morris (Syracuse, N.Y.: Syracuse University Press, 1966), 5. Chapter 1 deals with New Netherland.

22. For a listing of names of west central Africans enslaved in New Netherland see Heywood and Thornton, *Central Africans*, appendix, 346–52.

23. The use of *de* in Jan de Fort Orange's name is unusual and seems to reflect a Spanish or Portuguese influence, in which *de* is a preposition. In Dutch, *de* is an article; however, "John the Fort Orange" is clearly not the intended meaning. It is presumably "Jan" or "John of Fort Orange." Fort Orange, located on the Hudson River at the site of present-day Albany, was another settlement in New Netherland. Moreover, even when slaves had Dutch names, as in the case of men named "Jan," an additional name was included to suggest their status as slaves.

24. The use of *de* in Manuel de Gerrit de Reus seems to parallel the *de* in Jan de Fort Orange. Dutch usage in both cases would normally have been Manuel *van* Gerrit de Reus and Jan *van* Fort Orange. In both cases, however, the names seem to use *de* in a Spanish or Portuguese manner (i.e., as a preposition rather than an article). In the case of Manuel de Gerrit de Reus, the second *de* is part of the name of Dutch colonist Gerrit de Reus.

25. See Morton Wagman, "Corporate Slavery in New Netherland," *Journal of Negro History* 65 (1980): 34–42, especially 36.

26. See *New York Historical Manuscripts: Dutch*, trans. and annotated by Arnold J. F. van Laer and ed. Kenneth Scott and Kenn Stryker-Rodda. Vol. 1, *Register of the Provincial Secretary, 1638–1642* (Baltimore: Genealogical Publishing, 1974), 113.

27. For a preliminary assessment of family and community relationships among enslaved and free blacks in New Netherland see Joyce D. Goodfriend, "Black Families in New Netherland," in *A Beautiful and Fruitful Place: Selected Rensselaerswijck Seminar Papers*, ed. Nancy Anne McClure Zeller, with an introduction by Charles T. Gehring (Albany, N.Y.: New Netherland Publishing, 1991), 147–55; for a thorough discussion of society and government in New Netherland generally, see Jaap Jacobs, *New Netherland: A Dutch Colony in Seventeenth-Century America* (Boston: Brill, 2005).

28. See van Laer, vol. 4, *Council Minutes, 1638–1649*, 212–13. As we shall see, many of the company slaves who petitioned for manumission in 1644 had been among the group of defendants in a 1641 murder trial.

29. See ibid., 35. Oliver Rink assumed that Antony was a former slave at the time of his 1638 lawsuit; however, the records of the 1641 Premero murder case make it clear that Antony Portugues was a WIC slave. Further discussion of the Premero case follows in this chapter. See also Oliver A. Rink, *Holland on the Hudson: An Economic and Social History of Dutch New York* (Ithaca, N.Y.: Cornell University Press, 1986), 161.

30. For the debate over the nature of slavery in New Netherland see, for example, Ernst van den Boogaart, "The Servant Migration to New Netherland, 1624–1664," in *Colonialism and Migration: Indentured Labour before and after Slavery*, ed. P. C. Emmer (Dordrecht, the Netherlands: Nijhoff, 1986), 65–71; Joyce D. Goodfriend, "Burghers and Blacks: The Evolution of a Slave Society in New Amsterdam," in *New York History* (1978): 124–44; Morton Wagman, "Corporate Slavery in New Netherland," *Journal of Negro History* 65 (1980): 34–42.

31. Philip D. Curtin, *The Atlantic Slave Trade: A Census* (Madison: University of Wisconsin Press, 1969), 104–105; Thornton, *Africa and Africans*, 196; Jesus Alberto García, *La diaspora de los Kongos en las Americas en los Caribes* (Caracas: UNESCO, 1995), 19. Most recently, Heywood and Thornton have made an extremely persuasive argument

that west central Africans were by far the most numerous and culturally significant African group in North America in the first half of the seventeenth century. Heywood and Thornton, *Central Africans*.

32. See Postma, *Dutch in the Atlantic Slave Trade*, 18. Again, the lack of specific records that tell us where WIC officials bought slaves is frustrating; one would wish for more definitive evidence that the WIC sent enslaved people from its Brazilian colony to its New Netherland settlement. However, even though such evidence does not exist, the weight of circumstantial proof strongly points to two facts: first, that most Africans in any American colonies in this early period came from Bantu-speaking areas of west central Africa, and second, that some enslaved Africans in New Netherland probably lived for a time in other colonies, including the one in Brazil.

33. Thornton, *Africa and Africans*, 190–91.

34. See ibid., 205–206, for Thornton's argument contra Mintz and Price. More recently, Michael Angelo Gómez has demonstrated that many enslaved Africans lived among other people from their home region in North America. See Gómez, *Exchanging Our Country Marks: The Transformation of African Identities in the Colonial and Antebellum South* (Chapel Hill: University of North Carolina Press, 1998).

35. Thornton, *Africa and Africans*, 191.

36. Gómez has persuasively demonstrated the transplantation of ethnically distinct African communities in southern colonies and states. See Gómez, *Exchanging Our Country Marks*.

37. Heywood and Thornton, *Central Africans*.

38. Ibid.

39. Thornton, *Africa and Africans*, 202.

40. Ibid., 203–204.

41. Ibid., 204–205. On Atlantic Creoles see especially Ira Berlin, "From Creole to African: Atlantic Creoles and the Origins of African-American Society in Mainland North America," *William and Mary Quarterly*, 3d. ser., 53 (1996): 251–88; and Berlin, *Many Thousands Gone*.

42. See, for example, Heywood and Thornton, *Central Africans*, 263–64.

43. The records relating to this case appear in van Laer, *New York Historical Manuscripts*, vol. 4, 97–100. The original Dutch manuscripts are in the New York State Library, Albany, N.Y. This case appears in *Colonial Manuscripts*, vol. 4, folios 83–85. I am grateful to the New Netherland Project for its assistance with copies of the manuscripts.

44. Van Laer's translation denotes some of the accused men by English translations of the names given in the manuscript. For instance, he changed Cleijn Antonio to Little Antonio, Antonij Portugees to Anthony the Portuguese, and Manuel de Groote to Big Manuel. I prefer to use the men's names as given in the manuscript.

45. Van Laer, vol. 4, *Council Minutes*, 97, gives Gracia's name as "Gracia d'Angols" the first time it appears. The manuscript clearly reads "Gracia d'Angola," and the van Laer version correctly lists Gracia as "Gracia d'Angola" later in the translation.

Given the apparently female first name, it is possible that Gracia d'Angola was a woman; however, the weight of the evidence suggests that this person was a man. Seventeenth-century orthography may be at issue here: "Gracia" may have been a misspelling of "Garcia." More tellingly, a 1644 petition filed by many of the enslaved persons involved in this case includes Gracia d'Angola among the petitioners. There, the petitioning slaves requested their freedom because (in addition to other reasons) "it will be impossible for them to support their wives and children as they have been accustomed to in the past if they must continue in the honorable Company's service." Vol. 4, *Council Minutes*, 212–13. I am assuming that the court would have noted the fact if one of the petitioners had been a woman even if they did not think it worth noting that one of Premero's accused killers was a woman.

46. Van Laer lists Cleijn Antonio, or Little Anthony, and Paulo d'Angola together as if they were a single person named "Little Antonio Paulo d'Angola." The manuscript of the 1641 trial is difficult to make out on this point. However, a 1644 petition for manumission names most of the same men, and it distinctly lists Cleijn Antonio and Paulo d'Angola as two different people. Accordingly, I have assumed that the names refer to two men rather than to only one. See *Colonial Manuscripts*, vol. 4, entry for Feb. 25, 1644. Van Laer read the 1644 entry the same way that I have; see vol. 4, *Council Minutes*, 212.

The council minutes alternately use the terms "homicide," "manslaughter," and "murder" for the charge in this case; see van Laer, vol. 4, *Council Minutes*, 97–99. However, the actual terms given in the manuscript are *homisidio* and *dootslach*, and the council referred to the accused men as *dootslagers*, or murderers. The manuscript does not use any other term that might be interpreted as "manslaughter." Van Laer employed the English words "manslaughter" and "murder" in his translation; however, the original manuscript contains the term *dootslach* throughout. Accordingly, I see no reason for using the English word "manslaughter" in this case. Just as manslaughter was a lesser category of homicide than murder in early modern English law, Roman-Dutch criminal law distinguished between different kinds of homicide, the most important of which centered around intent and premeditation.

In this case, the council seems to have been considering the Premero homicide a case of murder. The term *dootslach* is not modified by adjectives or adverbs that might indicate accidental or mitigating circumstances. Thus I use the English term "murder" in my discussion.

47. For a study of early modern crime and punishment based largely on the criminal records of Amsterdam from 1650 to 1750 see Pieter Spierenburg, *The Spectacle of Suffering: Executions and the Evolution of Repression from a Preindustrial Metropolis to the European Experience* (New York: Cambridge University Press, 1984).

48. Van Laer, *Council Minutes*, vol. 4, 99. The manuscript reads as follows: "door de voorsieniheijt God"; *Colonial Manuscripts*, vol. 4, folio 84.

49. Van Laer, *Council Minutes*, vol. 4, 100.

50. In 1646, for example, the fiscal and the director general brought charges against Johan de Fries for a variety of challenges to their authority, including the accusation that he was "leading a scandalous life, highly dangerous in this infant republic." See ibid., 331–32.

51. See *Council Minutes, 1655–1656*, trans. and ed. Charles T. Gehring (Syracuse, N.Y.: Syracuse University Press, 1995), xiii, xviii.

52. In 1639 the council became the final authority for all criminal offenses, even capital crimes. Before that date the council was not legally authorized to punish capital cases. Prior to 1639 persons convicted of capital crimes in New Netherland were to be sent back to the United Provinces for punishment.

53. See Gehring, *Council Minutes*, xiii. After the establishment of a court at Beverwijck and Fort Orange in 1652, the council heard only appeals and some very serious criminal cases from the north Hudson community. See *Fort Orange Court Minutes, 1652–1660*, trans. and ed. Charles T. Gehring (Syracuse, N.Y.: Syracuse University Press, 1990), xxvi.

54. On offices devoted to enforcing law and order in New Netherland see Dennis Sullivan, *The Punishment of Crime in Colonial New York: The Dutch Experience in Albany during the Seventeenth Century* (New York: Peter Lang, 1997).

55. No list of council members has survived for 1641. La Montaigne was listed as being on the council for the years 1639 and 1642. The lists for 1640 and 1641 are missing. Because he was on the council in 1639 and still listed as a member in 1642, I am assuming that la Montagne was on the council during the 1641 Premero murder trial.

56. The WIC instructions for Willem Verhulst list those who were appointed to the council in 1624 and 1625. After listing several people by name, the instructions add that "the skippers who come there from time to time" would also be on the council. See *Documents Relating to New Netherland, 1624–1626*, trans. and ed. A. J. F. van Laer (San Marino, Calif.: Huntington Library, 1924), 90. Also, E. B. O'Callaghan noted that WIC ships' captains joined the council when they were on shore. Edmund B. O'Callaghan, *The Register of New Netherland, 1626 to 1674* (Albany, N.Y., 1865), 11; for an example of WIC ships' captains on the council in 1647, see p. 16.

57. Scott Christianson, "Criminal Punishment in New Netherland," in *A Beautiful and Fruitful Place*, ed. Zeller, 87.

58. See *Court Records of New Amsterdam*, vol. 4, 24. I thank Charles T. Gehring for drawing my attention to this court entry. It is also unclear whether Pieter was a slave, as his petition in 1662 was for payment for his services in executing two criminal sentences.

59. A. J. F. van Laer, trans. and ed., *Van Rensselaer Bowier Manuscripts* (Albany, N.Y., 1908), 835–36.

60. See Postma, *Dutch in the Atlantic Slave Trade*, 228, 68.

61. I assume that he was a man because "negro" is the singular masculine form of the Dutch noun. Moreover, I have never seen any records of women serving as executioners.

62. See Spierenburg, *Spectacle of Suffering*, for example, 13–24, and especially 18–19. Though Spierenburg describes authorities' efforts to recognize hangmen as their public servants and to raise their status through higher pay, executioners consistently came from the lower orders of society, and popular attitudes toward them retained considerable negative qualities.

63. Indians were of course an important presence in New Netherland. However, native peoples were not regarded by Dutch colonial officials as members of New Netherland's society, nor were they thought to be governed by the colony's laws to the same degree as free colonists, servants, and slaves. Their role, as the Dutch understood it, was either as allies and trading partners or as enemies.

64. During the 1640s (if not before) Dutch officials became increasingly aware of some of the dimensions in which Africans had formed a distinct community within the colony. A Dutch record notes that a man named Bastayen was a "Captain of the Negroes" in 1644, three years after the Premero murder trial; quoted in Heywood and Thornton, *Central Africans*, 264.

65. Van Laer, *Council Records*, vol. 4, 98.

66. *Buiten* could mean *without*, but more commonly it meant *outside*, while *zonder* was more often used to mean *without*. *Colonial Manuscripts*, vol. 4, folios 83–85.

67. Spierenburg's study is particularly applicable here because New Netherland modeled its laws and regulations after Amsterdam's municipal codes.

68. Spierenburg, *Spectacle of Suffering*, 188.

69. Ibid., 257n17.

70. See, for example, Edmund B. O'Callaghan, *Calendar of Dutch Historical Manuscripts in the Office of the Secretary of State, Albany, New York 1630–1664* (1856; repr., Ridgewood, N.J.: Gregg, 1968), vol. 4, 101, and van Laer, *Council Minutes*, vol. 4, 314, for a 1646 case in which the council ordered a defendant put to torture if he continued to refuse to confess.

71. Ultimately we know nothing of the accused men's motivations. It is possible, of course, that each man believed that they were all equally guilty of Premero's murder.

72. On justice day in the United Provinces see Spierenburg, *Spectacle of Suffering*, 46, 86. Moreover, English colonies in North America also established regularly scheduled court days based on English legal traditions.

73. *Simon van Leeuwen's Commentaries on Roman-Dutch Law*, rev. and ed. C. W. Decker (London: Sweet and Maxwell, 1921–1923), vol. 2, 278.

74. Thornton, *Africa and Africans*, 241.

75. Spierenburg, *Spectacle of Suffering*, 89.

76. New Netherland was indeed polyglot and heterogeneous. However, this argument also applies to other colonies that historians typically describe as more culturally homogeneous, such as the New England settlements. All North American colonies had inhabitants from cultures other than the governing one, and all of them had regular experiences with Native Americans.

Public displays of law, order, and colonial authority in those settlements were directed at the widest possible combination of audiences. Posting heads on pikes or palisades around colonial forts was common European practice in early colonial Atlantic North America and was intended to convey a message to those both inside and outside the fort.

77. On some unusual occasions the council could add members from among other officials and residents of the community. There are no records that the council did so in this case. See O'Callaghan, *Register of New Netherland*, 11.

78. Van Laer, *New York Historical Manuscripts*, vol. 4, 98.

79. Ibid., 98–99.

80. Ibid., 99.

81. Ibid.

82. Ibid.

83. Ibid. For a study of the ideological foundations of Dutch colonial punishment and its exemplary goals see Sullivan, *Punishment of Crime in Colonial New York*.

84. Van Laer, *New York Historical Manuscripts*, vol. 4, 100.

85. Ibid.

86. Ibid.

87. The council records do not indicate that the council ever asked the nine men why they committed the murder, only whether they had done it and who had struck the death blow.

88. Van Laer, *New York Historical Manuscripts*, vol. 4, 326–27.

89. The record notes that "after the previous examination of the aforesaid Jan Creoly, at present a prisoner, has without torture and while free of irons confessed having committed sodomy with the aforesaid boy and that he had also committed the said heinous and abominable crime on the island of Curaçao"; in ibid., 326–28.

90. Ibid., 327.

91. Cremation was not customary in New Netherland or the United Provinces. Therefore, the significance of burning Creoli's body to ashes provided a symbolic annihilation of his crime and his presence on earth. The connection to Sodom and Gomorrah would have been clear to early modern Europeans, if not necessarily to early modern Africans. Africans who were Christians, however, would certainly have understood the symbolism.

92. Van Laer, *New York Historical Manuscripts*, vol. 4, 327.

93. Ibid.

94. Ibid.

95. Ibid.

96. For a recent examination of the terrible costs of Kieft's war see Donna Merwick, *The Shame and the Sorrow: Dutch-Amerindian Encounters in New Netherland* (Philadelphia: University of Pennsylvania Press, 2006).

97. Ibid.

98. I have concluded that Africans in Manhattan regarded Manuel Congo as the victim of a crime rather than a participant (even an unwilling one) because Africans brought the Dutch judicial system into the situation and African witnesses explicitly testified that Jan Creoli had raped young Manuel. Their testimony made it clear that this was not a consensual act on the boy's part.

99. Van Laer, *New York Historical Manuscripts*, vol. 4, 328.

100. See, for example, "Report of the Condition of the Colony of New Netherland, 30 April 1638, Proposed Freedoms and Exemptions, 19 July 1640," in Edmund B. O'Callaghan, ed., *Documents relative to the Colonial History of the State of New-York: Procured in Holland, England, and France* (hereafter *NYCD*), vol. 1 (Albany, N.Y.: Weed, Parsons, 1856), 106, 107, 119. See also Rink, *Holland on the Hudson*, 134–37.

101. See "Report of the Board of Accounts on New Netherland, 15 December 1644," in O'Callaghan, ed., *NYCD*, vol. 1, 150; "Resolution concerning the Raritan Indians, 16 July 1640," in *New York Historical Manuscripts*, vol. 4, 87; "Interrogatories to be Proposed to Secretary van Tienhoven, 21 July 1650," in O'Callaghan, ed., *NYCD*, vol. 1, 410.

102. On Kieft's war see Merwick, *Shame and the Sorrow*; Paul Andrew Otto, "New Netherland Frontier: Europeans and Native Americans along the Lower Hudson River, 1524–1664," PhD diss., Indiana University, 1995, 167–207; Rink, *Holland on the Hudson*, 216–22; Trelease, *Indian Affairs in Colonial New York*.

CHAPTER 7: NATIONS INTERTWINED

1. Francis Jennings, "Glory, Death, and Transfiguration," *Proceedings of the American Philosophical Society* 112 (1968): 15–53; Barry C. Kent, *Susquehanna's Indians* (Harrisburg: Commonwealth of Pennsylvania, Pennsylvania Historical and Museum Commission, 1984); Allen W. Trelease, *Indian Affairs in Colonial New York: The Seventeenth Century* (Ithaca, N.Y.: Cornell University Press, 1960).

2. See, for example, James Pendergast, "Susquehannock Trade Northward to New France Prior to A.D. 1608: A Popular Misconception," *Pennsylvania Archaeologist* 62 (1992): 1–11 ; James Pendergast, *The Massawomeck: Raiders and Traders into the Chesapeake Bay in the Seventeenth Century* (Philadelphia: American Philosophical Society, 1991); Thomas E. Davidson, "Relations between the Powhatans and the Eastern Shore," in *Powhatan Foreign Relations*, ed. Helen C. Rountree (Charlottesville: University Press of Virginia, 1993), 151.

The mystery of the Massawomecks is still largely unsolved. No one is certain who they were, other than that they were an Iroquoian-speaking people and that "Massawomeck" is clearly the name given to them by Algonquian peoples. No one has yet satisfactorily explained why they disappear from the historical records in the mid-1630s, and archaeologists have found no sites that they can confidently identify as Massawomeck.

3. The English named Delaware Bay in honor of Sir Thomas West, third Lord de la Warre, governor of the Virginia Colony, after Samuel Argall first sailed into the bay in 1610.

4. For a discussion of some of the ways Dutch and Swedish record keepers transcribed the liquid *l* of Lenape languages and the ensuing challenge to scholars who use European-produced records to understand Native Americans see Robert Steven Grumet, "'We Are Not So Great Fools': Changes in Upper Delawaran Socio-Political Life, 1630–1758," PhD diss., Rutgers, State University of New Jersey, 1979, 119–22.

5. Francis Jennings has argued that the area that became "eastern Pennsylvania and all of New York were linked into one great system of intercourse by canoe and by trails through the valleys" for Native Americans. See Jennings, "'Pennsylvania Indians' and the Iroquois," in *Beyond the Covenant Chain: The Iroquois and Their Neighbors in Indian North America, 1600–1800*, ed. Daniel K. Richter and James H. Merrell (Syracuse, N.Y.: Syracuse University Press, 1987), 76.

6. Grumet, "'We Are Not So Great Fools,'" 130.

7. A number of scholars have argued that Native Americans on the eastern seaboard continued to exercise considerable power despite heavy disease mortality and related social dislocations. See, for example, José António Brandão, *"Your Fyre Shall Burn No More": Iroquois Policy toward New France and Its Native Allies to 1701* (Lincoln: University of Nebraska Press, 1997); Karen Ordahl Kupperman, *Indians and English: Facing Off in Early America* (Ithaca, N.Y.: Cornell University Press, 2000); Michael Leroy Oberg, *Dominion and Civility: English Imperialism and Native America, 1585–1685* (Ithaca, N.Y.: Cornell University Press, 1999). I made a similar argument in my PhD dissertation, "Negotiating Settlement: Colonialism, Cultural Exchange, and Conflict in Early Colonial Atlantic North America, 1580–1660," University of Connecticut, 1998.

8. John Hull, a Puritan colonist in Massachusetts Bay, heard about the Indian attacks on Manhattan during the peach war. See John Hull diary, 1624–1682, American Antiquarian Society, Worcester, Mass., Manuscript Department, octavo volumes "H." Hull made the entry under the year 1656; however, he was clearly writing about events that took place in the fall of 1655.

9. The Susquehannocks and the Senecas were enemies throughout most of this period. The Susquehannocks and the Mohawks clashed with each other throughout much of the 1650s; however, between about 1658 and 1662, they pursued parallel poli-

cies and seem to have developed an alliance. Susquehannock-Seneca antipathy continued, however. See, for example, Trelease, *Indian Affairs in Colonial New York*; Jennings,
"Glory, Death, and Transfiguration."

10. For research on the importance of the Susquehannocks in seventeenth-century
trade see, for instance, the work of Francis Jennings and J. Frederick Fausz. Although
Pendergast argues that the Massawomecks were the more important traders in the first
two decades of the century (and certainly in 1608, when Captain John Smith visited
the area), my argument here is focused on the 1630s and later. The Susquehannocks
certainly seem to have expanded their networks and influence by the mid-1630s. See, for
example, Pendergast, "Susquehannock Trade Northward to New France."

11. J. Frederick Fausz, "Merging and Emerging Worlds: Anglo-Indian Interest Groups
and the Development of the Seventeenth-century Chesapeake," in *Colonial Chesapeake
Society*, ed. Lois Green Carr, Philip D. Morgan, and Jean B. Russo (Chapel Hill: Published for the Institute of Early American History and Culture, Williamsburg, Va., by the
University of North Carolina Press, 1988), 47–98.

12. Karen Kupperman has pointed out the significance of early Susquehannock–New
Sweden contacts and first made the fascinating argument that the Susquehannocks were
the dominant member of the alliance. See Karen Ordahl Kupperman, "Scandinavian
Colonists Confront the New World," in *New Sweden in America*, ed. Carole Hoffecker,
Richard Waldron, Lorraine Williams, and Barbara Benson (Newark: University of Dela-
ware Press, 1993), 89–111.

13. *Archives of Maryland*, vol. 3 (69 vols., Baltimore, 1883–), 149–50, 276, 277. See also
Peter Lindeström, *Geographia Americae with an Account of the Delaware Indians, based
on Surveys and Notes Made in 1654–1656*, trans. and ed. Amandus Johnson (Philadelphia:
Swedish Colonial Society, 1925), 241–44.

Although Lindeström describes this as a battle between the Susquehannocks and
Virginia, he uses the term "Virginia" as a broad one for the whole Chesapeake Bay region,
and he mentions the Susquehannocks' capture of field artillery, which is consistent with
the reference in the *Archives of Maryland*. On this point see also Francis Jennings, "Glory,
Death, and Transfiguration," 20.

14. In reporting the details of the conquest of New Sweden to his superiors in Sweden,
Governor Johan Rising wrote the following:

> In a short time an Indian came in to us with a letter from Stüvesant, in which he
> arrogantly demanded the surrender of the whole river, and required me and all the
> Swedes either to evacuate the country or to remain there under Dutch protection,
> threatening with the consequences in case of refusal. Hereto I answered briefly, by
> letter, that, since so strange a demand was sent by him to me, I would reply by spe-
> cial messengers, and sent him my answer by the same Indian.

See "Relation of the Surrender of New Sweden, by Governor Johan Clasen Rising,
1655," in *Narratives of Early Pennsylvania, West New Jersey, and Delaware, 1630–1707*, ed.
Albert Cook Myers (1912; repr., New York: Barnes and Noble, 1967), 173.

15. In addition to the fact that the activities of many cultural mediators were not necessarily fully documented, many of the Dutch West India Company's records have not
survived. They were either destroyed as waste paper in the nineteenth century or lost in
the great library fire in Albany in 1911.

16. For additional information about Allerton see Cynthia J. Van Zandt, "The Dutch Connection: Isaac Allerton and the Dynamics of English Cultural Anxiety in the Gouden Eeuw," in *Connecting Cultures: The Netherlands in Five Centuries of Transatlantic Exchange*, ed. Rosemarijn Hoefte and Johanna C. Kardux. European Contributions to American Studies series, gen. ed. Rob Kroes (Amsterdam: Free University Press, 1994), 51–76; Van Zandt, "Negotiating Settlement."

17. I use the term "spokesperson" deliberately. Robert Grumet has argued persuasively that some Native American leaders whom scholars long assumed were men were in fact women. Men acted as spokesmen in contacts with Europeans more often than women did, but some women did fill this role. See Robert Steven Grumet, "Sunksquaws, Shamans, and Tradeswomen: Middle Atlantic Coastal Algonkian Women during the 17th and 18th Centuries," in *Women and Colonization: Anthropological Perspectives*, ed. Mona Etienne and Eleanor Leacock (New York: Praeger, 1980), 43–62. See also Grumet, "'We Are Not So Great Fools.'"

18. Charles T. Gehring, trans. and ed., *New York Historical Manuscripts, Delaware Papers: Dutch* (Baltimore: Genealogical Publishing, 1988), 35. An earlier translation appears in *Documents relative to the Colonial Period of the State of New-York; Procured in Holland, England, and France*, ed. Edmund Bailey O'Callaghan (Albany, 1856), vol. 12, trans. B. Fernow, 98.

19. Charles T. Gehring, "'Hodi Mihi, Cras Tibi': Swedish-Dutch Relations in the Delaware Valley," in *New Sweden in America*, 81.

20. Lindeström, *Geographia Americae*, 235–36.

21. Ibid.

22. Ibid.

23. Ibid.

24. Ibid.

25. Allen Trelease also thought it significant that the Indians singled out Allerton. However, he argued that they did so because of Allerton's New England connections and that the "northern Indians" whom the attackers claimed to be seeking were Narragansetts. Trelease also discounts Dutch suggestions that Susquehannocks participated in the attack. He finds those claims to be evidence of Dutch bewilderment at the surprise assault rather than of any real activity on the Susquehannocks' part. See Trelease, *Indian Affairs in Colonial New York*, 139–40.

26. Lindeström, *Geographia Americae*, 235–36.

27. The Susquehannocks' ongoing war with Maryland finally ended in the summer of 1652, but only when Virginia Puritan émigrés who were allied with William Claiborne negotiated with the Susquehannocks. See Fausz, "Merging and Emerging Worlds," 83.

28. See, for example, Kupperman, "Scandinavian Colonists Confront the New World," 89–111.

29. "Report of Governor Johan Rising, 1655," in *Narratives of Early Pennsylvania, West New Jersey, and Delaware, 1630–1707*, 159.

30. This population estimate includes colonists of both genders.

31. See Jennings, "Glory, Death, and Transfiguration," and Kent, *Susquehanna's Indians*, for discussion of the Lenape-Susquehannock wars in the 1620s and 1630s and the alliance they developed sometime in the 1640s.

32. "Report of Governor Johan Rising, 1655," 156–57.

33. Ibid.

34. Ibid.

35. Ibid.

36. The Hackensacks assimilated a number of refugee Susquehannocks and were active in the peach war. See Grumet, "'We Are Not So Great Fools,'" 112–14.

37. See Isaack de Rasière to the Amsterdam Chamber of the West India Company, Sept. 23, 1626, *Documents relating to New Netherland, 1624–1626, in the Henry E. Huntington Library*, trans. and ed. A. J. F. van Laer (San Marino, Calif., 1924), 192, 211. See also Francis Jennings, "Glory, Death, and Transfiguration," 17, for a discussion of the early Susquehannock-Dutch contacts. See also Trelease, *Indian Affairs in Colonial New York*, for a discussion of Susquehannock efforts to establish trade connections with the Dutch in the 1630s.

38. See Jennings, "Glory, Death, and Transfiguration," 22–23.

39. Francis Jennings has argued that the Iroquois wars against the Hurons from 1649 to 1652 had a great impact on the Susquehannocks and that the decisive defeat of the Hurons in 1652 led the Susquehannocks finally to make peace with Maryland. Jennings, "Indians and Frontiers in Seventeenth-century Maryland," in David B. Quinn, ed., *Early Maryland in a Wider World* (Detroit : Wayne State University Press, 1982), 220–21.

40. See Francis Jennings, "Susquehannock," in *Handbook of North American Indians*, vol. 15, *Northeast*, ed. William C. Sturtevant and Bruce. G. Trigger (Smithsonian Insitution Press, 1978), 362, 367; Kupperman, "Scandinavian Colonists Confront the New World," 104, 111n72.

41. Stuyvesant, for instance, arrived on the Delaware with a fleet of seven ships and more than three hundred men to conquer New Sweden. The conquering Dutch force was equal to or larger than the entire colonial population of New Sweden at that point.

EPILOGUE

1. See *Archives of Maryland, Proceedings of the Council of Maryland, 1667–1687/8*, ed. William Hand Browne (Baltimore: Maryland Historical Society, 1887), 157–239, for Claiborne's petition and supporting documents.

2. Ibid., 157.

3. Ibid.

4. Ibid.

Index

de Rasière, Isaack, 99–100, 127–29,
220n28, 220nn30–31
de Soto, Hernando, 49
Dee, John, 20
Deer Island, *90*
The Defence of Trade, 22, 193n13,
197–98n56, 201n90
Delaware Bay, 230n3
Delaware River
Allerton trade networks, 107, 110–11
claims to, 168
colonization of, 172
Dutch traders' kidnapping, 122,
219n17
Fort Nassau, 130
Fort Wilhelmus, 127
fur trade, 167
Maryland Colony, 168
New Netherland Colony, 151
New Sweden Colony, 168
Swaanendael, 133–34
trade pidgin, 59–60
van der Donck map, *146*
Virginia Colony, 168
Zuydt Rivier (South River), 168
Dening, Greg, 37, 194n16
depth soundings, 34
Dermer, Thomas, 56, 204n37
Dexter, Franklin Bowditch, 214n49
Dexter, Morton and Henry, 210–11n8
diaspora Africans. *See* Africans
Diggs, Dudley, 22, 193n13, 197–98n56,
201n90
Dike, Daniel, 26, 195n35
*Divers voyages touching the discouerie of
America*, 29, 196n43
Downing, Lucy, 103–104, 115
Drake manuscript, 36
Dutch States General, 37
Dutch West India Company. *See also* New
Netherland
Albany fire, 231n15
and Allerton senior, 177–79
and Blaeu, 32
Committee of Nineteen, 110
and de Fries, 226n50
and the Five Nations, 174
fur trade, 129, 174, 184

Kieft maps, 37
Kieft's war, 150, 165
and the Mohawks, 123–24, 184,
219n18
New Sweden Colony, 4, 171–72, 174,
176–77, 183–84, 231n14, 233n41
privateers, 141
slave population, 154
slave trade, 61, 138–40, 145, 222n8,
223n12, 225n32
and slavery, 147, 221n1
and the Susquehannocks, 127, 166
threats to, 148
and Verhulst, 127, 220n30, 227n56
Dutch-Algonquian war, 164–65
Dutch-Munsee war
and Allerton senior, 108, 215n57,
215n59
and Kieft, 108, 110, 165
New Netherland Colony, 161, 215n57
Staten Island, 165

East India Company, 194n18,
197–98n56
Eckhout, Albert, 36
Eight Men, 108–10, 215nn57–58
Eliot, John, 204n32
Elizabeth I, 35
Elmina (Mina), 141
Elswick, 113
England
Allerton senior as resident, 209n3
Anglo-Dutch war, 112, 216–17n76
and cartography, 20
civil war, 25, 103, 105–106, 110,
214n52
claims to New Netherland, 168
The Defence of Trade, 22
gender inequality in, 207n22
Gunpowder Plot, 93
maps as metaphors, 23–24
Powhatan-English alliance, 65, 67,
77–78, 84–85
Puritan emigrations, 92
Saxton map, 35
The Trades Increase, 21–22
women and trade, 196n47
Epenow, 54–57, 203–204n31